POPE JOHN XXIV

BY JOHN COGLEY

ISBN: 1461123623
ISBN-13: 9781461123620

Library of Congress Control Number: **XXXXX (If applicable)**
Library of Congress Control Number: X
CreateSpace Independent Publishing Platform
North Charleston, South Carolina

INTRODUCTION

All my life I have been a Catholic though not always an exemplary one. During my falls from grace the Church has always been there for me, sometimes in the guise of an understanding priest, sometimes in the guise of another struggling soul, rarely if ever judgemental, most often compassionate and healing. I cannot, despite scandals, abuses of power and a seemingly out of touch hierarchy, imagine myself as not being part of what Fr Hans Küng calls "This fellowship of believers". Like Dr Küng, the Catholic Church is my spiritual home. It has been this fellowship of believers, ordinary Catholics, clerical and lay, whose example has sustained my Faith as they have tried to grow closer to the Gospel in their own lives.

Many of us, perhaps most of us, feel that our Church is too authoritarian for the 21st century, that it wants to confine the "People of God" to a subordinate and obedient role, little different from that occupied by the majority in totalitarian states. Not that we want to dictate doctrine or ordain priests but we do want to contribute to the development of our Faith: to utilise our own experience, which is essentially different from that of many Church leaders. We want Catholicism to be lived less as a multitude of rules of dubious provenance and more as an embodiment of Jesus' instruction to "Love God and our neighbour". A simple enough message but one easily buried by manuals of instructions written in impenetrable prose, bearing little relation to everyday life and deviously implying infallibility while cautiously avoiding future hostages to fortune.

This authoritarian culture not only alienates many thinking Catholics and fellow Christians, but it sustains a leadership which does not believe itself accountable to the men and women in the pews. Those who are, in fact, the Church and who ultimately pay the bills, be they bills for Papal visits or for abused children.

This arrogance is evident when the Church, as an organisation, is elevated above the Church, as people, and is seen in the covering up abuses rather than admitting guilt and making amends. The penitent in the confessional has to confess guilt, renounce the sin and, wherever possible, make restitution. Should the same criteria not apply to those in Church leadership positions? The argument that the Church remains holy and inviolate, when its representatives misbehave, but claims the glory when they achieve sainthood, only invites accusations of hypocrisy, a sin which Jesus found particularly distasteful.

Psychologists sometimes use the metaphor of parent, adult and child to analyse the functional basis of relationships. Ideally relationships between mature, reasonably intelligent people should be conducted adult to adult: conducted with an openness to contrary opinion, a genuine seeking after truth and a reluctance to resort to the parent to child position of unquestioning obedience. In Cardinal Newman's terms, do I raise my glass "First to my conscience and then to the Pope?" Or do I reverse the procedure? That, in my view, is the question which most polarises opinion within the Catholic Church even if it is not usually stated in such general terms. A top down mind set is not conducive to a vibrant communion of believers.

Any organisation which wishes to retain committed and active participants must encourage continuing reflection and renewal. Failure to do so will result in a decline in membership, leaving behind those who comply mechanically together with those who demand absolute certainty and are thus vehemently opposed to any questioning of doctrine or process. Which is the better evidence of vitality, unquestioning certainty or honest enquiry?

The majority of human problems revolve round relationships and relationships are not well served by ignoring or glossing over the fault lines. Identifying the fault lines and seeking to repair them should be seen not as an act of sabotage but as a act of love.

Pope John XXIV is a work of fiction in which I have tried to raise some of the major issues which confront my Church. I believe, as do many of my fellow Catholics, that we have far more to lose by ignoring, denying or prohibiting than we do by re-examining in the light of 21st century knowledge. Pope John XXIV's predecessor, Pius XIII, is depicted as a Pope who embodied certainties and pursued his vision of the Church with courage and single-mindedness. His successor, Pope John XXIV, is less certain and less courageous, a flawed man but, then, Jesus often chose examples of flawed humanity to advance his ministry. John XXIV fits into that tradition.

Sydney 2012

CHAPTER 1

"I think it is too late to disturb the Holy Father, Eminence."

"I have my orders as you have yours." The Secretary of State replied flintily and the Monsignor retreated. He must learn quickly never to offer unsolicited advice, no matter how well intended, if he was ever to become a bishop.

Cardinal Peroni secretly agreed with his assistant but he valued obedience above all other virtues, both in himself and in the Church he served. Today vows were considered little more than statements of intent but, for him, chastity and obedience were fundamental to his vocation. If only the vast army of Catholics were as diligent: even if priests could be relied upon. He shook his head as he made his way to the Papal apartment.

Sister Maria, the Pope's minder, admitted him with ill grace. That she was aware of the Pope's instructions made no difference. Peroni pushed past her, noting that she looked more fearsome than usual at this late hour. At one level he recognised her devotion but he found her lack of respect for all but her master irritating. Thank God there would be no women priests during his lifetime. He expressed the feeling in his elaborate closing of the door to the Pope's chambers: the exclusion of a mere housekeeper from the centre of power.

Immediately his irritation was replaced by concern. Pius XIII was still in his chair looking frail and tired. Peroni wondered if he ever went to bed these days or whether he simply dozed and prayed. That this amazing man should be reduced to such a pitiful state seemed manifestly unjust. For a moment he had an image of the vigorous young Cardinal who had ascended to the Chair of Peter and who had subsequently chosen him to be a Prince of the Church and his Prime Minister. He made to genuflect as he always did but Pius waved him to his feet.

"Well, Stephano, what disturbance brings you here so late?"

"Holiness, I have sad news but not unexpected. Cardinal Harding died at 10.45pm this evening. He was heavily sedated and died peacefully." He watched the Pope for a reaction: Harding's death must remind him of his own rapidly approaching end.

Pius showed no sign of fear. He motioned to Peroni to assist him to his kneeler. "Pray with me, Stephano," was all he said. Peroni did as ordered hoping that the Holy Father would keep his prayers short as the hour was late. A faint hope as it turned out.

At 11.00am the next day Peroni had a further meeting with Pius. He presented him with a list which the Nuncio had prepared. It contained candidates who might replace the Cardinal Archbishop of Westminster. Months previously Peroni had briefed the Nuncio, given him a job description. The successor to Harding was to be mildly ecumenical, staunchly traditional and acceptable to the politicians of a country which, even today, held an historic suspicion of Catholics. He had used information, to which few were privy, to amend the list prior to presentation. The Nuncio had gone through the pretext of consulting the bishops but their views were of minor significance. Subsidiarity was, to quote Peroni, "The ordering of an army by its corporals".

"A quick announcement of the new archbishop is desirable, Holiness. You are aware that some of the bishops have been slow to speak out against lapses of the Faithful. A strong leader could do much to restore obedience."

Pius chuckled. "Stephano, I am sure you have already decided whom I should elevate. You are simply extending a courtesy to an old and fragile Pontiff." He laughed again and said something in the language of his youth. Several members of the Curia had observed his increasing tendency to revert to his native tongue. This gave Sister Maria greater power and was universally resented. "The Gate Keeper is a Polish peasant," one cardinal had remarked bitterly.

"I will pray about it so that the Holy Spirit will be permitted his imprimatur."

Later Peroni encountered Cardinal Kirst, Prefect of the Congregation for the Doctrine of the Faith. The two men represented the most powerful portfolios in the Vatican. Their relationship was cordial but not close.

"And how is his Holiness?" Kirst asked in his perfect Italian, product of almost half a century in Rome.

"I think he tires himself needlessly. He is still too involved in too much. He plans as though he will live forever yet all the signs are that he will be lucky to see Christmas."

Kirst shrugged. "We have tried to relieve him of decision making but he believes in his own accountability."

"It is a fearsome responsibility. Some of the decisions we have to take are burdensome enough but, the Holy Father....."

Archbishop William Carterton, wearing a rainproof jacket and boots, pushed his way through the wind which came ice-cold and wet off the River Mersey. Today, as so often, the river was grey-brown and singularly uninviting. He remembered how, as a boy, he had known the river teeming with ships: the bustling docks serviced by their own overhead railway. From Liverpool you could sail to anywhere in the world and miles of working dockland laid claim to the city's importance. Today the docks were silent, the railway scrapped and a few tiny boats plied the banks of the Mersey and the Irish Sea. Thatcher and Militant Tendency had achieved an economic devastation which the Nazi blitz had failed to accomplish.

So much had changed. As a boy he recalled the sectarian battles. The Protestant ghetto based on Netherfield Road and its Catholic equivalent based on Scotland Road. How the city had ground to a standstill each year as the Orange Lodge paraded to Exchange Station to celebrate King Billy's victory at the Boyne. Late that night the Lodge would return from Southport, the Catholics would be waiting and battle would be joined. As children, they imitated their parents.

"Say something in Latin?" They would demand of an innocent child. Failing the test was sufficient cause for a bashing. But it was not one sided. When crossing a building site one weekend, out of nowhere, a gang of boys emerged. "Are you a Catholic?" they asked menacingly. Since lying was a sin, the young Carterton told the truth.

Somehow he had managed to crawl home. No phone, no car. A neighbour called the doctor and he arrived, smelling of whisky.

"No bones broken but he'll have severe bruising.' Dr Jenkins announced. "I hope you gave a good account of yourself." Bill winced, not so much in pain as in the knowledge that he had surrendered without a fight in the hope that mercy would prevail. Jenkins misinterpreted and uttered a gruff "Well done! We'll dress these then we'll find the bastards."

His mother retreated from this unprofessional display. Bill was bundled into the doctor's car and joined by his father, just home from work. Together they combed the streets but they never did find the louts. Had they done so the two men would have administered their own brand of justice? How times had changed.

Now the prejudice and the self-reliance had long departed. Derek Worlock and David Sheppard, a Catholic and an Anglican Archbishop, had shown that the Gospel could overcome history: where bigotry was let tolerance be. He felt like a pigmy in a giant's footsteps. He turned away from the river and walked for a while through what seemed to be a war zone. Boarded windows, businesses gone broke, litter and weeds. He had been their archbishop for five years and what had he achieved? He had inherited an archdiocese renewed and failed to maintain the momentum. A third of all births were illegitimate (to use a politically incorrect term). His priests were demoralised: one was even in prison and his cathedral had concrete cancer. New vocations were at an all-time low. The Faithful were only too faithful in their resistance to the closure of inner city churches and Catholic schools and were conspicuously unfaithful in their attendance at Mass. Congregations were divided into hostile camps, those who demanded a crusade for social justice and those who wanted a Marian shrine on every street corner. It had been known locally as the Cruel See, when presided over by John Carmel Heenan, surely it now qualified as the Dead See. Perhaps the regular catharsis of fist fights had been a vital incentive to religious practice.

Even the weather seemed violently set against hope. Theoretically it was spring but pensioners were still dying of hypothermia. As he brooded, he noticed a figure in a doorway across the street, an African woman sheltering against the cold. One of New Labour's asylum seekers, a Section 55 pauper. He crossed towards her and the woman cowered further back in the doorway. She probably had good reason to fear men. He wanted to reach out and touch her, make some small gesture of humanity. Instead he gave her what money he had and went on his way.

Returning to the Wigwam (as the Cathedral of Christ the King was usually known) he knelt for a long time before retiring to his study. Easter was close and his mind wandered to that first Easter: the terrible death of the saviour; Peter's betrayal; the disarray of the disciples. He identified with Peter. His time as Archbishop had not been without its betrayals. Was what he had excused as shyness and humility more honestly described as cowardice? He looked up at the cross.

"Father forgive me. Help me to do whatever I must do."

The depression which always lurked close began to overwhelm him. Rationally he knew that the Church everywhere was going through a period of decline: falling Mass attendance; child abuse scandals; an absence of vocations; above all a failure to communicate the 'good news'. He recalled a young, vigorous Pope who had declared: "We are the Easter people and hallelujah is our song". Did the now aged Pope still believe his own assertion? What would the African woman have made of these words?

He despised himself for his own failure of hope. Faith and charity remained easy for him but, hope, in the present climate? Yet, if the leaders did not convey hope what chance was there for the flock? Hope came courtesy of the lottery, reality TV, symbiosis with the lives of celebrities. Jam tomorrow was no longer enough. The people hadn't yet given up on charity, still clung to aspects of faith but, unfortunately, there were three Cardinal Virtues. Somehow he had to re-establish hope. A sense that this creaky, two millennia-old Church was not a bedridden geriatric but a still pulsating, evolving organism. This, he now realised, was not the work of a theologian but the work of a shepherd. Why had it taken him so long?

Ten days later he opened the side door to his house and admitted a rather dishevelled figure who smelled strongly of beer and who hastily discarded a cigarette.

"Good of you to come, Joe. How was the match?"

"Bloody awful! You were wise to stay away. Now if I was the manager.........sorry.....but it's the third loss in succession."

"I know and you'll need a drink to console you. Jamieson's OK on a cold night?"

Joe nodded vigorously. "And maybe just a chaser too, Bill. I think I have the 'flu coming on."

The old friends settled companionably in front of the fire and raised their glasses. "To the next cardinal."

Carterton laughed. "I don't think so but I appreciate the thought."

Joe Shelley looked annoyed. "Why ever not? You've got more degrees than a vice-chancellor and you are a product of the most Catholic city in England. What's more important you played soccer for Everton."

"Actually I had a trial for the reserves. That was as far as it got."

"Don't split hairs. You're my choice anyway and if those bastards in the Curia choose anyone else I'll slaughter them in my column."

"Your column, Joe! That's what I want to talk to you about. I want you to do something for me."

Joe raised an eyebrow. "Promote your cause!"

"Not quite. Rather the reverse. I want you to do something that will put me out of the race."

"Well I won't do it. It's your bloody right to go to Westminster. Harding was a good man but he was too quiet. We want a cardinal with a voice." Shelley's own voice trailed off and his host did not miss the significance.

"You mean I used to have a voice….a long time ago."

Embarrassed Shelley started to object.

"Joe, it's no good. I've been doing a spot of introspection. I've looked back over my five years here and asked myself what have I achieved? The answer is very little." He held up his hand as Shelley was about to interrupt. "I appreciate your unconditional support but the fact remains that I have been too timid. Partly because I'd hate to be considered a grandstander, partly because I believed that subtle pressure could produce change, partly because I didn't want to stick my head over the parapet. Yet if I can't speak out for the poor and voiceless I might as well resign now."

"You're depressed! It's the weather. I can name half a dozen issues which you've influenced."

"So can I but they're all small beer. Now, for better or worse, I am going to say what I believe Jesus would say if he walked the streets of Liverpool and many of our other cities. I'm going to give you a copy of my Easter Sunday sermon and I want you to publish it in your column immediately afterwards. Not because I want personal publicity, but because I fear how it could be made to read if parts are taken out of context. Will you do it for me?"

"Of course. I'd be honoured."

"Perhaps you'd better read it first. Mine may not be the only job on the line."

Shelley read rapidly and chuckled occasionally. "Well I must say you'll manage to offend a broad cross section of the community and probably endear yourself the rest. Unfortunately the former wield power and the latter wield little except their suffering. Not that I don't agree with you. It's a bit lengthy for my column but I can précis it without compromising the message but it is bound to get misquoted. You can just imagine what the right wing press, which means most of them, will do with it. I can see the headlines already: the Red Archbishop, Carterton's Communist Credo, Militant Tendency replaced by Belligerent Bishop."

"That's why I want you to publish first so there is a true record before any distortion begins."

"Bill, you are a lovely man but a little naive. The Liverpool Echo doesn't have quite the circulation or the influence of the national tabloids. What is more, the tabloids are not interested in reporting you honestly. They'll be out to create an impression of someone who is, at best, dotty and at worst malevolent. If you plan to go ahead I think we should put the full text on the internet. Then anyone actually interested in the truth can access it unadulterated.

Archbishop William Carterton looked round his crowded cathedral. If only it was so well filled on a normal Sunday. He wondered whether his sermon would lead to a greater or lesser congregation in the future or whether, as he suspected, it would be a nine days wonder. As always, the enemy within was apathy.

"As we all know, today we celebrate the resurrection from the dead of Jesus Christ. An event which is unique in history and the cornerstone of the Christian faith. As Catholics we believe that it is both a physical event and a metaphor. Today I want to speak about its metaphorical significance. There are two aspects of the metaphor, death and rising above death.

In our world we are only too familiar with death. The last century saw more needless slaughter of human life than any other century. At times I suspect we became numb through the sheer scale of slaughter and our perceived inability to affect events, often far from these shores. But there are other forms of death which are far crueller than the bomb and the bullet. I refer to death of the human spirit, to the steady erosion of hope. We live in an affluent country. We have one of the largest economies in the world, yet we see all around us manifest injustice: poverty amongst children, homelessness amongst the mentally ill, run down council housing, pensioners without heat, women forced into prostitution, refugees treated like criminals. You are as familiar as I am with the litany. Yet we have politicians who speak of their humanity and their desire to eliminate poverty and despair. A spell in a condemned flat in Dingle might challenge such hypocrisy. Bankers who tell us that we must be more productive and work harder. How many of them have worked on an assembly line night shift? Company Directors who cry that wage rises are impossible if we are to remain competitive except, of course, when it comes to their own remuneration. Bankers whose bonuses accrue from short term profits but who leave the ordinary citizen to pay for long term losses. Some would argue that we are witnessing the behaviour of a worldwide superrich, tax cheating cabal whose only allegiance is to personal greed.

History can be viewed as constant struggle between an 'in group' which wishes to retain power and use it to control 'out groups' which are often the source of the 'in group's' wealth and prestige. We all know the story of Magna Carta, when the feudal lords of England took power away from the king. We also know that they did not re-direct that power to the people. In the centuries which followed the people tried to take some power for themselves. Often they were unsuccessful and many died in the process but, gradually, power was diffused. Arguably post World War II Britain, despite the huge debts incurred during the war and the need to maintain a high Cold War defence budget, was the fairest society we have ever known in these islands. Many of you in this congregation will recall the relative egalitarianism of that time but it is now no more than a memory.

We have experienced a sustained campaign to put the working man back in his place, and not just the working man. Contracts and casualisation have resulted in a workforce that fears for its employment. Men and women accept conditions which would have been unacceptable forty years ago because they live in fear. The union movement has been emasculated and marginalised. The media has ceased to be a 'free press' and a 'free press' is essential to make democracy work. Democratic governments have used tactics which they would have condemned as abuses of human rights if used elsewhere.

At this point a minor commotion broke out in the front pews and several people left the cathedral muttering words like 'communist' and 'lunatic'. The Archbishop merely paused and smiled.

So what went wrong? Why do we not now enjoy a society where all share in its prosperity? Why do we allow ourselves to be controlled by people who, no matter how often they appear in the Honour's List, whatever titles they hold or however much wealth they accumulate, bear no higher loyalty than to their own preferment? The answer, I fear, is because you and I have failed to speak out and to act. We have been asleep on our watch. We have been too busy becoming respectable. There is even seductive talk now that the Act of Succession should be amended to allow for a Catholic to rule the United Kingdom. To some that may seem as though the Catholic Church in England has come of age. In one sense I believe it tells us that we have sold our soul."

Yes, my friends we have become respectable. Yet the man whose resurrection we celebrate today died because he refused to become respectable. A few well-chosen words to the Sanhedrin, a blind eye to hypocrisy, a retraction of the Sermon on the Mount and he could have been a powerful rabbi in Jerusalem. He paid a price far higher than you or I are likely to pay and he did it for love of those who will continue to betray the ideals for which he stood and for which he still stands. We can conspire with his crucifiers if we choose to ignore the wrongs we see all around us. We can participate in his resurrection if we choose to do something about them.

You would not be human if you did not charge me with hypocrisy. I live in a nice house. I have a housekeeper. I eat well. People largely treat me with respect. I have no family whose welfare I may jeopardise by talking sedition. I cannot be as vulnerable as many of you are but, to the extent that I can live less opulently, I intend to do so. I should have done so long ago. As of Easter Monday I shall vacate Archbishop's House and I will move to the presbytery attached to St Kevin's Church. Fr Nolan has been kind enough to offer me a home and it will do me no harm to return to the realities of parish life. I have made separate provision for my staff and they will not be accompanying me. I will continue to serve as your Archbishop for as long as I am permitted to do so or for so long as I feel I have something to offer you.

I hope you will take my words today to your hearts and consider what contribution you may be able to make to ensure that we do build a New Jerusalem in England's green and pleasant land. And remember, the apostles were not without fear despite the knowledge of the Son of God in their midst.

Essentially I am encouraging you to embark on a crusade. Not a crusade which aims to conquer land but a crusade which aims to conquer the fear we feel when we dare to challenge power which is being misused. Recall the apostles on Lake Galilee when Jesus walked towards them on the water and his words 'Fear not, it is I'. Let us bear those words in mind for if we act in a truly Christian manner, he will be with us.

May God bless you all and a very happy Easter."

For a moment the cathedral was silent, and then the applause started. Spasmodic at first for it is not the Catholic tradition to applaud sermons. Then it grew and stifled completely the angry voices of dissent as perhaps a tenth of the congregation departed in disgust. Carterton returned to the altar, weak at the knees and light headed. A terrible realisation dawned. He felt that he had started something without any idea of where to go next. He had anticipated that a few people would respond in some way, expand the social justice group and develop from there. What he had unearthed was far more visceral. Why, he wondered, did he not use the word exciting? He knew he was a victim of the very fear of which he had spoken. Sacrificing his house for a bed sitter at St Kevin's was going to be the easy part of his transition. Just for a moment he hoped the Curia would hear of his outspokenness, sack him and he could return to academe. He looked up at the crucifix and asked for forgiveness.

CHAPTER 2

"Archbishop Stanford for you, Eminence."

Peroni showed his annoyance. "What does he want this time?" The Monsignor shrugged and hoped that he would not be blamed for the bad news which Stanford usually heralded. Peroni was not exactly a moderniser but Stanford was an arch revisionist.

"Yes?" Peroni said in his most unwelcoming voice. The Monsignor applied himself to the file on his desk and tried to become invisible. Out of the corner of his eye he saw his master grow red with annoyance.

"You have written proof of this? It is on the internet! Are we running a circus? You can be sure I will."

"Get me this site will you." He passed an address to his assistant and paced the room. Pleased to demonstrate his talent, the Monsignor obliged and the full text of Carterton's Easter sermon was revealed. Peroni glanced at it and demanded a print. Ten minutes later he was striding towards the Pope's apartment clutching the papers.

"Holiness! We can delay no longer. We must fill Westminster with someone reliable. Someone who can deal with Archbishop Carterton quickly and firmly. We cannot be seen as enemies of social justice, or some such platitude, but nor can we be seen as promoting anarchy. We have always achieved by diplomacy what anarchy could never accomplish. The British Prime Minister has conveyed his concern about an Archbishop who has developed a taste for political interference. He told Archbishop Stanford that he was considering a speech to Parliament on the subject of Church teaching and its anachronistic character in the modern world. While I feel sure he is joking to make the point it is, none the less, a matter of concern."

The Pope seemed amused. Peroni wondered if he was degenerating mentally as well as physically. Developing a sense of humour at the eleventh hour of his pontificate was a frightening prospect. He hoped he would not have to witness such an event.

"I do not think the Gdansk shipyard workers had studied diplomacy."

"Not Poland!" Peroni shuddered. He wanted to keep the matter at a rational level.

"No, Holiness. But they were fighting a manifest evil. The whole of the free world sympathised and, as we now know, many in the unfree world. I do not think there is a comparison."

"I'm sure you are right Stephano. I should not tease you. What have you decided?"

'Not more humour!' Peroni prayed. "The list I provided was in order of merit, as advised. However, in view of the Carterton manifesto I believe we should send a clear signal to the British Government and beyond. That the Vatican favours a cardinal who believes in slow evolution of society rather than instant revolution. With this in mind I think Archbishop Stanford's name should move to the top of the list. He is staunchly conservative and, through his connections with the Organisation, is able to influence opinion where it actually matters. What's more he never makes a move, no matter how trivial, without my blessing. " Inwardly Peroni winced. In promoting Stanford's cause and that of the Organisation he was placing the good of the Church ahead of his personal feelings. "But, as ever Holiness, I will carry out your orders, whomsoever you select."

"Thank you, Stephano. Loyalty is your most admirable quality. I will decide within two days."

Peroni left the chamber reflecting on the Pope's comment on loyalty. Was it a further example of his reawakened sense of humour? Perhaps popes as well as cardinals should retire at 75.

Pius read Carterton's Easter sermon and understood Peroni's concern. It was certainly not the voice of a diplomat, seasoned by years of Curial service. Perhaps that accounted for its freshness and its accessibility. He recalled his only meeting with the Archbishop. Clearly something had changed the man. He only hoped it was grace and not ambition or self-destruction."

A small gathering of well-dressed men, two of whom were in formal clerical garb, met at the home of Desmond Delile. After a few brief pleasantries Delile called them to order.

"Gentlemen welcome! And a particular welcome to Fathers Garcia and Parkes. Now, Father if you would lead us in prayer." They bowed their heads. After the prayer, Delile continued.

"As you know there is much concern about the Easter Sunday sermon of Archbishop Carterton. We all share that concern. Already representations have been made to the Holy See through our usual channels and many of our Liverpool brothers expressed their total disagreement by walking out of the cathedral. However acts of mass public outrage, no matter how well intentioned, undermine the unity of the Church more than they assist our cause. To-night Father Garcia will give us the benefit of his experience in dealing with such sensitive matters."

"Thank you, Desmond. All of us in this room have pledged ourselves to a return to the traditional morality and concerns of the Church. We have given our time, our money and, sadly, some have given their health in the cause of re-instating what we have lost since the Second Vatican Council. In many areas we have made much progress and, with the inspiring leadership of Pope Pius XIII, have been able to reassert doctrine in its clash with fashion. Our struggle has been recognised by the promotion of some of our clerical members to high positions in the hierarchy, even to cardinal. I say this not because it is new to you but to remind you how far we have come and how we are determined not to surrender ground to the wishy, washy pseudo liberal wing of the Church. Now, gentlemen, is not the time to rest on our successes."

"The sermon to which Desmond referred and which you have all read, could appear to be no more than the unrealistic ravings of an academic who inhabits a world of odd ideas. In fact it is far more dangerous. The Organisation recognised from the start that power does not rest with the masses and that to possess it we have to either occupy positions of power or be able to influence those who do. In practice we do both. We recruit Catholics who are or will become leaders in society and we seek association with non-Catholics elites. While Carterton's views, if applied, might be detrimental to some of our brothers they will unquestionably alienate the non-Catholic elites whom we currently espouse. I am sure you have already picked up the rumblings which herald an avalanche to come, unless we act decisively."

"I realise that I preach to the converted but you have only to look at my own country to see how dysfunctional it has become since the Generalissimo's death. To be sure, he had his human failings, even in his treatment of the Church but at least he maintained Christian standards: today we have moral anarchy. Humanity has not yet evolved to a state where it can operate without strong ethical imperatives backed by powerful sanctions. And what did the Archbishop of Liverpool have to say on the subject? Did he condemn sex outside of marriage in a city where one third of all births are out of wedlock? Did he remind the congregation of the reality of sin and the need for regular confession? Did he mention that unfashionable topic of Hell? Did he endorse the rhythm method as the only acceptable means of birth control? Did he suggest that men and women would be better employed praying for the grace to bear the sorrows of this life rather filling their minds with an unobtainable utopian dream? I think you know the answer. He most emphatically did not. So in one Easter sermon he has managed to both alienate those outside the Church whom we seek to influence and, at the same time, focus the attention of those of the Faithful who took him seriously towards Cloud Cuckoo Land and away from the basic practices which lead to salvation."

"So what is to be done? First, gentlemen, we must make it very clear to other bishops and to the clergy in general that the Archbishop is speaking for himself and, while he may reflect the opinion of some nominal Catholics, he is completely out of step with committed Catholics. Second, we must allay fears in the wider community that he has any support worthy of consideration. Third, we must renew our efforts to ensure that the new cardinal is a man of traditional values, in step with the Holy See and capable of dealing promptly with self-indulgent prelates, regardless of their rank. Finally, we should not shrink from any legitimate action which reduces the credibility of the Carterton position, to the extent that it has any credibility"

"And now, gentlemen, I must take leave of you but Father Parkes will remain to provide any necessary spiritual guidance. May we thank you in the name of our blessed founder and exhort you to keep up God's work."

The Chancellor's press secretary was quick off the mark and his master had a copy of the sermon before it was picked up in Number 10. Though it was late at night he had orders to deliver anything controversial immediately. Number 11 enjoyed being ahead of Number 10. The prime number outwitting the Prime Minister, as the Chancellor was apt to remark.

Cardinal Harding had been of the old school of non-political clerics, at least in so far as his public image was concerned. He had occasionally tried to influence the political process but discretely, some might say ineffectually and generally only on matters of sexual morality. The only time he had come close to open opposition to the government his wings had been quickly clipped by the PM's threat to abolish denominational schools under the guise that they were an affront to EU Anti-discrimination Laws. The Chancellor laughed. He might not like the man next door but he admired his ability to engage in blackmail while citing the very highest moral principles, a modern version of the iron fist in the velvet glove. 'We are the absolute monarchs of old, re-costumed for the twenty first century.' At the same time he rather revelled in the approaching discomfort. Everyone knew he believed in nothing more spiritual than the pound sterling but the PM had made rather a production of his deep religious convictions.

The Chancellor picked up the phone and put himself through on the PM's personal line. He was the only member of the government so authorised. Authorised by him as one of the many quid pro quo for withdrawing from the leadership contest. In reality, he liked to think, most things the government did were authorised by him when they weren't actually initiated by the 'Government in Exile' as Number 11 was increasing known. He did not consider the PM a strategic thinker: he was a salesman and an ambulance chaser, gifted with a quick tongue and an amazing capacity to believe his own propaganda. He might think he was running the country but Brian Fellows was the effective force.

"Not disturbing you, I hope?"

"Of course not. Never get to bed before one o'clock. What's on your mind?"

"Something you need to read. I'll come through."

Alex Trent would not give him the satisfaction of a show of emotion but Fellows knew the blow would be felt and at two levels. Trent would see it as a betrayal of a card carrying Christian, himself, as well as a political threat.

"Dear Doctor Harding. Such an easy man to deal with. Kept the rabble in check. We need a replacement with a killer instinct before this gets out of hand."

"Killer instinct!" The PM mused. "Ah! I see! You're after his job"

Fellows laughed. Trent should know better than to joust with him. "I would be if I looked as good as Freddie in a dress." This was a reference to Freddie Maybury who had been the PM's Minister without Portfolio and general hit man until The Star had photographed him in drag in a bar in Morocco, wrapped round a youth of about thirteen.

Alex Trent felt back footed as he so often did when dealing with his Chancellor. It was a clever response, taking up his joke and playing it back with just enough intimation of his Achilles heel.

"Well if you aren't after his job?"

"It's a question of who may get it. I've heard of one or two dark horses recently and I don't think we want a man who lacks conspicuous enthusiasm for the Third Way." He looked at the PM as though questioning whether he understood the point and for clarification added. "We don't want a Catholic primate armed with a social agenda more radical than a French lorry driver."

Now it was the PM's turn to feel superior. "You have no need to worry about Carterton getting a red hat. I'll have a word with my friend, Archbishop Stanford. Rest assured he'll be kept in the Wigwam until retirement."

"I hope you are right. Having amputated the Left Wing of the Party we don't want it transplanted to Westminster Cathedral."

"You really are a pessimist, Brian. You should be like me and go to church more often. Keeps you spiritually and politically healthy. Good night."

Alex Trent regretted the loss of his transvestite Minister without Portfolio. Freddy would have dealt with the whole issue of the Westminster appointment and Carterton's political interference without him having to waste time on the matter. He needed a replacement who was totally trustworthy and totally devious, two qualities which rarely went together, especially if their possessor became redundant.

He was interrupted by Mike Doran, his Press Secretary, with the daily media synopsis. "Nothing worth worrying about today.... unless you happen to be the Leader of the Opposition....the temporary leader, that is."

"Not too temporary, I trust. He's our best guarantee of being re-elected." Trent motioned to Doran to sit. "Mike, I'd like you to turn your mind to the Archbishop of Liverpool. You know the social conscience of the North. He's probably just a harmless old buffer who alienates more than he influences but a spot of insurance could be in order. Anything which suggests that he's a bit dotty."

Doran laughed. "You mean like a resurrection of the Red Dean of the last century. The tabloids had lots of fun with him and they were relatively restrained in those days."

"You know, I had forgotten all about him. But you're right. The Anarchic Archbishop sounds like a suitable successor."

The following day Doran was the PM's first visitor. Trent had sent for him and had The Star, The Chronicle and The Post spread across his desk. "The Star should pay me for christening him 'the Anarchic Archbishop'." He pointed to the banner headline of page 5. "And look at the Herald....'Wigwam Warrior' but only in 24 point. As for The Chronicle, they've made him an Anglican."

He looked at Doran and saw his disappointment. "I'm not worried, Mike. You've done a pretty good job and I especially like your theme in The Star of a resurrection in Merseyside linking Carterton with the Red Dean. I think we can both claim some journalistic credit."

"Do you want me to keep up the pressure?"

"No need. Stanford has been on the phone to Rome since Monday and I'm told the Organisation is mobilising. I think we can leave the civil war to the professionals."

Peroni was distinctly unamused and his Monsignor was displaying even greater signs of concentration on the file in front of him.

"What is this man playing at? The last thing we want is adverse publicity. We are just beginning to get over the scandal of priests who interfere with children and now we have one who excites the British tabloids by attacking the government. I would not normally trouble the Holy Father with such ill tidings but it adds increased urgency to the Westminster appointment."

Monsignor Fanelli was not sure whether he was required to respond or ignore the outburst: Peroni was a mercurial master. He attempted both actions by nodding sagely and continuing to stare at the file. Not for the first time, he misread the situation.

"Don't distress yourself, Monsignor," Peroni remarked sarcastically. "A relaxed disposition is a good indicator of long life but not of rapid preferment. It would seem that you have made your choice."

Fanelli coughed. "But Eminence I am not yet skilled in interpreting the significance of such events. I do not yet have your ability to place them in the big picture." If in doubt, use flattery, had long been his motto.

"Monsignor! The whole purpose of a Curial posting is to provide you with the big picture, as you put it. Decisions here have to take into account the whole structure of the Church. It is not just a religious reality; it is also a practical reality. What can be seen, naively, as the right action at one time in one place may be totally in contradiction of our best interests in a dozen other places on a variety of time scales. The Church, Monsignor, is a multi-national corporation which just happens to be the mind of Jesus Christ on earth. The Curia is the international boardroom and the cardinals are the directors. The Holy Father is the president. It is we and we alone who have sufficient information on which to determine policy worldwide. Of course, there are those who resent this centralisation of power but without it the barque of Peter would be a rudderless ship. Men like Archbishop Carterton, often well intentioned, are like rocks in the ocean. They endanger the whole voyage. Men like you, Monsignor, are given a unique opportunity to prove that you have the capacity to become a navigational officer on this sacred ship, maybe even a future first mate or captain. I suggest that you look to your manual of seamanship a little more attentively."

Peroni set off in the direction of the Pope's apartment without waiting for a reaction. Fanelli wondered if the life of a simple parish priest might not be his true vocation. Perhaps the peccadillo's of holy women and the smell of poverty were no more injurious to one's health than a Curial posting. Conversely, an ability to mix metaphors might guarantee him a red hat.

"Sit, Stephano. Please sit."

Peroni reluctantly did as he was ordered, fearing that sitting might undermine the urgency of the situation.

"The Westminster appointment, Holiness. It is now most pressing. Archbishop Carterton has moved from Archbishop's House to St Kevin's Presbytery. He has dispensed with his staff and now lives with a Fr Nolan. A man of eccentric character to say the least. He owns a dog called Kyrie, has Guinness delivered by the crateful and says a monthly Mass for prostitutes. The Nuncio is appalled by the situation and the tabloids are in hot pursuit. We need an English primate to call him to account."

Pius seemed to only half hear him. Peroni waited, and then prompted. "Holiness?"

The Pope held up his hand. "Please, Stephano. How would you describe my appointments to the College of Cardinals?"

"Wise, well considered, sound." Where was this all leading? "Conservative?"

"In the main. Reflecting the need for a return to tradition."

"When I was elected. What did you think then?"

Peroni smiled. "I was amazed, Holiness. Amazed. A non-Italian! A Pole! Even more amazed when you chose me. Your election was an unexpected choice which turned out to have been an inspired choice."

"Inspired!" The Pope seemed distracted. "Yes! All our choices should be inspired. When you use the word 'inspired' to describe my election and the word 'sound' to describe my appointments you are telling me something. Something I needed to hear. Thank you, Stephano, for all you have done for me, for our Church." Curiously the Pope then blessed his Secretary. "When you do something for the last time, you must be sure to get it right."

Kirst phoned. "Well? Has he decided?"

"Who knows? I haven't seen him like this before."

Kirst was annoyed by Peroni's seeming resignation. "How am I supposed to safeguard doctrine with loose cannon like Carterton going unchecked?"

"May I remind you, Cardinal Prefect that I, too, am concerned for a speedy resolution but I am not the Holy Father. If

you believe that you can expedite a decision, feel free to do so."
Peroni cut the connection.

The Pope asked Sister Maria to join him in prayer. When
they had concluded he said to her.

"Maria, we Poles have suffered much for our faith. Not just in
the past but recently. Our sufferings travel always with us."

"Yes, Holiness."

"In all those years, what kept us going? Why didn't we capitulate to communism as did so many others? Why did the Poles
stay pure?"

The old nun reflected. "I think, Holiness, I think because we
had leaders who spoke out for us. Who rejected publicly what
the communists wanted us to believe. Who would not say that we
were living in a people's paradise when all reason told us we were
not?" She felt proud of the memory.

Thank you, Maria. "Please arrange for Archbishop Carterton
to come to Rome. Let him be told that it is urgent. I don't have
much time left."

CHAPTER 3

Archbishop Carterton sat down with Father Patrick Nolan to his first evening meal at St Kevin's. The cook was Father Nolan himself. He looked down at the assorted items on his plate and found it difficult to identify any of them. Any hint of hunger deserted him but, clearly, not so Patrick Nolan.

"Will ye be sayin' grace, Your Grace?" He asked in a brogue which had resisted thirty years of Scouse colonisation.

"I'm sorry...and call me Bill. Don't forget I'm the lodger and you're the landlord. Bless us O Lord and these gifts which we are about to receive from thy bounty through Christ, Our Lord. Amen."

Father Nolan was shovelling away as though his salvation depended upon it. "Don't mind me, Your Grace....Bill. Living alone is no good for the table manners." He returned to his plate with even greater vigour. Meanwhile Carterton extracted a minute piece of grey matter which might have been meat or vegetable or even something more sinister and did his best to appear convivial.

"Do you do all your own cooking, Pat?"

"Mostly. Sometimes the Mothers' Union send in a casserole or a pie....if it looks like I'm fading away."

The Archbishop assumed this to be a joke since whichever of life's dangers threatened the good father, fading away was not one of them. How could one grow spherical on such a diet? Nolan seemed to read his mind.

"Not to your liking, Bill?"

"It's not that. I think I'm a bit overwhelmed, what with the move and causing all that drama. I've been cloistered for too long."

"You've finished then?"

"I'm afraid so."

"Then just pass your plate across, I'd hate to waste a fine Irish stew." He cast his own plate to one side and began on Carterton's. Suddenly he leapt from the table and disappeared into the kitchen, returning with two bottle of stout. "Get that down you, Bill. There's no better remedy for an upset stomach." He patted his own lovingly. "Mine never lets me down thanks to the Guinness."

Carterton reflected. Twenty four hours previously he had enjoyed a meal of lightly grilled lamb cutlets with croquette potatoes, green beans and buttered carrots accompanied by a half bottle of claret and with sherry trifle to follow. A few days prior to that he had been exercising his episcopal functions in relative tranquillity. He had slept in a bedroom the size of a dormitory and written at a desk made of solid mahogany. He stopped himself. He could go on about the trappings he missed but they were no more than trappings, the Gospel was very clear on that point. He had made his decision and there would be no back sliding.

After dinner he washed the dishes while Pat walked his dog. It was an ancient brute, rather smelly and far friendlier than the Archbishop would have wished. "Wonderful companion. Keeps me fit." While the former might well be true the latter was less evidently so. Pat's walks scarcely lasted ten minutes and the brute, whose name was Kyrie, had to be forced out into the street and returned in a state of collapse.

"If ye don't mind, Bill, we'll watch the Nine O'clock news. I like to be in bed by ten. Ye never know what the night will bring."

"As I said, you're the landlord. You make the rules."

Nolan presented him with another Guinness. "One isn't enough for a grown man. Two is the absolute minimum. Cheers."

Nolan did not so much watch the news as comment upon it. He held strong views on a range of subjects and, Carterton assumed, was unused to anyone disputing his opinions after years of having only Kyrie for an audience. He also appeared to be rather deaf and had the volume turned up so that the bric-a-brac on top of the television occasionally rattled. When the Prime Minister was shown visiting a hospital Nolan fairly shook with rage.

"That sanctimonious idjit. He wouldn't know a bed pan from a frying pan. Prostitutes! That's what they all are and he's the biggest whore of the lot. The girls on Lime Street are better looking and a damned sight more honest." He stopped himself and turned to Carterton. "Sorry, Bill. I'm forgetting I've got company."

"Don't apologise. I tend to agree with you though I'm no expert on how good looking your girls are."

"We'll soon fix that. I'll introduce you. I say a special Mass once a month with confession before and after. I get a good turnout but they're not too strong on confession."

"I never knew that when I was Archbishop."

"You still are....aren't you?"

"Yes. I suppose I am. But I feel different."

"Let me ask you something, Bill. Did you always tell the Cardinal or the Curia everything you were doing as Archbishop?"

"Not if I thought they'd try to stop me."

"Most parish priests are the same. We don't deal in abstractions, we deal with people. We try to help them make sense of their lives, to be kind to each other and, if they have any spare capacity left, to worship God in a more traditional way. Quite often that means cutting the odd corner or turning a blind eye. It also means not attempting to formalise some of our more pragmatic decisions. Just imagine asking the Congregation for the Doctrine of the Faith if it is permissible to give communion to a prostitute. 'Only if she repents and gives up her sinful ways,' would be the stock answer. Putting the same question to the bishop would only make him piggy in the middle. So we lowly priests make a pastoral decision to 'do unto others as we would have done to ourselves'. I hope I haven't shocked you?"

"You've given me food for thought. I spent too long in academe and I think you were sent to de-program me. You've also given me something else."

"What's that?"

"A taste for Guinness. Now good night to you, Pat, before you tell me you buy the stout out of the Poor Box."

"God bless, Bill. And by the way, tomorrow being Friday there's a special treat for dinner....fish fingers."

Carterton said his Office and fell asleep soundly. At one point in the night he though he heard a phone ring but it scarcely disturbed his rest. He woke refreshed and optimistic. Any doubts about his decision to move to St Kevin's Presbytery had vanished. He looked forward to breakfast with Nolan: he could hardly deconstitute toast.

However, Nolan was absent and only Kyrie was available to eat with him, a problem since he had no idea what dogs ate or even if they did eat breakfast: his days of insulation from the real world were surely over. At last he found a tin which bore a dog-like name and Kyrie expressed his appreciation in hearty gulps. He was about to attend to his own needs when there was a knock on the kitchen door and a middle aged woman entered without waiting to be asked.

"Where's Fr Pat? And who are you?"

Carterton looked up from the toaster and rather delighted in his new found anonymity. "The answer is that I don't know....to both your questions."

"Are you a priest?"

"Yes."

"Then you'd better get into the church we're waiting for the seven o'clock Mass."

The Archbishop entered St Kevin's unshaven and in vestments more suited to his corpulent host than to his own narrow frame. However, any embarrassment he might have felt dissipated when he saw his congregation. It reminded him of pictures of emigrants to America about to disembark on Ellis Island. The only difference being numerical. By a certain symmetry, seven o'clock Mass at St Kevin's attracted exactly seven people. But, within minutes, the familiar words had removed all strangeness and he was simply a priest performing an age old ritual.

As his ancient acolyte read the lesson he wondered whether he should give a short homily, unaware of Nolan's custom. Used to preaching in a cathedral, seven of the Faithful seemed a more rigorous test. He would be talking with rather than to his audience.

"My dear friends." He began. "I am new here and so I don't really know you. I don't know which aspect of today's readings resonates best with your lives but two points certainly resonate with mine." He paused realising his language was unsuitable. "I mean which bit strikes a chord best. For me it is the fact that Jesus actually spoke to the woman at the well. To most Jews of the time her non-Jewishness made her inferior and her way of life added to her disgrace. Yet here we have the Son of God asking her for a favour. I take away two lessons for myself. First, God, in this case Jesus, actually does ask us for favours. In His gift of free will He has given us a power, a power which we often misapply, to act as his agents, his delegates. In a sense He can only act through us. Second, He often asks that favour of the least powerful, the despised. What they can deliver may be minute in the scheme of things but the opening of their free will to God's will enables Him to act with all His power. Any act of love, no matter how trivial, is like a crack in the dam through which the Holy Spirit can penetrate the world. We are all called to be Dam Busters. May God bless you all?"

In the sacristy Carterton shook hands with the acolyte and thanked him. The old man, Bob Lewis was his name, maintained an unnerving silence as he tidied the vestments away. After several minutes he spoke.

"I've been thinking about what you said in there. It wasn't bad for a first sermon. I hope you can stay with us. Fr Paddy needs a break and someone to walk the dog. He paused. "You know, I think I've seen you somewhere before."

Carterton returned to his cold toast and found Fr Nolan tucking into bacon and eggs. "Would you like some? Sorry I couldn't wait."

"No thanks. Toast is fine."

"Thanks for saying Mass. I've been at the hospital. Young mother, died at 5.00 am this morning. Hope I didn't wake you."

"So there was a phone call?"

"Ay there was. At 2.15am exactly. Bugger of a time to get out of a warm bed."

"You should have called me."

"Don't worry, I will."

CHAPTER 4

William Carterton had scarcely unpacked his bags at St Kevin's when he was installed as Archbishop of Westminster having been confirmed as cardinal by Pius two days before the latter's death. Alex Trent was present as were several cabinet ministers, some minor royals and representatives of the Anglican and other denominations. Presence in Westminster Cathedral was by invitation only and security was tight in view of the terrorist threat.

Carterton had simplified the ceremony as much as possible and asked Fr Nolan to act as one of the concelebrants, the only parish priest amongst the bishops. Far from welcoming the opportunity he had tried to avoid it but Carterton had bought his acquiescence with the promise of Guinness galore to follow.

Conscious of his recent sermons in Liverpool, there was an air of expectancy when he began his homily.

"I am deeply honoured that so many of you have, today, taken precious time away from urgent matters to be a part of this investiture. I am deeply moved that we have learned to set aside religious differences which have bedevilled civilisation for centuries. Not only have other Christian denominations graced the occasion but also representatives of our Jewish, Moslem, Hindu, Sikh and Buddhist communities. It is to these religious leaders that I particularly wish to appeal today.

We all carry baggage from a past when we interpreted our respective faiths as being hostile to one another rather than complementary. What we share is vastly more important than any differences we may uncover. All our holy books tell us to act with justice and charity, not just towards our own but towards mankind in general. Whatever the future holds for me in this office I hope and pray that fraternal dialogue with other creeds will always be a priority.

When we survey our world we still see examples of appalling bigotry, of men, women and children suffering or being taught to hate in the name of religion. We see poverty, not just in the developing world, but in our own cities. We often accept the material benefit's which result from accident of birth, or intelligence, or other chance events without accepting that these are gifts from God and that He demands that we share his gifts. We are not their owners, we are merely their trustees. One day we will have to account for that trust.

My own experience of life reinforces the old saying that 'virtue is its own reward' and not just in a sense of having done the right thing but in a very practical sense. Acts of self-sacrifice today often bring blessings or avert potential disasters. Giving alms to the poor, as all our great religions command us to do, fulfils a moral obligation though it would be nice to think that we did so out of a real compassion for the less fortunate. But, at a lower level, it goes some way to avoiding an angry under class with the potential to explode against being condemned to poverty in a world of plenty.

Each year vast sums of money are spent on defence. Money which could otherwise be used to provide reasonable standards of nutrition, housing, health and education worldwide. If that money was so allocated, the need for defence would largely vanish. Indeed, the belief that greater quantities of ever more powerful weapons can provide security is quite fallacious. A few fanatical terrorists can create mayhem in the most powerful nation on the planet, bypassing its nuclear arsenal. The phrase 'war against terror' may sound powerful. It may help convince an electorate that its leaders are averting danger. In reality they are doing no more than attempt to deal with effect while the causes remain unresolved and ever resurgent. A more realistic and a far more moral defence must arise from the fact that people who feel fairly treated and have a real stake in life, no matter how humble, are disinclined to make war.

I recall the Victorian era cartoons which depicted the starving peering in through the window at the rich family feasting. Today television pro-

vides the world's starving with the same window on the rich man's table. The miracle is not that they protest too loudly but that that they protest too quietly. Large armies and missile systems can do little to protect the teeming cities of the developed world from the wrath of angry men with little to lose. We can, of course, spend still greater sums on internal security and restrict the freedom of our own citizens in order to make acts of terrorism more difficult. But if we just have the generosity, or even the self-interest, to ensure a more even distribution of wealth and a less flagrant use of power to bully weaker nations, these measures become unnecessary.

For fear that you would think me hypocritical I admit that the Catholic Church in this country has often failed to provide an example of generosity in terms of both its dealings with other religions and with the poor. I hope to play some small part in making good these omissions. Within the next few weeks I intend to make certain changes in my personal living arrangements which will reflect a desire to live more simply and to be freer to practice what I preach. I also intend to speak out for our fellow humans, be they here or abroad, who lack an advocate. I say this not because I see myself as some knight in shining armour but because it is what I believe the Gospel commands me to do. I am only too conscious of Lazarus who begged at the Temple gates and of the rich man who was condemned to Hell for ignoring his needs. If we continue to ignore such needs we will create our own hell as recent events have so amply demonstrated.

I realise that, in speaking like this, I may cause offence to some in high office. If I do so, I hope they will accept that I am acting out of conscience and not out of malice. Above all, what I would like to achieve in the weeks ahead is an ecumenical grouping of religious leaders from across the spectrum in order to establish a common purpose in attacking those injustices which are manifest in society. If our politicians are unwilling to do so for fear of an electoral backlash. If they do not trust the generosity and common sense of their electorates then we, the unelected, must speak out."

Traditionally it has been the role of the fourth estate, the media, to maintain a critical eye on politicians, business leaders and, indeed, church leaders. Today, with some admirable exceptions, we can no longer rely on the media performing this duty. Globalisation and amalgamation have ensured that there are just a few major media conglomerates. This control of information has put extraordinary power in the hands of a few, largely unaccountable individuals. This power often exceeds that of national *governments and extends far beyond national boundaries. Politicians are afraid to promote policies detrimental to media magnates for fear of reprisals. It has been said that the price of freedom is eternal watchfulness. It might just as well be said that the price of freedom is access to unbiased information. This process of near media monopoly has gone a long way towards denying the electorate that access. The self-serving views of one man can be disseminated through a multitude of outlets, worldwide if necessary, and woe to that politician who dares cry 'foul'. The nexus between the people and the parliament has been replaced by a new and sinister nexus between the media mogul and the politician, the media mogul and the people. He is the new puppet master and we are the puppets: the political puppets are controlled by fear, the people puppets by disinformation. In my Easter Sunday sermon in Liverpool I referred to the flow of power away from ordinary people to politicians over the past decades. That remains a danger but politicians are at least periodically accountable though the ballot. Not so the near-invisible men who decide what we shall be told and how it shall be told.*

I draw these matters to your attention, not out of any sense of despair but out of a real sense of hope. Acting together in a multitude of small ways we can re-shape our own country and ultimately our world. But remember this. God created us with free will. He could have fashioned a different creation. One in which humanity was programmed to behave according to His will with no other option. In a sense God surrendered power to us, the believers of whatever faith. He acts through us. We are His necessary agents. That is why we have to harness our own meagre talents as a conduit for His grace.

Finally I ask your prayers as the Catholic Church begins the process of electing a new pope. Pope Pius, by his courage and determination, achieved the seemingly unachievable. May his successor display the same virtues in tackling the unfinished business.

May God bless you all."

Brian Fellows caught the gist of the new Cardinal's homily on the six o'clock news. He immediately phoned Alex Trent.

"How did you enjoy the sermon?"

"Sermon! It was an indirect diatribe against the government and highly offensive to the United States. The man's quite mad. That extraordinary performance when he was Archbishop of

Liverpool contained sufficient evidence for him to be put away quietly but no! Pius must also have been mad, himself, when he promoted him. As though that wasn't enough, he fired another salvo at Sebastian Hart and others like him. Someone must have pressed his self-destruct button."

Fellows suppressed his enjoyment of the PM's discomfort. As with most leaders he had noted an increasing tendency towards paranoia. They became prime ministers rather in awe of their task. They gathered confidence, not least from the supine behaviour of lesser mortals. They began to believe in their own omniscience and, when this came under challenge, their only plausible explanation had to be a plot since simple misjudgement was no longer logically possible. Trent was heading down that particular road.

"You don't think he had a point though, scarcely an original one. After all we are supposed to be the party of the under privileged."

"That is exactly what we are. Why I've increased spending on social security, on hospitals, on housing. Given the pensioners a Christmas bonus. Added a winter fuel supplement. We're an example to the rest of the world. If he had any sense of justice he'd have held this government up as a shining example."

"Are you going to point that out? I think you should issue a press release."

"You issue it. You're the Chancellor." Trent was not one to cause unnecessary offence, not if he could pass the ammunition to someone else.

"Very well. I'll give it priority. I wonder what he meant by unfinished business? Ominous don't you think?"

Trent relaxed. It was not often he got one over on his Chancellor. However, his satisfaction was short lived when he saw the morning papers. The Post ran with the headline.

Chancellor praises Cardinal's recipe for Justice
Government abandons Ideals

Brian Fellows, Chancellor of the Exchequer, commenting on the inaugural homily of the new Roman Catholic Cardinal

Archbishop of Westminster, William Carterton, said that the Cardinal showed "A strong social conscience and a determination to lead by example". Asked whether he felt that his remarks about the unequal distribution of wealth in this country were critical of the present government, he replied, "Emphatically not, we have simply carried out the Prime Minister's pre-election pledge to maintain a responsible economic policy. This means spending according to our means and not according to our ideals".

The Economics Editor of The Star wrote that, "The Star will never abandon its ideals of defending the ordinary citizens of this country. We have never taken an economic rationalists approach, preferring to put people before doctrinaire theories".

Trent was furious. Fellows was unfazed. "I did what you told me."

"I didn't tell you to give our opponents a free kick, which is exactly what you have done. Not living up to our ideals! A line more in keeping with the opposition than a senior cabinet member."

"Unfortunately I agree but they edited the press release. My press secretary has spoken to their editor. There'll be a retraction tomorrow."

"Fat lot of use that will be. The damage is done." He gave Fellows a stony glare. "Either you're losing the plot or you're plotting. Which is it?"

"Alex, I'm going to pretend I never heard that remark. We have too much to achieve to let a misunderstanding mar our working relationship."

At Prime Minister's Question time, the Leader of the Opposition rose and looked smugly across the Chamber.

"Can the Prime Minister assure the nation that he is not about to disband our armed forces and distribute the savings to various Third World dictators in the faint hope that a little of his largess may trickle down to their poverty stricken subjects?"

"Clearly the Leader of the Opposition has been reading science fiction again and confusing it with fact. No! I have no intention of disbanding or even reducing the number of Armed Forces personnel or their weaponry."

He was rewarded with loyal chuckles and "Hear, hears".

"Then does the Prime Minister categorically reject the advice of the Roman Catholic Archbishop of Westminster?"

"I am always happy to receive advice on religious matters from the clergy but I do not feel constrained to consult them on matters of defence."

"I find your reply unconvincing and so, I fear, will our NATO allies. Talk of unilateral disarmament from influential sources in this country cannot be passed off with glib phrases. A prime minister with any strength of character would denounce such talk in the strongest terms. If you are not up to the job you should resign. I'm sure your Chancellor would be prepared to replace you."

Trent was angered by this further reference to Fellows. "The honourable member may not have noticed that we have in this country a tradition of free speech. I believe that Cardinal Carterton has that right and I have no intention of engaging in chest beating when he chooses to exercise it. The fact that you raise the issue demonstrates your own disregard for that tradition and gives the British people a clear indication of the fascist policies you would implement if elected. Fortunately for democracy, your party is never likely to be elected while you remain its leader and I can suggest any number of your front bench who would willingly take over a task which is beyond your meagre talents."

There was merriment on the government benches but Trent's victory was soured by these regular references to the Prime Minister-in-Waiting. This feeling was exacerbated when Fellows leant across and said.

"Well done, Alex. Did you notice how his loyal deputy almost applauded? But don't demolish him completely. We need him to win the next election for us." He appeared to become aware of the double entendre. "Not that I'm saying you couldn't win it single handed.

CHAPTER 5

Obituaries for Pius XIII and analysis of his long pontificate kept the Western media busy for days. Sebastian Hart, his conservative views even more firmly entrenched following the Cardinal's sermon, made sure that his editors had a clear indication of the type of man who should succeed Pius and connected this with a eulogy to the Polish Church. It is interesting to compare a feature from Hart's London broadsheet, The Post, with that of the Catholic weekly, The Sentinel.

The Post Religious Affairs Correspondent, Phillip Stowe, after a good deal of editorial guidance, wrote the following piece.

Pius XIV

The legacy of Pius XIII cannot be overstated. Faced with a Western world practicing an increasingly subjective morality, he stood resolutely for traditional Catholic values. While other mainstream Christian religions seemed unable to agree on something as fundamental as the divinity of Christ, Pius was never wavering in his message to Catholics. For some this proved his arch conservatism but, for most, it re-emphasised that Christ had founded his Church on a rock. Two millennia previously that

rock was Peter. No one could doubt that Pius was the contemporary embodiment.

Pius knew only too well the inhumanity of atheistic communism. He also loved Poland, almost as much as he loved his God. Unquestionably the greatest achievement of his pontificate was the freeing of the Polish people from their oppressors and, with this bloodless revolution, the beginning of the end of communist domination of Eastern Europe. Clearly forces other than the Pope contributed to the downfall of the Soviet Empire but it was he who launched the most effective assault, the spirit of the Polish people, that lethal mixture of Catholicism and nationalism. This victory was not, however, without cost. One of the Pope's great sorrows was to see his country turn away from the very Church which had maintained its cohesion. Joining the West involved more than just defeating communism. It meant, too, a defeat for traditional Catholic values, notably over contraception and abortion.

Pius used the papacy in a way in which it had never before been used. He made it an international brand with his face as the logo. Was any other face so universally recognised for such a long period of time? Enemies would argue that this exposure simply replicated the communist style personality cult but this is far from the truth. Pius realised from the outset that a Faith of one billion people spread across five continents was too amorphous to be summarised in a sound bite: it needed a logo. As one critic has argued, he could have used St Peter's as a universal logo. What rot! St Peter's is essentially static and very Western. With himself as the logo, Pius could bring instantly recognisable Catholicism to the four corners of the world. It was a public relations master stroke. Had he chosen a career in marketing he would have made a fortune.

However, the establishment of Pius XIII as the logo of the Catholic Church carried an inherent danger. We have seen, in recent times, how a well-established brand can self-mutate when it changes the formula which made it a success, even when such change is minor. Coca Cola was a case in point but, fortunately for the company, the change of formula was quickly abandoned when sales began to plummet. Not so with an injudicious choice of pope. The church might wait years, decades even, before such an error could be undone. In choosing Pius's successor, the cardinals must choose very carefully. Despite criticisms of conservatism, the late Pope carried his people through the period of greatest change known to man. Each year the world is faced with ethical dilemmas previously unimagined. The new pope must be able to lead on such matters without being sidetracked by the various international fringe movements which preach a vague, humanistic creed. He must, to quote Kipling, be able to "Keep his head when all about him are losing theirs". Two days before his death Pius appeared to deviate from the whole direction of his pontificate by appointing the radical Archbishop of Liverpool to the See of Westminster. It would be unwise for the Conclave to see this last act of a frail and probably confused Pope as other than an aberration and certainly not as a pointer as to the nature of his successor. To do so would be to disregard the consistency of previous appointments in favour of one inexplicable variation.

That is why the new Pontiff must be a man who embodies the strength and moral inflexibility of Pius XIII. Long live Pius XIV.

Arnold Senior, a laicised priest and religious affairs writer, was commissioned to write The Sentinel's obituary.

A NEW POPE FOR A NEW MILLENNIUM

There will be few, no matter how sharply opposed to Pius XIII's leadership, who do not recognise the passing of perhaps the most influential man of the twentieth century. A century in which men such as Hitler and Stalin changed the lives of many, almost always for the worse, but they were simply bit players compared with Pius. Today their insane contribution has largely passed and they are disowned by the nations from which they sprang. Not so the contribution of the 263rd Pontiff: he may not have spoken 'ex cathedra' but his legacy will be permanent.

At a time when many Catholics were embracing a New Testament Jesus, Pius could come across as an Old Testament prophet. His condemnation of moral turpitude and, more divisively, of open debate on non-doctrinal matters pushed many Catholics to the limits of their faith and, sometimes, beyond. Yet even those who lapsed, out of conviction rather than sloth, testified to the man's innate holiness. This became more apparent towards the end of his long reign when he was reported as spending more and more time in private prayer. Nor could those who rejected much of his traditionalism fail to be impressed with his obvious love of youth with all its pretensions, its pimples and its potential.

It is sometimes said that saints are simply ordinary people (with all the failings that this implies) who do extraordinary things. By that description, Pius is clearly a saint. But, like most of us, he was a prisoner of his experience. He had the siege mentality which comes from formative years under an atheistic, totalitarian regime magnified by the uniquely Polish prism of religion and nationalism. It is dangerous to claim insight into the workings of another's mind, too often we are unconscious even of our own mixed motives. However, there is a widespread agreement that Pius saw himself as a warrior Pope, a Commander-in-Chief and, in so doing, he never lost sight of two fundamental principles of war: maintenance of the aim and concentration of force. Thus such burning issues as the poor of South America and the associated liberation theology had to be sacrificed in order to defeat communism. How much moral anguish such decisions cost him we will never know but they cannot have been easy. However Pius had seen how territorial wars could be lost by attempting to fight simultaneously on too many fronts. One might even say that Adolf Hitler was his inadvertent mentor.

As with all successful military commanders he had to both enforce strict discipline whilst fostering high morale: an army divided within its ranks is an army inviting defeat. The silencing of the theologian, Hans Küng; the unilateral decision to dismiss Father Arrupe, the Jesuit Superior General, the favourable treatment of the Organisation, all speak of his determination to 'steady the ranks'. It seems likely, too, that the most influential members of the Curia rejoiced in a Pope who appeared to be demolishing the remains of Vatican II and actively encouraged his conformist agenda. Pius might want democracy for Poland but he did not accept it as relevant for his Church.

This paper has often tried to reflect the more liberal side of Catholicism without resorting to a facile criticism of either the Vatican or its master. It has done so in the belief that any organisation which attempts to stifle internal debate will ultimately decay like a dead carcass. At the time of the Reformation, Luther charged, "The hungry sheep look up and are not fed". Many modern Catholics must experience some resonance with his claim.

A different pope could not have achieved what Pius achieved and his achievements were staggering. The world is a better place for his pontificate but the time has come for a new style of pope. The battle has been won, discipline can be relaxed. The essential tenets of the Magisterium are not at risk but the Faithful should be free, nay encouraged, to debate non-core issues and to re-set the Petrine compass for the 21st century. What is needed is a new pope for a new millennium, not a clone of Pius XIII, no matter how much revered.

Alex Trent informed Phillip Stowe, through the medium of his Press Secretary, that he was most impressed with Pius's obituary and would welcome a series of articles promoting the argument in favour of a successor who would 'continue the good work'. It was hinted that a mention in the next Honours List was a distinct possibility. Stowe developed a migraine. He had sacrificed integrity by amending his original obituary under indirect pressure from New York. Now he was being asked to prostitute himself still further. He had moved into religious journalism because it seemed less subject to editorial interference than political reporting: less prestige, greater autonomy. No longer.

In 2 Fantail Gardens, Wimbledon, he confided his dilemma to his wife. Another mistake. Felicity Stowe, a woman who had quit the Church over its anti-feminist bias, viewed Pius's pontificate as an anachronism and his demise as a cause for celebration. As an admirer of Mo Mowland and her courage as Northern Ireland Secretary, she held the Prime Minister responsible for gross treachery towards his former Minister. By his article, Stowe had managed to accommodate two of the men she held in deepest contempt. Her husband may have endeared himself to the powerful, without, but he would pay a high price to the powerful, within. Felicity, in full pursuit of justice, left the Archangel Michael a poor second.

CHAPTER 6

"My dear Desmond, have you read the Sentinel?" Archbishop Stanford's patrician tone was unmistakable. Delile knew the question was rhetorical and waited for him to continue. "Not that I read it myself but the obituary was faxed to me. What have we come to when an unfrocked priest is employed by an allegedly Catholic paper to provide unsolicited advice to anyone stupid enough to read such balderdash?" Stanford laughed. "Not that anyone of importance reads the rag but still.....it is a sign of the lunatic times in which we have to preserve our faith."

"I'm sure you are right, Your Grace. I have always thought of Sentinel readers as rather like Guardian readers. The latter believe that they should be running the country, the former that they should be running the Church. Since there is no danger of any of them running anything more taxing than a cake stall they can propose the pottiest of ideas without fear of having to put them into practice."

Stanford always enjoyed his chats with Desmond: reinforcing one's prejudices was one of life's sweetest pleasures. "Of course, we can't afford to be complacent. Even in our lifetime we have seen the havoc which can be caused by an unfortunate choice of pope and, on the secular scene, madmen have been regularly accorded the highest office. However remote the chance of the College of Cardinals being influenced by voices which are barely Christian let alone Catholic, we must take precautions. And you, my dear Desmond, have long been a fighter for the true faith. I know we can rely on your influence in the Organisation."

"But of course. The leadership has the matter firmly in hand and I think I can promise you an increasingly vocal chorus. But that is not the only matter of concern. Closer to home there is the matter of Cardinal Harding's successor. The Organisation was quite unanimous that you were the most desirable choice and had reason to believe that the Holy Father and his Secretary of State were of similar mind, but now....."

Stanford adopted a tone of surprise. "Of course I am flattered and, unworthy though I am, I must admit to grave misgivings about the new Cardinal." Neither he nor Delile could bring themselves to use Carterton's name.

"It is a travesty! Your Grace, humility has its place but not at the expense of the greater good of the Catholic Church in this country. Cardinal Harding was a saintly man but scarcely a strong leader. We needed a cardinal at Westminster who resembled the late Holy Father, a man of strong conviction, not afraid to proclaim the gospel even when it offends the proponents of situational ethics. You had all the right qualifications. Pope Pius's decision is inexplicable other than in terms of his mental decline. I hate to say this of a Pope whom we admired so much but his last act was a negation of his papacy."

Stanford reflected on what he had just heard. Privately he had to admit that he had been the perfect choice. Some of his fellow bishops and archbishops acted as though offending their fellow man was a more heinous crime than offending God, not a disease from which he, personally, suffered. At the other extreme, Carterton seemed to revel in offending just about everyone.

"Thank you for your kind words, Desmond. Let us pray that the cardinals at the Conclave are in possession of all their faculties. Now that we have a lose canon in Westminster we have an even more pressing need for a sober voice in the Vatican"

Trent invited Carterton to dinner at No 10. He was not unaware of the seductive power of his office. He felt certain that an offer of friendship and a suggestion that he was always willing to take the Cardinal's views into account, provided that they were delivered in private, would be sufficient bait.

It was to be an intimate dinner. Just Trent, his wife Sarah, the Home Secretary and his wife, the Chancellor and his current girlfriend, Serena Page, and the Cardinal. At the last minute Carterton phoned and asked if he could bring his press secretary. Trent was angry but could not easily refuse. So it was that a rather scruffy Shelley joined the illustrious group. To the Cardinal's amazement Shelley had made no effort to dress for the occasion. It was not as though he had dressed down. He had simply worn his normal dress, a tired Donegal tweed jacket and a pair of ancient corduroy trousers. The only item which suggested that he was aware that invitations to Downing Street were highly prized was a tie in the red of New Labour but also bearing the Liverpool Football Club motif.

As practised politicians and the spouses of politicians, there was no hint of Shelley's faux pas except from the Chancellor's girlfriend. As Trent remarked afterwards, she looked twenty one in the face and forty two in the bust. Despite her obvious attractions, Brian Fellows paid her little attention and concentrated on Carterton. Slighted, Ms Page, having ruled out all other potential candidates, decided to flirt with Shelley. It was an unfortunate choice as he remained stoically unresponsive, enjoying instead Trent's rather obvious courting of the Cardinal. Her efforts irritated Shelley while their lack of success infuriated her. If he could not be seduced, he could be humiliated.

"Tell me, is that tie you are wearing the latest style on Merseyside? I've heard that Liverpudlians are consummate trend setters." For a moment all conversation stopped and Shelley was heard to reply. "No love. I'm doing a retrospective for the sixties. You know, when girls like you were fashionable."

Trent noted Fellow's failure to come to the rescue. Ms Page might have invited the retort but Fellow's indifference was another thing. He could not fault his Chancellor's competence but his emotional detachment was a different and worrying matter. While he remained high in the polls he was safe but, one stumble, and he could expect no mercy.

The Cardinal disappointed himself by feeling embarrassed at Shelley's behaviour. His friend was being himself, even to drinking beer with dinner. He realised that he must develop a much tougher hide if he was to encourage an atmosphere of trust in which people behaved naturally and felt it unnecessary to act a part.

Trent had briefed the Home Secretary on the agenda he wished to pursue and, over coffee, he opened the batting.

"I welcomed your initiative in inviting the leaders of other faiths to your investiture. As you realise, recent events have made it all the more important that religion is not used as a tool for fermenting unrest and violence."

"Thank you. I think most faiths have been guilty of self-righteousness, my own included. I just hope we are entering a new era where we will respect what others believe even if it does appear curious from the outside as Catholicism must to many non-Catholics."

"Excellent! As a Christian myself, I couldn't agree more. Here I think the churches and politics have much in common. There is always a strong temptation to use the cause as an excuse for blurring the truth and exploiting the electorate. I think New Labour has generally acted in an ethical fashion and, if I may say so, set a new standard for all politicians. I would like to see us as partners who are steering our respective organisations in the same direction. What do you think, Cardinal?"

Carterton was tempted to prevaricate but he had set himself a goal of honesty. "I am, of course, flattered that the Prime Minister should consider a partnership with a novice cardinal but I am not sure that I could always be relied upon to deliver in the way that a partner must be relied upon. Certainly I would welcome the opportunity to receive your advice and maybe to reciprocate if I felt the Church had a legitimate view. But I suspect this should be a more of a transient arrangement than a concordat."

Trent recovered with practiced skill. "I'm sorry, I used the word partner loosely. Clearly there are many matters on which I would never dream of troubling any church leader. I refer only to those issues where the sacred and the profane overlap. Rather the situation which you have just described."

His Chancellor felt a warm glow. He realised only too well how angry Trent would be at this jumped up cleric rejecting a partnership with his Prime Minister, no matter how one-sided that partnership was intended to remain. He would have to work at maintaining Trent's annoyance. New Labour had monopolised the Christian vote in the last election and the party would be merciless with a leader who alienated such an important constituency.

Driving away from Downing Street, Carterton asked Shelley his impression of the evening.

"I thought it was great. You had him, Trent, back footed. He thought you'd be so flattered by the idea of partnership that you'd roll over for him. Mind you, he'll make a formidable enemy."

"I had no intention of making him an enemy. I just felt I had to begin by stating how I believe relations should exist between Church and State."

"I don't think politicians value honesty or principles. They deal in pragmatism and they sort of expect other leaders to do the same. I mean they've got the Church of England over a barrel with the power of patronage and most of them think the Catholic Church is responsive to the promise of respectability. Do what Trent wants and he'll hold out the promise of a bill to enable a Catholic monarchy to reign over the United Kingdom. Pretty much as you predicted in your sermon"

The Cardinal laughed. "Bow down and adore me and I will give you power over all the nations. I don't think the gospel permit's a pragmatic response."

It was Shelley's time to laugh. "A Prince of the Church who emulates its founder. We're in for a rough old ride."

Trent was undressing for bed and Sarah was removing her makeup.

"Do you think there is any chance they might make him pope and get him off my patch?"

Sarah laughed. "About as much chance as Brian renouncing all claim to your job."

"He'll learn to regret to-night. A man who has alienated Consol needs allies not enemies. I've done my Christian duty in offering the hand of friendship. I can do no more."

Sarah turned out the light quickly. Alex was at his most hypocritical when he invoked religion but her cynicism was hidden in the dark.

"I think another word with Archbishop Stanford may be in order before things get too out of hand."

In the weeks which followed his investiture, Carterton was encouraged by the response from other religious leaders. While there had been some past liaison, formal working parties had only existed between some of the Christian Churches. Now there was sufficient impetus to establish some which included all the major faiths and, more importantly, initial meetings had been characterised by good will.

Following his Liverpool precedent, Carterton had moved out of the Archbishop's House and established himself in more humble surroundings. Shelley believed that it was this determination to live the Gospel which underpinned the response to his initiative. There was no contradiction between the man and the message. That, coupled with the racial riots and their inevitable religious overtones, had provided the catalyst. Conversely, the National Front and fellow travellers maintained their overt hostility towards all religious groups but especially towards non-Christians.

Within the Catholic Church reactions had been mixed. Part of Shelley's job had been to find out the nature of that reaction so that Carterton could aim to maintain unity as he steered a more radical course than any of his predecessors.

At first, without ever admitting ownership, the Organisation had promoted the line that the new Cardinal was moving too far, too fast and without having allowed himself sufficient time to assimilate the complex nature of his role as the Catholic Primate of England and Wales. Again, without any public acknowledgement, Cardinal Peroni had indicated that a groundswell of opinion, contrary to Carterton's ideas, would not cause offence in Rome. At least not to himself and Cardinal Kirst.

Archbishop Stanford was sufficiently encouraged by this hint of Curial policy that he preached a sermon on the subject of inter-faith dialogue. One excerpt gives the flavour of his homily.

"When Our Lord expressed the wish that we should all be one, what exactly did he mean? Did he intend that we should confess an outward unity which masked internal differences arising out of centuries of separate development? Or did he intend that through patience and prayer, our separated brethren should gradually see and embrace the Church as the embodiment of God's will on earth? We are all aware of times when, in order to reach a desirable destination, we have driven too fast for safety. We have to thank God's patience that our intemperate haste has not led to catastrophe. Today we face a similar dilemma. Are we not, perhaps, testing God's patience too much if we rush headlong towards some all-embracing ecumenical association, ignoring or skating over radical differences? Are we not adopting the false logic that the ends justifies the means? God's wisdom is eternal. Unlike us, He is not subject to a human timetable. To try to impose such a timetable, no matter how well intentioned, may be no more than a form of human arrogance. Believe me, I do not speak as an opponent of moves to increase our contact with other faiths, quite the contrary. I welcome such moves but caution the use of the accelerator in favour of a less cavalier but safer use of the cruise control."

Karl Maier was nominally Operations Director at Consol but, in practice, he was much more being effectively the Chief of Staff. The situation was strongly resented by his fellow directors but Maier always seemed a step ahead of the rest so rumblings of discontent took place behind closed doors. Maier's rise within the conglomerate was a source of mystery. He had appeared out of nowhere and risen like a rocket. His background in media was sketchy and his private life unknown. As a relative newcomer, he showed no wish to ingratiate himself with his colleagues or, quite remarkably, with Sebastian Hart, the autocratic Chief Executive and virtual owner of Consol. While much about Maier remained obscure, two things were strikingly evident: his almost intuitive ability to sense danger and his complete lack of conscience. "He's the brother the boss never had." Was the closest anyone had come to explaining his authority.

Karl Maier was alerted to the content of Stanford's sermon. It vindicated his judgement to hold fire following Carterton's only lightly veiled attack on Consol. A schism within the English Catholic hierarchy was ideal. Let the enemy shoot each other while he provided some encouragement. Accordingly he instructed Consol's editors to "Exercise their editorial independence", code within Consol which translated as, using all means to discredit or promote any person, organisation or viewpoint, in line with Hart's thinking or increasingly his own. As usual, the editors obliged.

Shelley produced a synopsis of the press comments for the Cardinal. The Post and the Star shared a common theme expressed in language suited to their very different readerships.

The Post's opening paragraph began:

"The British public has become used to Anglican clerics arguing in public over almost every point of received doctrine. Indeed, it is hard to find a statement in the Apostle's Creed which is not disputed by some Church of England theologian. While it may be possible to be agnostic and remain a member the Church it seems somehow contradictory to claim atheist status and continue to remain a minister. Such inclusiveness may reflect the democratic nature of Anglicanism but its seeming fluidity of recent years has failed to attract Sunday worshipers.

On the other hand, the Roman Catholic Church in most countries (The Netherlands being an aberrant case) has always exercised strong discipline and avoided, at least in public, any hint of serious schism for many centuries. But for how much longer? The newly appointed Cardinal Archbishop of Westminster seems determined to push the boundaries of British Catholicism to new extremes. While some will admire his dispensing with the trapping of office and his openness to other non-Christian denominations, concerns are already being raised that he is something of a loose cannon. Even his appointment was controversial, the last act of a dying and, possibly, mentally enfeebled Pope.

Cardinal Carterton appears to be taking the example of the Gospel to heart in a way that has rarely been practiced by his predecessors. Some Catholics see this as exemplary, others as implied criticism of previous office holders. Some would go so far as to say that the Carterton lifestyle is a challenge to the lifestyle of popes, fellow cardinals, bishops and not a few parish priests.

Are we witnessing simply a naive academic trying to come to terms with an office for which he is unsuited by experience? Or are we witnessing a populist cleric who may have ambitions far beyond Westminster? Having a web site devoted to one's sermons suggests that the Cardinal is aiming for a wide audience and may be seeking an individual power base.

Already Archbishop Stanford, recently tipped for the Westminster appointment, has raised concerns about the Primate's accelerating rate of change. In this he has the support of the powerful but secretive Organisation which commands the loyalty of some of the most committed and influential Catholics. But for Archbishop Stanford to speak out publicly, albeit in general terms, it seems likely that he must have received encouragement from within the Vatican Itself.

Though there is no longer serious enmity between Anglicans and Catholics in England, Catholics have taken a quiet satisfaction in watching the civil wars within the Anglican community. Perhaps the time has come for Anglicans to savour the co-religionists copying their behaviour. If some sort of truce is not concluded quickly, one of the first tasks of the new pope will be to discipline his turbulent sons.

Cardinal Carterton's remarks about the media suggest a sense of paranoia which is not open to rational argument and, on this basis, they are to be ignored rather than challenged.

The Star took a more brutal approach:

"First we had New Labour, now we have New Catholicism. But can the trick work twice on an already disillusioned public? New Labour promised us politicians without sleaze and signally failed to deliver. New Catholicism promises us bishops who live in council houses, ideally as close as possible to the local mosque. Cardinal Carterton may well be an A plus academic but he is not an A plus student of human nature. The people do not want their leaders to live in conditions which many of them endure. At a practical level they know that the work of leadership is enhanced by decent accommodation. At a personal level they need to feel that their own efforts or those of their children will lead to a legitimate improvement in their conditions of life, not a voluntary rejection of a little greater comfort.

Jesus of Nazareth is a shining example of a good man who shunned personal possessions in order to be free to preach his message. But he lived two thousand years ago, in a different land, without a family to support and amongst a conquered people. His life was very different from life today as we experience in the United Kingdom. The ordinary people of this country, the people to whom this newspaper is dedicated, have suffered enough. Many of them have known war and rationing, crippling inflation and high unemployment. They have been told that yesterday's enemies are today's friends and they must adjust to the fact. They have been told that they are now more European than British even though for years they were rejected by Europe: a Europe they had saved from fascism.

As for his attacks on the media. They have become only too common when politicians or business leaders are trying to place responsibilities for the world's ills on shoulders other than their own. It is sad when a church leader chooses the same debased currency. The Star believes that its reputation needs no additional defence.

So we say this to the British people. Let us enjoy the fruits of our labours and sacrifices and not be plagued by a false guilt that we should live poorer and embrace beliefs which are quite alien to our character. Let us be proud to be British and not blackmailed into believing that we are either unworthy or that we should are obliged to sacrifice our unique culture in the cause of European sameness.

The Chronicle took an opposite view:

Christianity defines the cardinal virtues as faith, hope and charity and we now appear to have a Cardinal who believes in them. His rejection of an affluent lifestyle is surely a concrete illustration of his faith in the values inherent in the Gospel. His appeal to all religious leaders to unite behind their core beliefs is certainly a statement of hope in an area previously considered too controversial. His concern for the poor and oppressed, manifest in his sermons as Archbishop of Liverpool and repeated on his accession to Westminster, underwrite his charity. In short, Cardinal William Carterton is something of a rarity, at least in the developed world. We have seen his like from time to time in South America but rarely in Europe or the United States.

Already he is being identified as a threat by some, both inside and outside his own Church. For others he is the true face of Christianity. The man who appointed him was himself a contradiction: a Pope who undermined the Soviet Union yet who was opposed to liberation theology in South America. A deeply spiritual man but a consummate actor. A priest and a politician. Too conservative to permit ordination of women yet his last act was wildly radical in his appointment of Cardinal Carterton. Perhaps he would have been safer to permit women priests! But then the founder of Christianity also lived dangerously.

CHAPTER 7

The formal procedure following the death of the Pope had begun. Though not entirely unexpected, the suddenness of the news did come as a surprise for, as one observer has noted, the pope's health is not usually admitted to be of concern until rigor mortis is well advanced. The Camerlengo, Cardinal Gaspari, had verified the death in the prescribed manner by calling the Pope three times by name. Having received no response he had authorised the death certificate and notified the Cardinal Vicar of the Diocese of Rome. The Church then embarked on the nine day period of mourning. The papal seal and the Pope's ring, known as the Ring of the Fisherman, were broken. The Pope's death had, in effect, rendered the Curia redundant. However, this did not mean that prominent cardinals lost both the prospect of reinstatement and interim influence. Peroni fitted this category.

During the hiatus, the government of the Church fell to Gaspari assisted by three cardinals, elected by the College of Cardinals, and replaced every three days with three new cardinals. This regular turnover is stipulated to prevent any faction from obtaining excessive power, especially where an election is delayed.

Already the cardinals were beginning to assemble in Rome for the first Conclave of the new millennium along with representatives of the world's media. Peroni had made it clear that, to paraphrase a wartime expression, "Loose lips endanger the dignity of the process" by which Pius's successor would be chosen. If the Secretary of State could not control the secular media, he intended to control the College of Cardinals. Monsignor Franelli had been given the task of ensuring that no cardinal or other senior cleric did other than refer media requests to the Vatican Press Office with its conservative filtration mechanism. Peroni knew it was an impossible task and Franelli knew it was an impossible task and the latter believed that it was a prelude to his dismissal. However, the Monsignor's capacity for fear appeared to have peaked and less and less did he live in terror of Peroni's power. If the worst thing that could happen to him was a posting to Sicily, then so be it. Peroni detected his assistant's uncharacteristic sang froid and it added to his own sense of impending doom.

He paid a visit to Cardinal Kirst and hinted that the atmosphere surrounding the Conclave was ominous. Kirst responded in his usual non-committal manner.

"In what way do you feel that, how shall I say it, that this Conclave is special……..dangerous even?"

Peroni did not want to be drawn. "That is precisely why I am asking for your opinion. I simply have a nebulous feeling and I wondered if you shared it?"

"I think that all Conclaves produce a tension and the interval between Conclaves has been so long. Perhaps we are just out of tune."

"It is more than that. There is a sense of radicalism in the air. The Church in Asia, in Africa and in South America has long felt sidelined. Such views are understandable but they are also parochial. Our late Holy Father saw the big picture and we do not want a successor who is locked into a world view conditioned merely by local issues."

Kirst remained inscrutable. "What do you intend to do about this perceived crisis?"

Peroni was losing patience. "First I had hoped to reach an agreement with some of the Vatican cardinals that we face a real danger and enlist their help. Of course, if they consider me as simply paranoid I can expect no such support. That is why I turned to you in, the first instance, to test the reality of my beliefs. I would value your advice. So Cardinal Prefect, am I being alarmist or do we have something to fear?"

"Of course, I am not so well informed as the Secretary of State. I do not have access to your intelligence network." A snub to Peroni's renowned secrecy. "But from what little I do hear, I think there could be a groundswell to appoint a non-Curial figure, possibly someone from the Third World and, if that is the case, it is hard to believe that the Conclave would choose a conservative. To do so would be to send out mixed signals. Why raise expectations by making a radical decision which turns out to have a conservative outcome. So, on balance, I think you have cause to be anxious."

"Thank you, Helmut." It was the first time Peroni had ever used his Christian name, a sure sign that he must be worried and seeking allies. "May I go a little further and ask if you see such a choice of pope, should it ever occur, as placing the Church at great risk?"

"I have always believed in hastening slowly."

"Then would you be prepared to use your influence to educate those fellow cardinals who might, from the very highest of motives, be contemplating such a hazardous course of action?"

"I am not sure that my influence is sufficient to sway anyone but you may regard me as of similar mind to yourself."

Peroni clasped Kirst's hand in his with a warmth never previously displayed. "Thank you again, Helmut. I knew I could count on you. And now I must do a little more consulting. Good night."

The logistic of transporting one hundred and forty cardinals to Rome, accommodating them and feeding them cannot be done in twenty four hours. Consequently there is a loss of control until the Conclave Itself gets under way. This period of relative freedom is sometimes known to old Vatican hands as 'playschool'. A reference to the fact that all sorts of silly games are entered into only to be abandoned because no one can agree the rules. On one infamous occasion, as Peroni liked to quote in his rare light hearted moments, a French cardinal had suggested sarcastically that the next Holy Father should have an Asian mother, an African father, live in South America with a Harvard degree, speak French with an English accent and wear an Akubra hat. That way he would be truly representative of the Universal Church. The joke was taken seriously by a fellow cardinal who received a poor translation. In an unguarded moment he passed this on to a journalist posing as a Curial messenger. Soon afterwards, the public was made aware that the French cardinals were likely to vote for Cardinal Pasquami of Uruguay on the basis that he had a lineage which included an African slave, a Chinese market gardener, was multi-lingual and had a degree from the Sorbonne. The absence of an Akubra hat was ignored.

Cardinal Murengo hosted a small meeting of African cardinals in his room. Not noted for subtlety he came straight to the point.

"Brothers! It is time that Africa had a pope. Our late Holy Father had a unique experience which enabled him to concentrate of the demise of the Soviets and the emancipation of the Poles, amongst others. Now it is time for the long suffering peoples of Africa to enter Christian consciousness as never before. We, of the second largest continent, with a population heading towards 1000 million are virtually invisible on the world screen. An African pope can command that sort of visibility. We owe it to our people to ensure his election at this Conclave." His eyes raked the room, half in challenge, and half in menace. "Are you with me brothers?"

Cardinal Sawola of Mozambique asked, disingenuously: "And whom did you have in mind, Thomas?"

"That is for the Holy Spirit to decide. I am merely raising the issue in principle."

The meeting lasted for several hours. All agreed that it should be Africa's turn but as to whom? Murengo's guests departed into the Roman night leaving their host confused more than angry. 'It is so obvious,' he mused. 'I represent the most populous nation in Africa. I am the senior African cardinal. I speak four languages and a variety of dialects. I served for three years in Rome as a monsignor. I am the clear choice yet no one was prepared to state it publicly.' Murengo decided to sleep on the events of this evening before beginning the telephone assault.

Cardinal Jose Luca took a less public approach. One by one he telephoned his South America colleagues. His message was simple. Liberation theology was alive and well and biding its time. It was waiting only for a wink from the new pontiff before re-emerging as a force in Latin America. While the thrust of the doctrine resonated with much of the Gospel, in the hands of a few hot headed priests it would surely lead to anarchy followed either by brutal repression or economic disaster or both. It was essential, therefore, that the new pope fully understood the dangers in uncaging the beast which, in turn, meant that a South American of compassionate but conservative bent was the ideal choice.

He was gratified that several cardinals expressed not only strong agreement but also proposed that he was the obvious choice. However, Luca was cynical enough to believe in the old adage that 'whoever enters the Conclave a pope comes out a cardinal'. On this basis, he was adamant that he did not see himself as a candidate though he declined to suggest a suitable alternative. Unfortunately for him, too many interpreted his reticence as genuine.

Cardinal Duffy had once been uncharitable described as having the good looks of a potato and the brain of a turnip. The journalist who had been unwise enough to write these words did little to enhance his career.

Duffy might have lacked finesse but he did not lack cunning. He was realistic enough to know that he would never survive even a first ballot but he intended to ensure that a North American ascended the throne of Peter. He had little time for the whining Curial Europeans who claimed some sort of intellectual remit in doctrinal matters but were only too happy to have their American brethren assume the financial bailout of Vatican finances which occurred with monotonous regularity throughout the 1980s. 'The Power without Responsibility Club' as Duffy referred to them. It was a great pity, he reflected, that there was not a current financial crisis to increase his leverage. In its absence he would simply rely on the Chicago technique of hinting that there was much dirty linen in the ecclesiastical laundry and that he was doing his best to keep it well hidden.

Duffy made a phone call to a senior North American partner of Andrews Robinson, International Accountants. He raised the hypothetical and strictly confidential question as to whether the prestigious firm would be interested in undertaking an audit of some America dioceses on behalf of the Vatican. Having taken out a spot of insurance he made some further calls. His plan worked well and a sample conversation will illustrate the point.

"Just a friendly call, Jim, to see which direction you are taking when the Conclave meets."

Cardinal Powell was cagey. "I'm still considering a short list, Pat. It's a difficult call."

"A word in your ear then, Jim. There's a rumour that the Curia is planning to investigate several North American Sees on account of complaints as to lose accounting procedures." He paused to let Powell appreciate the implications. "Bloody nerve after that Vatican Bank business and a few other peccadilloes. If you ask me its revenge for all the times we bailed them out. You know how it is. People resent their saviours."

"It's still a worrying suggestion."

"It's more than a suggestion. I've found out that Andrews Robinson have already been approached and that only the Pope's death put the matter on hold."

"But can they do it? I mean it's never been done before. There must be a Cannon Law on the matter."

"I'm afraid that they can but, and this is the good news, the new pope may be more of a realist than the late Holy Father was at the end." He laughed sympathetically. "Don't worry, Jim. You and I have cut a few corners in our time but it was always for the good of the Church. We Americans understand the modern world. We just need an American pope to teach the Curia how to do business. What do you reckon?"

"I'm 100% behind you, Pat. Do you have any suggestions?"

"Well I wouldn't want to influence what goes on between you and the Holy Spirit but I think our friend from California could be the man. Mexican mother and Marine Corps father. Speaks Spanish and Portuguese. Could be an attractive candidate on both sides of the continent."

Peroni made a number of personal visits to his Curial colleagues and several phone calls within Italy. Though their numbers had steadily declined over the years the Italians were still, at around 25%, the largest national block in the College. Acting collectively they could seriously promote or undermine any candidate for the papacy. They did not, however, have the power to appoint. For this they needed alliances and alliances were proving more difficult as the non-Italian Church became increasing self-confident and critical of the disproportionate influence of the Holy Mafia as they were sometimes known.

The Curia, too, had shrunk as a collective force. At the time of John XXIII's pontificate they held 37% of the College, this was now reduced to by about half, insufficient to appoint but more than enough to influence.

Peroni sought to use the potential block votes to influence the final choice. An Italian would be ideal but he would accept another nationality, provided the man had strong conservative credentials. He was shocked to find that he could count on less than half of his fellow nationals and, even those who promised to act collectively could always waiver as the Conclave progressed. As for the Curial cardinals, not a few had old scores to settle.

Peroni regretted his past overt contempt for some of his fellow bureaucrats. Franelli tried to remain inconspicuous as the cloud of his master's anger sought a place to settle.

It is little wonder that a Conclave attracts the world's media. The pope is the leader of some one billion Catholics worldwide, one sixth of the global population. He is the head of an organisation which, despite scandals of gargantuan proportions, has survived for two millennia. Pius XIII had achieved a higher recognition factor than any other contemporary leader whereas several of his recent predecessors was scarcely recognisable to half the Curia. A pope can be as famous as a pop star or as unobtrusive as a hermit.

To add a sense of pageantry, the pope wears funny clothes as do the men who elect him. He conducts strange rituals in public. He is, in a sense, one of the world's dictators, sharing with some of them the claim to be infallible. To Catholics much of this is a given but, to the outsider, it is a matter of curiosity, madness even. In recent centuries the conduct of popes has, in general, been less bizarre than that of Idi Amin or Colonel Gadaffi but step back into history and they compete on equal terms. Add to this already exotic brew the fact that the Holy Spirit is supposed to guide deliberations during the Conclave. No one claims to have seen the Holy Spirit at Conclaves since the middle Ages but, none the less, he/she is presumed to be present. Whether all the cardinals subscribe to this belief is not known, though the intense lobbying which accompanies a Conclave would suggest that they take precautions just in case he/she is otherwise engaged.

The election of Pope John XXIII, followed by his rather radical approach to the papacy led to a joke about the Holy Spirit's influence. The Camerlengo, who summoned the Conclave which elected him, dies and goes to heaven. He is interviewed by St Peter who requires character referees. The Camerlengo cites the Holy Spirit and St Peter telephones for confirmation. In response to St Peter's request, the Holy Spirit becomes embarrassed. "Of course I'll vouch for him but please give him my apologies. He sent me an invitation to a Conclave not long ago and I was so busy I forgot to attend."

A Conclave has all the elements of melodrama. A fabulous prize. A secret gathering locked in a room, protected by Swiss Guards in medieval costume. Participants speaking a variety of languages and many far from fluent in Latin. Intrigue, perhaps double dealing. An invisible guest. Media saturation. Smoke signals to announce a winner or lack thereof. Occasionally a death. However, as research continually reveals, a digital public has an ever diminishing attention span so both the media and the Vatican Press Office hope that the Conclave will not be too indecisive. To elect a pope on the first ballot is undesirable in that it allows insufficient time for tension to mount. Some students of Conclaves believe that a clear choice on the second ballot is the ideal outcome. Others maintain that the 'best of three' ballots results in optimum degree of tension with the minimum loss of interest. Most agree that procrastination beyond three disengages the public and undermines the authority of the eventual victor.

As the opening of the Conclave approached, Peroni became increasingly agitated. His enquiries told him that the voting was potentially all over the place and might well follow racial or, more accurately, geographic lines. At least that seemed the case for North and South America, Africa and Asia. Only the European cardinals seemed open to an extra-continental candidate. Peroni tried various permutations but could only conclude, and it was a highly speculative conclusion, that if the cardinals voted in geographic blocks he was unlikely to get his conservative candidate. On this basis he began to lobby against a geographical split. Dependent upon the recipient of his advice, he painted various pictures. To one cardinal he expressed concern that the new pope should not be seen as a compromise candidate who emerged only when the geographic contest had failed to produce the required majority. To another he stressed the difficulty of preventing the Italian cardinals from forming a racist rump if they believed similar continental blocks were being formed. His diplomacy proved only too effective in separating the factions but not in his ultimate aim of uniting them behind a candidate acceptable to the Secretary of State.

In the course of Peroni's discussions he, himself, was lobbied. Cardinal Sabatini congratulated him on his farsightedness in promoting the need for a conservative pope and, after many flattering allusions to Peroni's success in eroding the influence of Vatican II, made a suggestion of his own.

"I believe, Cardinal Secretary, that we would be best served by a Holy Father who is not only conservative but who is aligned with the most effective conservative force in the Church. The pope can achieve only so much. He can personally supervise only so much. Even with the support of a man like you, with so many years of accumulated wisdom, there are many aspects of governance which cannot be controlled. To be blunt, Cardinal Secretary, if we are serious about re-setting the compass for the new millennium then we must exercise control at the micro level as well as the macro level."

Peroni laughed. "I have no illusions about the difficulty of ensuring conformity at all levels of the Church but the fact that this is impossible does not mean that we should not try to influence the micro decisions, as you choose to call them."

"But we can. That is the whole point. We already have a dedicated group of men......and women who are pledged to restoring certainty and eliminating ambiguity. Our late Holy Father gave several signs that he approved of their activities. As you are well aware he even established a personal prelature to enable him to have direct links with these dedicated Catholics."

Peroni winced internally. He had advised against the appointment for two reasons. At a personal level it undermined his control of access to the Pope and at a professional level he saw it as the establishment of a church within the Church. Whatever Peroni's faults, he would never support any idea which led to division. However, he suppressed his feelings and asked Sabatini to continue.

"Please realise that I do not seek any personal preferment. In any case, who would vote for a man of 73 years? But I have two names for you who are secret admirers of the Organisation and who have indicated a powerful role for it, should they be in a position to create one. I realise that one is not yet eligible to join the Conclave but that does not mean he is ineligible for election.

There are precedents. " He passed a piece of paper to Peroni and departed.

The names revealed just why you needed realists at the heart of the Church...and well informed realists. The cardinal candidate had had some very dubious relationships with at least one South American dictator and Peroni could just image the media dragging up every unsavoury allegation, proven or unproven. He was clearly unelectable. The second was equally surprising but for a different reason. Few outside the Conclave itself were ever elected pope and while an exceptional candidate with a strong block vote might make the lists, Archbishop Stanford was little known outside of the United Kingdom though rather too well known to Peroni. His conservative credentials were excellent but with only two cardinals from Great Britain it was unlikely that that country would ever provide another pope. In Stanford's case it was even less likely. Carterton was a card carrying liberal, almost a communist, and the eccentric from Scotland would be more swayed by prowess on the sports field than by notions of sanctity.

Later that same day, Cardinal Murengo approached the Secretary of State. He was still simmering over the seeming rejection of his fellow Africans. During his term in the Curia he had had a nodding acquaintance with Peroni then, also, a humble monsignor. Indeed, as Murengo recalled it, Peroni and many others had been somewhat in awe of this powerful black man who dwarfed the stunted Italian clerics. He had already developed the technique of standing rather too close for comfort so that his physical mass could intimidate, as the situation required.

"Forgive the intrusion Cardinal Secretary, I realise you are burdened and have no time to spare."

Peroni's attitude gave little encouragement. None the less Murengo continued. "I merely want your opinion. As you may be aware several cardinals have approached me in the belief that it is time for an African pope and that I, despite my woeful inadequacy, am their preferred candidate. I don't know how to respond. I am, of course, flattered but I must not allow my own ego to get in the way of what is best for the Church. So who better to advise me than yourself?" Murengo seated himself, uninvited, and looked directly at Peroni. Peroni starred fixedly at the wall for what seemed an eternity. At last he turned to Murengo.

"You are right to put the Church before personal ambition. We who have been favoured by His Holiness must always keep that foremost in our minds. So the question becomes: is the Church ready for an African pope? Sadly I think the answer must be no. As to why or, in this case, why not?"

Peroni noted Murengo puffing up his huge chest as if to threaten him from the chair before rising as if to leave. He rather relished the man's discomfort. Clearly, having failed to receive Peroni's endorsement, he had no further business but the Secretary was not about to release him.

"Why not? Africa is in turmoil. A combination of civil wars, coups, dictatorships, AIDS, tribalism, superstition and a Christianity tainted with paganism provide its image to the outside world. Why we had to hide a voodoo Archbishop away in an Italian monastery in order to avoid further scandal from within the African Church and reach an expensive accommodation with his alleged wife. At least one bishop is openly siding with a murdering dictator. A pope from such a background would somehow be expected to create order out of this chaos rather as our late Holy Father did for Poland. I realise that the comparison is unfair. That Africa is to Poland as calculus is to simple arithmetic but, for better or worse, the pope is now seen as a political mover and shaker. The secular world leaders are at a total loss as to what to do in Africa and, hence, they now do nothing beyond a few pious statements of intent. They would love to have an African pope so that they could flag all the troubles of the continent for his attention and so excuse their own inaction."

Murengo was becoming increasingly restless. Peroni gave him a look which implied compassion mixed with insight. "I realise that the honour of an African pope would be well received by your flock and someday, sooner rather than later, I hope it will occur. But my view, which I believe is shared by many, is that the time is not yet ripe. I am sorry but there it is."

Murengo was about to depart with as much good grace as he could exhibit when Peroni added. "You can still provide an important influence on the direction of the next pontificate. What we need most of all is a further calming of the expectations that Vatican II aroused. If your African cardinals were convinced of the need for a conservative pope you would have made a major contribution to the Church's future, and with your own Curial experience such a pope might well show his gratitude and good sense by appointing you to an important position on his staff. What better counsellor as to the needs of the African Church than Africa's pre-eminent cardinal at the pope's right hand. I would certainly be able to guide him in that regard."

Peroni felt well pleased with the day's progress to the extent that he told Franelli that he had been working too hard and should take it easier. "You know Monsignor, the Holy Spirit has to work though simple men. Even one such as myself." He smiled at his own mock humility.

Franelli in his new mood of optimistic-fatalism was bold enough to respond. "Eminence, you express my own deepest feelings."

Had Peroni been present at a meeting of some of the European cardinals he might have been less sanguine. Had one of the other Italian cardinals been present, he might have been better informed. In the event he was as unaware as a rock fisherman caught by a freak wave.

The Belgian, Cardinal Anvers, had convened the gathering. He spoke respectfully of the late Pope and his achievements before coming to the point.

"It seems to me that we have two decisions to make. First, do we choose someone with conservative credentials or do we choose a progressive pope? Having made that decision, do we have a consensus as to whom? Personally, I believe that the time has come for a progressive pope. He laughed quietly. "Yes! I know that past Conclaves have elected apparent progressives only to find that the weight of office or circumstances, or both turn them rapidly into revisionists. But that should not cause us to waste our votes. We should aim for the man most likely to meet the current needs of the Church based on whatever information is currently available to us."

"It seems, Pierre, that you have already decided that we need a liberal pope."

"Not entirely. Certainly that is my general feeling but I am open to persuasion. I hope we all are."

A French cardinal took up the theme. "I am of similar mind to Pierre but I, too, have come to listen. However, it is important to bear in mind that the European Church and, to a lesser extent, the universal Church is not composed of a bunch of ill-educated, semi-literate peasants who are too exhausted by the end of the day to think for themselves. Paternalism may have worked in the past, may have even ensured that the Faithful remained childish in their attitude to religion, but that is no longer the case. One reason, one major reason that our congregations are shrinking, is because we have rules which no longer make sense even assuming that they ever did make sense."

"If that was the whole story, then why is the Organisation so strong?" A Spanish cardinal interjected.

"Because." The Belgian held the floor again. "Because there will always be people, and that includes educated people, who cannot cope with uncertainty. Who defend against it by attaching themselves to a strong leader or by trying to enforce immutable rules? Their problem is psychological, not spiritual."

As the evening progressed it was apparent that the Europeans favoured a progressive pope. At that point Anvers second question came up for discussion. If progressive, whom?" The initial reaction was to suggest Anvers himself.

"No, my friends. I am overwhelmed but over age. Our late Holy Father had a quarter of a century to impose his vision on the Church. We need a man with a minimum of a decade of vigorous activity ahead of him. Anyone over seventy will be seen as a caretaker and have little impact. I served my apprenticeship in the Curia and know how easily minor impediments become problems, how problems become difficulties and how difficulties become impossibilities. Time and energy are needed to effect radical change and I fear that I am blessed with neither."

The Cardinal Archbishop of Cologne became the next contender. He, too, declined on the grounds that a Pole followed by a German was just too close in geographic terms and, probably, in terms of recent history. "Germany has been very careful to avoid using its political and economic might to intimidate other European countries. I believe this has been a wise policy and has helped with the rehabilitation of Germany but it has, by no means, healed all the scars of Nazism. In any case, what about the Russians? If the Catholic Church is to foster increasing ties with Russia and the Orthodox Church, a German pope would be an additional obstacle."

The meeting ended with a consensus for electing a reformist pope but no nearer deciding who might best fit the bill while remaining papable.

CHAPTER 8

The voting system for a new pope is complicated, largely to ensure that the actual process is beyond suspicion. Even though the government of the Church is in the hands of the Camerlengo and his assistants, during the hiatus between the pope's death and his successor's appointment, their powers are limited. They cannot, for example, change the rules of the forthcoming election or make decisions which bind the new pope.

The Conclave must begin between fifteen and twenty days after the pope's death, a precaution which it owes more to the days of sea travel than to modern transportation. In 1922, the American cardinals missed the Conclave due to the slowness of their ship. Today voting is restricted to cardinals under 80 years of age but this restriction did not apply until the second millennium. For most of the first millennium, popes were usually chosen in their capacity as Bishop of Rome by both the clergy and laity of the diocese. Though theoretically democratic this system was far from perfect. Mobs fought over rival candidates and deaths at election time were by no means uncommon. Calls on the civil authorities to maintain law and order merely removed power from the mob and passed it to the city fathers. As the prestige of the Bishop of Rome grew so did the temptation to influence his selection. In the sixth century Vigilius was elected Pope due to the influence of the Empress Theodora. When he failed to deliver on an election promise he was arrested. His efforts to regain the royal favour led to further alienation amongst his fellow bishops who responded by excommunicating him. He died shortly afterwards, probably from trauma occasioned by this dramatic fall from grace.

Though most recent papal appointments may have failed to find favour with everyone, in terms of personal probity they have been light years ahead of some historic occupants of St Peter's Chair. The Italian Renaissance popes acted as though responsible neither to God nor to man. The Borgia's, the Medici, the Riario and the Della Rovere ruled the Church like a personal fiefdom. Celibacy for the lower clergy and unbridled licence for themselves. The Della Rovere, Sistus IV, may well have promulgated the Immaculate Conception but he espoused nepotism with even greater enthusiasm. He appointed six relatives as cardinals including his cousin, Pietro, who died of debauchery while still in his twenties. The Borgia, Alexander VI, excommunicated Savonarola for preaching penance while he gaily fathered numerous children and practiced simony. Leo X received a healthy boost to his ascent towards the papacy when promoted cardinal by his uncle, Innocent VIII, at the age of thirteen. The same Innocent who encouraged witch hunting with as much enthusiasm as he celebrated the marriages of his illegitimate offspring in St Peter's. Today's papacy may have its faults but it is relatively stain free.

For students of coincidence there is fertile ground in the papacy of the Johns', the coincidence being their ability to attract misfortune or bad publicity or both. John VII was murdered by members of his family at the young age of 26 having been elected Pope at the age of 18. John XI was also murdered, not by family but by a cuckolded husband. John XXI was sleeping soundly one night in 1277 when part of the papal palace collapsed on him and ended his reign after less than a year. The first John XXIII ruled but briefly in the fifteenth century. Accused of murder, adultery (with his brother's wife) and incest he was deposed by the Council of Constance but remained a cardinal-bishop. Undeterred, he continued to ravish legions of women including a number of nuns. In recognition of his scandalous career the Vatican decided to 'unmake' him and he was struck off the register of popes. It was not until the twentieth century that Angelo Roncalli, perhaps exercising his irreverent sense of humour, chose to become the second John XXIII. Some consider his convening of the Second Vatican Council a further example of his bizarre sense of humour. But the ultimate accolade for misfortune goes to Pope John XX, the pope who never was, for he exists only as an omission in the panoply of popes.

Pius XII was not just controversial with regard to the holocaust. He suffered from hypochondria and what would now be called obsessive-compulsive disorder. Not only did he claim about a dozen psychosomatic illnesses but he made a fetish of incessant teeth cleaning using a specially prepared paste. Obsessed with flies, he carried a hidden fly swat and regularly attacked these unwelcome visitors. Curiously, he adopted a Buddhist attitude towards other small creatures. He was also the only Pope known to plan his resignation, not on grounds of personal competence but to avoid having a pope captured by the German forces, then encamped outside the Vatican City. A further eccentricity was his de facto appointment of the German, Sister Pasqualina, effectively as his chief of staff. An action which proved manifestly unpopular among many of the cardinals.

Pasqualina became known as La Popessa and was more powerful than many a cardinal. She is variously credited with delaying the elevation of Archbishop Montini (later Pope Paul VI) to cardinal when he was Archbishop of Milan and ensuring the promotion of Cardinal Spellman, the Archbishop of New York. Such was her influence that she was involved in a major diplomatic intrigue to enable Mussolini to escape from his hitherto allies, the Germans. Also starring in the same intrigue were the Pope, Il Duce's mistress and General Eisenhower. As history tells us, the plot failed and both Mussolini and his mistress, Claretta Petacci, were hanged by angry Italians.

The average length of a papacy over the two millennia is between seven and eight years though recent papacies have, generally, been longer. One commentator claimed, without any supporting evidence, that this was because popes were no longer married. Though St Peter is often credited with a papacy of around 35 years, the undisputed record for longevity belongs to Pius IX who, despite a weak constitution, was in office for 32 years and prompted one cardinal to remark that, "We thought we were electing a Holy Father not an Eternal Father". Not only does Pius IX hold the longevity record but he also holds the record of declaring himself Pope in his capacity as a scrutineer at the Conclave which elected him. The shortest pontificate was that of Pope Stephen II which lasted only four days.

In the early Church, marriage was no barrier to papability nor, indeed, was an absence of Holy Orders. There have been numerous married popes including St Peter. There has been at least one convict pope, Pope Callistus who served time in a Sardinian salt mine. Allegedly one woman pope, Pope Joan. Several rival popes during the Avignon Papacy. Even a warrior pope, Julius II, who led his own troops into battle. Finally, demonstrating equality of opportunity, there have been at least two illegitimate popes.

As recently as the nineteenth century, the Austro-Hungarian Emperor is said to have vetoed a potential papal appointee. So while election by a small, select group may appear regressive in an age when democracy is seen as the ideal, it does have the benefit of excluding some of the more bizarre practices of the past. It does not as a system exclude, nor is it ever likely to exclude, undue influence even from beyond the grave. A liberal pope is likely to appoint liberal cardinals, a conservative pope conservative cardinals. A long lived pope is certain to have greater influence on the election of his successor than one who leaves behind a College largely appointed prior to his pontificate. A pope who increases the number of cardinals and who is also long lived will have an even greater effect on the next election. If, in addition, he changes the rules of the election he can further influence the process which will fill his empty shoes. Pius XIII met all the criteria for post mortem electioneering.

For centuries the pope required a two thirds majority vote. Pius XII increased this to two thirds plus one. Such a requirement can lead to over long elections with many votes being taken before a conclusive outcome is reached. It can also lead to a compromise candidate being chosen or, in extreme cases, to no candidate being chosen. In the thirteenth century the election of Innocent IV was preceded by eighteen months of procrastination until the Romans locked up the cardinals as a means of encouraging a rapid resolution. Failing to learn from history, it took three years to elect Gregory X. By this time the patience of the people was exhausted. Not only did they lock up the electors but they further motivated them by reducing their diet to bread and water and by tearing the roof off the building in which they were confined. Gregory appears to have been so impressed by the experience of his own election that in 1274 that he formalised the process and decreed that, in future, cardinals would be locked in the room where they would vote, eat and sleep. Food supplies would decrease over time, with bread and water only being served after eight days of inconclusiveness. While superficially attractive, these practices were potentially dangerous, especially considering the age and, not infrequently, the physical conditions of Princes of the Church. In the eighteenth century some eight cardinals died during an especially hot Conclave.

Making the Conclave as uncomfortable as possible does seem to concentrate the collective mind of the College. Whether it has the same effect on the Holy Spirit is questionable. Though more recent Conclaves have been known to last for many weeks, occasionally months, a few days is usually sufficient. Despite this, Pius XIII decreed that, if after a specified number of ballots, no one had received the necessary two thirds plus one, an absolute majority of the cardinals could vote to elect by absolute majority.

While superficially a means of breaking a deadlock this revision undermines the two thirds plus one rule. Assuming a candidate obtains an absolute majority on an early ballot and the same block maintain solidarity throughout all subsequent ballots, this is the candidate who is virtually certain to be elected. Thus a pope who has appointed perhaps eighty per cent of the cardinals eligible to vote stretches a very long arm from the crypt.. Again Pius XIII met this criterion.

If the influence of the dead Pope as a force had waxed prior to his demise other forces had waned. The number of Curial cardinals had declined significantly since Vatican II as had the number of Italian cardinals. Third World cardinals had increased in the past half century and those from Eastern Europe during the last pontificate. The United States had also moved up the pecking order and was the largest block after the Italians.

All these factors and more were well known to Vaticanologists and to most of the cardinals with the exception of a very few unworldly prelates. As a result the days prior to the commencement of the Conclave saw much lobbying and many rumours. Promises were made in the clear knowledge that a new pope is freed by Conclave regulation from any promises made before his election. A regulation, less strictly respected, forbad the discussion of candidates until after the pope's death. One Vatican observer has pointed out that an examination of Frequent Flyer Points in the period when a pope's tenure is seen as coming to an end is a sound indication of those who seek to replace him. As with profane elections, the recognition factor is highly valued.

Then, as George Weigel has noted, there is the Pignedoli Principle based on the story of the late Cardinal Sergio Pignedoli. A clear favourite with the Roman press corps to succeed Pope Paul in 1978, he had all but disappeared by the end of the second ballot. Thus, the principle contends that electability decreases in proportion to media promotion.

As the Conclave opened, Roy Sanderson, an ex-priest turned journalist, wrote the following article for the Chronicle.

THE KEYS TO THE THIRD MILLENNIUM

Decisions made in Rome over the course of the next few days will be a clear signal to the world as to whether the Roman Catholic Church is able to shake off a medieval past and become relevant to the future or whether it is to become a rump organisation, notable for its curiosity value rather then it's relevance to ordinary lives.

When Pius XIII was elected the world sat back and took notice. It seemed such an imaginative decision. A Pope from a communist country. A Pope who was not a Vatican bureaucrat. A Pope with both an intellectual and physical presence. A Pope who would face down injustice. A Pope who represented the unheard majority of the oppressed and impoverished and not the elite. A Pope who might kick-start the dynamic of Vatican II. Hope had never soared higher.

Alas! Though Pius had many qualities and was a major player on the world stage he was essentially of the siege mentality. For all his travelling, he made few real incursions into the modern world. Ironically, at one level he was rather like the servant in the Gospel who is entrusted with his master's talents while the master is elsewhere. On the master's return the servant proudly informs him that his talent is still safe as it has been buried. Far from being grateful the master punishes the servant for not exploiting the talent, at the same time rewarding the other servants who have been more adventurous and so increased the master's treasure.

Pius has handed over a Church which has been unable to reach a modus vivendi on questions of birth control, on women's' rights, on sexual identity, on divorce, on clerical celibacy: to name but some of the issues which effect everyday lives. He has silenced theologians who have tried to open up the debate on such issues. He has failed to support, in any tangible way, South American priests who have demanded a better distribution of wealth and fought for the people of the favelas and not infrequently died for them.

Pius XIII was, I believe, a holy man. I do not think for a moment that he trod his chosen path other than with the highest motives. But, I do believe that he could rationalise his decisions and so embrace a double standard which the Gospel explicitly condemned when practiced by the Pharisees. How can one support the actions of the United States in Afghanistan, when it embarks on a crusade against those responsible for the deaths of a few thousand of its citizens, and fails to support action for the millions who die prematurely because they are effectively the slaves of the elite of their own country or of global capital. Is a South American life less precious than a North America life?

If the CEO of a multi-national company was losing his junior managers at a rate far in excess of their recruitment, surely his shareholders would ask questions. If the Corporate Headquarters issued instructions which most members of the firm disregarded as impractical, surely the decision making procedures would require re-evaluation. If tradition stated that the directors and especially the CEO could never be wrong, regardless of the evidence to the contrary, surely a paradigm shift would be long overdue.

My own case is interesting only in that it is typical. Like so many seminarians I was caught in a trap. I believed that I had a vocation but little in my priestly training engendered a sense of excitement. Much of what we were taught seemed light years away from the concerns which affected the lives of our families back home. Rules seemed to govern even the most mundane of issues: rituals surrounding the blessing and composition of Holy Water were given greater attention than the counselling of the bereaved and the sexually ambivalent. Despite this steady disillusionment most of us persisted in the hope that it would be different in the field. Then came the fresh winds of the Second Vatican Council and, suddenly, we were flying, desperate to spread the Good News which it had resurrected from the cellar. But the exhilaration was short lived. The forces of reaction proved too powerful. John XXIII legacy was slowly but surely interred.

Perhaps it would have been better for the Church if he had never inspired such hope. Perhaps seminarians like me would have exchanged our moribund training for a moribund priesthood. Having been immersed in the status quo we would have continued to deliver the status quo. But being offered vinegar when you have tasted claret was never going to prove a selling point with the result that, today, most of my contemporaries have abandoned a ship which seems on course for the rocks. Do the cardinals now meeting in Rome have the courage and realism to initiate a change of direction under a captain who will break the grip of the reactionaries?

On the basis of the first vote of the Conclave it would seem that the answer was a resounding 'No'. In order of precedence each cardinal approached the altar, knelt in prayer and, on rising, swore that, "I call to witness Christ the Lord who will be my judge that my vote is given to the one who before God I consider should be elected". Each cardinal then placed his vote, in disguised writing, onto the paten and thence into the chalice

Once all cardinals had voted, the chalice was covered by the paten and shaken to mix the ballots. The three elected scrutineers checked the cards, the last reading out the name before threading it with a needle. When all cards were in place the three revisers checked the accuracy of the process. Since this first ballot had not been conclusive, the votes, together with any notes taken by the cardinals, were immediately burned with a chemical to ensure that the smoke rising above the Vatican was black, alerting those in St Peter's Square and beyond to the fact that the Church still lacked a pope.

Peroni was well satisfied with the first ballot. He was only too aware that, despite the oath, some cardinals would have cast their vote as a mark of public respect for an otherwise unelectable colleague and would become serious only on the second and subsequent ballots. Others might be playing a more tactical game by trying to disguise their true intentions at this early stage. These thoughts aside, Cardinal Spinola, Archbishop of Naples, had received 51 of the 118 votes cast. While this was no guarantee that he would become pope it was a strong indicator that the Conclave was favouring a conservative. Of the remaining 67 votes, 25 had gone to Cardinal Lorenzo of Sao Paulo, 11 to Cardinal Murengo, seven to Cardinal Murray of Pittsburgh, six to Peroni himself, six to Cardinal Montalban of Lyon, four to Cardinal Carterton, the balance consisting of single votes.

Peroni was astonished that Carterton had attracted any votes. He was the most junior cardinal as well as being among the least mentally stable. He could only assume that those who voted for him did so in order to disguise their real intentions or out of respect for Pius's last act. An irritation at most and certainly not a tragedy.

With luck, Peroni reasoned, Spinola might get up on the second ballot. If he was perceived as the next pope even cardinals who did not favour him might vote for him. In so doing they would be proclaiming to the Faithful that he enjoyed strong support: no one benefited from disunity in the ranks. Perhaps they would have a new pope in time for lunch. With this in mind he switched his own vote from himself to Spinola, as the second ballot was called and he waited eagerly for the results. Yet his long curial career warned him against premature conclusions. Spinola had entered the Conclave as a front runner and that was historically a bad omen. While it was true that he was a conservative, he had also established a reputation as an advocate for the poor of Naples, who endured appalling conditions in a country with the tenth largest GDP in the world. Spinola was a candidate who should be acceptable to the majority. Lorenzo, on the other hand, had protested vehemently to Pius over his intolerance towards Liberation Theology and had taken a gentle line with Brazilian priests who were its advocates. But if conservative and liberal blocks were emerging, the conservatives held a comfortable majority. One not too far short of an absolute majority and Pius's rule change discouraged the strongest block from thoughts of compromise. Cautious optimism was in order.

The results of the second ballot proved less conclusive. Spinola's vote dropped from 51 to 43 and Lorenzo's' rose from 25 to 29. Murengo was down three to eight. Peroni down three. Murray constant at seven. Montalban up one to seven. Carterton up eight to 12. The balance in single votes. More black smoke. That Carterton should have received one vote yet alone twelve caused Peroni to reflect that a compulsory psychiatric assessment ought to be added to the existing age qualification of the electors.

According to the rules, the Conclave now adjourned and would re-convene in the afternoon for a further two votes, should two prove necessary. As the cardinals walked the 350 metres from the Sistine Chapel to lunch in their new, hotel style accommodation in the Domus Sanctae Marthae, Peroni went into overdrive. He was determined to block Lorenzo's candidature at all costs. He held a hurried conversation with Kirst, in order to enlist his help, and between the two of them they concocted a scheme to ensure a conservative, even if Spinola had to be abandoned, to achieve their aim. Given more time they could have used more subtle tactics and more subtle tactics might have caused less resentment. As it was they alienated more than they persuaded. The North American cardinals in particular, still smarting at being summoned to Rome to explain their seeming reluctance to deal with paedophilic priests, needed little provocation to suspect more Curial high handedness. Murengo had not forgotten his unsatisfactory meeting with Peroni and was not about use his influence as directed by the Secretary, even with the vague bribe of a Vatican appointment. The European and Asian cardinals had no conspicuous leader and were not, therefore, accessible in the time available. Thus the post-prandial vote was conducted in an atmosphere of panic, resentment or confusion, depending on who had said what to whom and how it had been interpreted.

Of course, no one can be sure why the cardinals voted as they did in this third and final ballot, though many in the media have offered opinions based as much on their own prejudices as on the scant facts which were available. To the extent that there was a consensus, it saw the vote more as a protest against the increased centralisation of the Church under Pius XIII and his bureaucrats together with a need to distance the institution from the scandals associated with sexual and financial misconduct. Whatever the motivation, at 4.07pm the Monsignor of the College of Cardinals asked the traditional question, "Do you accept your canonical election as supreme pontiff?" At 4.08pm, having received an affirmative reply, he asked, "By what name shall you be known?" In asking this question, the Monsignor was harking back to the sixth century when the newly elected Pope felt that Mercury, the name of a pagan god, was somehow inappropriate. "John XXIV" was the reply which sent a visible shiver down Peroni's spine and, indeed, the spines of many other cardinals but there was little left to do other than signify obedience to will of the Conclave - or was it the will of the Spirit?

Soon the white smoke rose over St Peter's Square and the crowd roared it's welcome to the new leader of the billion Catholics. The late Archbishop of Westminster gave his blessing and a few words of appreciation in rather rusty Italian. He recalled how he had been seized with panic after his first provocative sermon in the Liverpool Cathedral of Christ the King. Now it was more of a trance. Was this really happening? Could it be a dream? Why him? Why had he accepted? Why had he not followed the precedent of St Philip Benizi, fleeing the Conclave and hiding until another pope could be elected? He was unsuited to the role. He would be paralysed by fear. A sacrificial lamb to the Curia. He had only four changes of under clothes and was almost out of shaving cream.

CHAPTER 9

In New York Sebastian Hart was holding his weekly briefing. As usual he displayed a visible impatience, especially with those who stated the obvious, waving them on to closure. Today, Karl Maier ignored his autocratic boss with characteristic disregard for his career.

"But I am coming to the point however, without the background, there is no point."

Hart reddened. He was not used to insubordination. "It may have escaped your notice but I have three other directors waiting to brief me and a surprisingly finite amount of time."

"It had not escaped me." Maier replied, unchastened. "And that knowledge simply underlines the importance of what I am trying to communicate. May I continue."

His fellow directors almost gasped at his effrontery while inwardly calculating what prizes his demise might bestow on them. At worst it allowed the old man to ventilate his spleen on Maier, leaving them less vulnerable.

"We all know that the phenomenal growth in your media empire has not occurred unopposed. However, you have been largely able to neutralise opposition by depicting opponents as, variously, mad, dangerous, degenerate or incompetent. At the same time you have been able to promote factions favourable to your cause. However, the same tactics cannot be expected to work all of the time. People become wise to them even though they may feel powerless to intervene. We have already seen evidence of this in some European countries where similar vested interests have prevailed but without your subtlety of style. A strong and universal voice speaking out against....not just you.... but vested interests in general....would be speaking to a highly receptive audience. To label the itinerant rabble, protesting at the G8 and similar meetings, as a drug-crazed minority worked well in that context but will not necessarily prove effective when dealing with a middle aged, middle class population with an outspoken leader."

Hart yarned ostentatiously. "I really don't need a lesson in manipulating public opinion." He smiled. "It has always been, you might say, our core business. Recall what happened to the Voice of the People in South America, twenty five years in a rat infested gaol....if he lives that long. The same was true in East Africa except that he was killed in that tragic air disaster."

Maier seemed unmoved. "Knocking off a few nignogs who appear to represent mobs of savages in second hand clothing is one thing. Knocking off a pope is another."

Hart spluttered. "Have you gone mad?" He looked at his other directors who hastened to express visible doubts as to Maier's sanity. "Somehow knocking off a pope is not part of the Consol business plan. Must be an oversight on my part."

Maier looked supremely self-satisfied. "I can assure you it is......let me explain."

"You'd better...and convincingly."

Hart had dismissed his other directors and was alone with Maier. In the corridor outside the Chairman's suite they whispered together.

"If that slimy bastard is getting his cards, well and good." The Australian was his usual vitriolic self. Maier, it was alleged, had poisoned Hart's mind against him when the antipodian operation was being allocated. Bruce had never forgiven him.

The Swiss exhibited all the caution of a Zurich banker. "Maybe he is, maybe he isn't. Time will tell. For me, I prefer to get along with everyone."

They shook hands and went away to contemplate each other's weaknesses while Maier received Hart's full attention.

Hart held mixed feelings regarding Maier. He disliked his lack of deference while admiring his ability to think strategically and to railroad the opposition. Maier was much like himself thirty years ago and, he had to admit, he would have liked to have a son like Maier. Instead he had sired a playboy and a mystic. Maybe there was still time for another crack at a decent heir but that required some personal readjustments, notably the acquisition of a new wife and the discarding of the old one. He would hear Maier out first and then turn his mind to the succession.

"Well Karl, what do I have to fear from the papacy?"

"Well, for a start the CV for the new pope as defined in the Consol media was scarcely an identikit picture of Carterton but, leaving that aside, one look at his website when he was a mere Archbishop will tell you. John XXIV is something of a maverick. As I am sure you are aware he has an agenda that reaches far beyond obscure points of doctrine and the immorality of the pill. Despite your usual indifference to religion, I think you had better start taking an interest."

Hart laughed mirthlessly. "You don't exactly see me in the role of St Francis then?"

"Genghis Khan was more what I had in mind. He never pretended to be out to do good and nor do you. But the fact that you cannot be accused of hypocrisy is unlikely to save you from the crusading Pope."

Hart tried to conceal his anger. "I try to keep my mind focused on the modern world and avoid paying too much attention to a product of the Dark Ages."

"Dark Ages or not, there are a billion Catholics in the world. Most of them don't attend church regularly, some cannot read, some would put de Sade to shame. But, and the research proves it, most still subscribe to what might be termed the Church's social agenda. We have seen the effect of a vocal right wing

Christianity in this country. Think what the effect of a vocal left wing Christianity might be if it had a strong leader and used its universal voice. Whatever divisions Pius has opened up with his neo-conservatism on matters of sex he caused little dissent with his statements on human dignity. But just consider what problems this new, seemingly activist Pope might conjure up if he continues to identify rampant capitalism and globalisation, supported by a disingenuous media, as the major threats to humanity. It is an ideal platform, it avoids internal controversy and unites the Faithful against an external foe. It might even bring all Christianity into one fold and haul Islam on board. We can't expect the dream run of recent years to continue forever. The right wing international consensus amongst the powerful was bound to create its own backlash. All it needed was a feeling of alienation amongst the plebs and a strong, universal leader. Now they've got one and one who increasingly targets the media and, without too much subtlety, Consol. What he began Westminster is likely to survive the transition to Rome."

Hart was impressed. Impressed that he had personally chosen Maier against strong opposition and impressed at the coherence of what he had argued. However, Hart liked to check the data for himself, well aware of how often he had furthered his own cause by persuasive reasoning based on false premises.

"Leave it with me. We'll talk again...soon. Let me have your thoughts on a pre-emptive strike."

"I have already prepared them." Maier smiled at his boss and passed over a purple folder: the one reserved for director's top secret material. ` "And by the way, I think you should invite Archbishop Kowalski to spend a weekend at Cedars."

"Who the hell is Archbishop Kowalski?"

"The Papal Nuncio. A man noted for his refined palate and his expertise with a twelve bore."

Consol 1H landed at Cedars late on Saturday morning. Archbishop Kowalski levered himself out of his seat and, with the assistance of the attractive flight attendant, crouched his way towards his host. The chopper was airborne almost immediately

The next passenger would be in an entirely different line of business from the portly cleric, but one equally important to Consol.

"Welcome Archbishop. I trust the flight was to your liking?"

"I have no complaints but my preference is for ground travel." Automatically he held out his ring for the customary respect but, just in time, turned the gesture into a handshake. Hart noted the error and smiled to himself.

"I am delighted you could make it at such short notice but, as you may guess, there are few weekends when I can enjoy the New England countryside and the companionship of distinguished guests."

The Nuncio was accustomed to flattery. "I must say I was surprised and flattered that a humble priest should receive an invitation from one of the world's most prominent businessmen."

Kowalski lived up to his reputation, both as a gourmet and as a marksman. Hart was amazed that the man could consume so much and still remain awake let alone manage a full afternoon's shoot. He had intended to let his guest bag the most birds but such subterfuge proved unnecessary. The corpulent cleric outclassed his host with seeming ease and demolished an afternoon tea as an encore.

"I'd like you to call me Seb. My friends do and even my more adventurous employees, especially those wanting a career change." Hart joked.

"I'd be honoured. My friends call me Kol, short for Kowalski."

"Kol! Are you sure. I'm quite happy with Archbishop or Your Grace."

Kowalski waved away the offer of respect. What was this man?" He wondered.

"Kol, then. I must tell you how much I, an unbeliever, admired Pius XIII. No, not just him, but the Polish people. Their extraordinary sense of self. You can invade them, partition them, oppress them but nothing can put out the flame of nationalism. Who would have predicted that the Poles and their Pope would have slain the Soviet dragon. For me, someone who is essentially a media man, it is the most remarkable story of the twentieth century by miles and, as you know, the competition has been fierce. You must be inordinately proud to have sprung from such robust roots."

"Yes, I am. Even though my vocation has kept me away from home for almost two decades, my heart is always there and I know the late Holy Father shared that same longing. I appreciate what you have just said. Recent history is easy to overlook. Unfortunately the Polish people seem to have forgotten their benefactor and turned towards the ways of the modern world."

"It is ironic." Hart leaned forward. "That you and I should see things in such a similar fashion while coming from totally different philosophical positions. You are distressed by what you see as sin and I am distressed by what I see as ingratitude. Pius deserves the respect, homage even, of the free world for achieving what could have cost millions of lives or even left a devastated planet."

Kowalski maintained his diplomatic mask. He did not trust Hart and yet it was just possible that the man may be genuine. Ruthlessness in business did not automatically mean that he had no finer feelings. "It is good to hear you express such sentiments, even in private."

"Don't misunderstand me, Archbishop. I have stated this view in public. However, your comment makes me think that I should be far more public in airing it." He paused and appeared to search for something. "I have it. I will endeavour to repay society's debt to Pius by encouraging my editors to give greater weight to his achievements and the perceived failure of gratitude on behalf of some members of his Church and the broader community. I am also impressed, intrigued, by his very different successor, the Pope of Surprises." Hart smiled at his little joke. "You see, Kol, though the media has no moral mission per se, it cannot remain a moral vacuum. So, even for people like me and my editors, the Pope's teaching can be a source of education. In that spirit I would like the Holy Father to know that the media can be his unlikely ally. He has had some harsh things to say about the media, not all of them without foundation. However, we may not be quite as evil as he currently appears to believe and, possibly, the Pope is more open minded than some of his remarks would suggest"

Hart continued to elaborate his theme but it was unnecessary. The Nuncio understood only too well where his host's advantage lay, but he was not going to let that stand in the way of an offer which might, just might, deliver major benefits.

"That is a most interesting insight and one important enough to convey to the current Holy Father. You have never met him have you?"

"Unfortunately no and I am sure he has better things to do with his time than exchanging idle chatter with press barons."

"But if he didn't feel that he had better things to do...what then."

"Then I would be immensely proud to meet the very different successor of Pius XIII, if I may put it that way."

Once his guest had left Hart phoned Maier. "I think I am going to get an audience with the Pope so you'd better do your homework. It's an opportunity unlikely to recur."

Maier seemed impressed. "How did you manage it?"

Hart summarised his meeting with Kowalski. "I pressed the Polish nationalism button and lamented that Pius's vision of a staunchly Catholic Poland, at the cross roads of Europe, being able to evangelise both east and west was fading fast. Kowalski agreed that it was to have been the model for the twenty first century and now it looks only too like the semi pagan hinterland. Then I dropped the odd hint about our interests in China: evangelising over a billion Chinese must be a temptation even for the Pope. If Pius was prepared to cooperate with a United States, which was backing proxy wars in South America, in order to defeat European communism I don't think an alliance between Consol and his successor will be too difficult to achieve."

"I wonder? English Catholicism is a different beast. Carterton is from a lesser siege mentality. We might do better trying to influence some of the cardinals, after all Pius appointed most of them and not for their liberal credentials. Then, of course, we can always have a crack at the Holy Spirit or so the rather quaint theory goes."

"Well I can't fix an audience with him...her." Hart taunted.

"Just as well, he has been out of favour ever since they elected John XXIII. Don't under estimate the influence of Pius, even from beyond the grave. I shall await the results of your audience with considerable interest. If anyone can deflect his progress.........."

Again Maier niggled him with this patronising comment: expression of faith should be top down. Maier was walking a narrow line. Hart valued his advice and would tolerate him for the time being but for no longer.

Maier laughed as he got off the phone. He could just imagine Hart's annoyance but, unlike his employer, deep down he knew it was all a game. Sometimes a profitable game, sometimes a dangerous game, even a deadly game....but still a game. He refused to compromise himself by taking it seriously. He knew he was good at it but he had seen how the game had devoured the over dedicated. Those whose whole persona was dependent upon winning every round. Inevitably the time came when they lost a round, the persona collapsed and they found that that the personality which had once hidden behind it was no longer there. Depression, suicide, domestic violence, even murder. All were possible with a non-person. Maier admitted to a persona himself but he took care to maintain the real self beneath. He was still in daily touch with the mocking, anarchic and risk taking teenager who had run away at fifteen and lived on his wits for a decade before joining the suits. He knew he could do the same again if need be, although a series of numbered bank accounts made this an unlikely scenario. And what was money for anyhow if it didn't bring you the confidence to wave two fingers at anyone who annoyed you?

Hart may come across as an urbane and no nonsense businessman who used both his wealth and his power with discretion. Who preferred to talk softly than to rant and rave. Of course, he was at heart an amoral monster who would use anyone to the point of exhaustion and then throw them away without a thought. But the cultivated veneer was sufficient excuse for his senior staff to claim loyalty to an inspired leader. I suppose, Maier reflected, men could not be blamed for failing to embrace the truth when the truth meant saying 'I have sold my soul to a man whose only ethic is the furtherance of his own ambition'. Faust was alive and well and living in corporate America."

Maier kept such happy delusions at bay both in relation to Hart and to himself. He acknowledged that he shared Hart's lack of ethics but the difference between them was that he did not really care whether Consol or any other organisation rose or fell. To him a job was something to keep boredom away, not a means to establish a personal empire. He despised the poor prisoners who were wedded to the company. He could be fired or resign tomorrow without a moment of regret. Psychologically he travelled light and his bag was always packed.

CHAPTER 10

John XXIV slept badly. He was woken by Peroni and together the Pope and the Cardinal Secretary celebrated Mass. He asked Peroni if he could spend some time in prayer before confronting whatever lay ahead. He was assured that the business of the Vatican could be left safely in the hands of experienced officials and that His Holiness should take as much time as he needed. Sister Donella would attend to his meals and to any housekeeping needs.

Peroni continued: "I trust your quarters are to your liking?"

"More than adequate. Maybe that's why I didn't sleep too well. I've been used to rather less luxury of late."

"There is also your private garden." Peroni pointed to the roof. "It is very secure and effectively invisible from within and without the Vatican City."

Peroni departed and Sister Donella served a hearty breakfast, a definite improvement on Pat Nolan's cuisine but not on his company.

Kirst, in an uncharacteristic change in habit, actually approached Peroni. "Cardinal Secretary." He addressed him, returning to a previous formality. "The Spirit has again taught us a lesson. At least that is the way I am determined to view the situation. But, of course, my office is not one in which the Holy Father offers regular guidance. With you it is different."

Peroni sensed Kirst distancing himself and wanted him to remain an ally in whatever difficulties lay ahead. "Helmut, as always your wisdom is most welcome. The Holy Father directs and we obey. As you point out, my own office is particularly sensitive to the will of the Pope but none of the great offices of the Church are immune. It is my fond hope that old Curial hands like you and I can guide the Holy Father so that his pontificate is one of renewed certainty. We have seen how easily the sheep are led astray when traditional beliefs are undermined. Evolution not revolution must be our guiding principle. Don't you agree?"

For a humourless man Kirst was rather enjoying himself. "Of course I agree but it was neither you nor I who was elected pope. While we may agree with each other, the question remains, does the Holy Father agree with us or does he intend to follow a more liberal agenda? His pronouncements as Archbishop of Liverpool and of Westminster suggest that may be the case."

"Very true, but it is one thing to open Pandora's box in a country with a relatively small Catholic population and a history of tolerating eccentrics and quite another to do so as leader of a billion believers. As Archbishop in the United Kingdom he might antagonise the Prime Minister and a few Cabinet Ministers. As Pope in the Vatican he can alienate a whole galaxy of VIPs to say nothing of half the Faithful. A Pope at war with the world is not going to have a productive pontificate. That is the message I am hoping to pass onto the Holy Father and I am relying on senior cardinals, such as you, to reinforce the message."

Kirst decided to play Peroni a little longer. "I read that he was very well received by the Church of England. That he and the Archbishop of Canterbury were planning a major joint initiative in terms of social policy."

Peroni laughed. "My dear Helmut, the Church of England has long since ceased to stand for anything remotely connected with Christianity. It ordains women. It ordains homosexuals. It has bishops who deny the divinity of Christ and others who deny the Resurrection and some who deny both. To be endorsed by the Church of England is not the sort of entry one would willingly place on one's CV. It has all the discipline of an eight year olds' football team."

"Very well, Stephano. Forgive my little attempt at humour. I am not well practiced in such matters. I do agree. John XXIV must be given all the guidance that is at our disposal. It is our duty to him and to the Church. You and I are used to making difficult decisions in the interests of the Church."

The two men shook hands and departed.

John XXIV was almost catatonic with fear. He had scarcely slept since the Conclave. He had eaten little and, with the exception of Peroni and Sister Donella, he had had no human contact. He had tried to pray but his mind churned randomly. For an instant he would know, with absolute clarity, where his first priority as Pope must lie: moments later he would be unable to recall the thought. By day three of his Pontificate he was convinced that he was going mad....was already mad. He knew he must talk to someone but he had already begun to fear Peroni and the good Sister spoke little Italian and even less English.

At about 4.00am he woke from a fitful sleep and, somehow, a decision had been made. Out of courtesy he waited until 5.30am before he phoned Father Nolan. The gruffness of his friend's voice was balm to his spirit.

"Who the hell is that phoning on me day off?"

"Pat! I'm sorry I'd quite forgotten."

"Who is that?"

"It's me. Bill Carterton. I'm phoning from the Vatican."

"You silly bugger. If I find out who you are you'll be phoning from the cemetery. Now clear off and leave me in peace." He slammed the phone down.

The Pope paused and dialled again.

"Bloody hell. What's the matter with you?"

"Pat! It really is me. I lived with you at St Kevin's. You must know my voice."

"Be God it is...Forgive me.....Holiness........I'm kneeling down......Is that the right thing to do?........I've not had a phone call from the Pope before."

The Pope roared with laughter. "You've done exactly the right thing. Not kneeling down. Just being Pat Nolan. " There was a silence. "Look, I'm sorry to phone on your day off. I'd quite forgotten. The election was a big surprise and I haven't been able to think straight or even believe that it really happened. To tell you the truth, Pat, I've been in a papal funk. Too frightened to venture out of my apartment and unable to concentrate suffi-ciently to make a simple decision.........other than to phone you."

"Then I'm truly honoured. The very first phone call from the new Pope. Now it's me who can't believe what is happening. Wait till I tell the girls. By the way they were thrilled when you got the job. We had a special Mass to celebrate."

"I wish I hadn't."

"Don't talk like that. It's the best news we've had in years. Now we....I mean you.....can give this old Church of ours a good shaking. Get rid of some of the cobwebs and arthritic limbs."

"Pat! I'd like to ask you a big favour. A very big favour."

"You don't have to ask Holiness. I took a vow once and so did you."

"I know but I won't have it any other way. Either you agree voluntarily or I will have no part of it."

"You're the boss. What's the favour?"

"I want you to come to Rome. To work in the Vatican. To help me..... and I need help so badly."

"Me! Amongst all those cardinals. Why they'll think you've gone mad."

"I don't care what they think. What I do care about, at least what I am now remembering to care about, is a chance to show Christ's human face to the world. I don't think we've been too good at that recently. When I was in your house I felt I was a part of that, I was learning something. I need you here to keep me grounded and to sharpen me up if I start to crumble. So, an honest answer, will you agree voluntarily?"

"Of course I'll agree. I'm flattered. First a phone call and now the offer of a job with the leader of the Church. It's more than I usually digest in one day but I'll manage. When do you need me?"

"The sooner you get here the sooner I can start behaving like a pope and not like a frightened school boy."

"I'll be there by the weekend. But what about the girls. I won't get to say goodbye. What about Kyrie?"

"We'll hold a special audience for them and you can show them the Vatican. The girls I mean, not Kyrie."

Pat laughed. "That'll be nailing you colours to the mast. I think I'll enjoy working for the Pope of the Prostitutes. It's as though things have come the full circle.

"Cardinal Peroni I owe you an apology. I have been too concerned with my own inadequacies these past few days and neglecting my duties. However, I believe that time of retreat is now over and perhaps you can advise me what engagements have been planned and what decisions need to be taken."

"Holiness, in view of your predecessor's failing health, we avoided any future engagements since last minute withdrawals caused disappointment to the Faithful and speculation in the media. Of course we are already receiving invitations for the new Pope to visit both within Italy and abroad. However, no one will expect an early answer on such matters. As to decision making, we made a major effort to clear Pope Pius' 'in tray' so to speak in order to give his successor a clean start. So, Holiness, you are under no immediate pressure either to visit your flock or tax your mind with matters of moment."

"I appreciate your efficiency, Eminence, but I can scarcely sit back and do nothing."

"Of course not. May I suggest that you spend some time getting to know the workings of your civil service, the Curia. As a Pope who has not worked in the Vatican, such a initial briefing will be invaluable and will be work enough. My assistant, Monsignor Franelli, would be an admirable guide to the organisation and I will place him at your service. Would tomorrow be too soon to start?"

"Tomorrow will be fine but I do have a couple of pressing issues. I have asked an English priest....actually he's Irish but based in England, Father Pat Nolan, to join me as a personal adviser. He will arrive this weekend. I would like him to have quarters close to mine and be given access to the usual facilities."

"A personal adviser, Holiness? It is unusual for a Pope to have a personal adviser...at least one from outside the Curia. This Father Nolan, I take it he has not worked in the Vatican?"

"Definitely not. He is the quintessential parish priest. I don't think he has ever worked outside of Liverpool Archdiocese. I'm just grateful that he agreed to come. It will be a big wrench for him."

Peroni smiled. "Holiness you have a natural humility, if I may say so. Most priests dream of serving in the Vatican. To be part, even a small part, of the executive body which governs one sixth of the world's population. Why it is a tremendous honour. I think the good father was, as you English say, tongue in cheek if he expressed reservations about such an appointment."

"No! Pat was perfectly genuine. His major concern was in not being able to say his weekly Mass for the local prostitutes. As I said, he is the quintessential parish priest. And as for not having worked here before, I am hoping he will provide me with some balance in the face of all you experienced diplomats......no offence intended."

"He sounds an interesting man, Holiness. I am sure he has much to teach us diplomats." Peroni paused then said. "There is the matter of the See of Westminster, the vacancy caused by your own election. I have prepared a short list of possible candidates with brief biographical details. I have taken the liberty of placing them in a rank order based on such criteria as loyalty to the pope, access to influential members of the British establishment, unequivocal adherence to Church doctrine and, I hope without causing offence, knowledge of Curial procedures."

"You don't mention the opinion of the clergy of Westminster Diocese.

"I don't understand."

"Surely they will be more likely to work effectively for a man of whom they approve rather than one thrust upon them? "

"I think our vow of obedience causes us to work for whomsoever the Church appoints as our lawful superior."

"Agreed ! But do we work as well for someone we fear or fail to respect? In English there is a saying: 'Tell me and I won't, ask me and I might, involve me and I will'. Why, I wonder, should we have a democratic procedure for electing a pope but not for appointing a bishop?"

Peroni looked puzzled. "Holiness, the Church has evolved over two millennia. Our means of filling appointments did not just happen. They reflect the wisdom which only develops over time and in response to other methods which have proved less satisfactory."

"But surely we have not yet reached a Golden Age in which our procedures are so perfect that they should never be improved. Sometimes I think we confuse procedure with dogma and the former becomes as immutable as the latter."

"Holiness, I do not claim that our procedures are perfect but neither are they imperfect. I advise most strongly against immediate and radical change. This consultation process! How would it take place? Would candidates produce an election manifesto? Would they hold public meetings? Be interviewed on television? Debate each other in public? Make promises in order to be elected which, like their lay equivalents, they would hastily forget on achieving office?"

The Pope laughed. "Stephano you remind me more and more of Sir Humphrey."

Peroni did not share the Pope's amusement any more than he understood the analogy. Life in the Vatican was meant to be serious and he was the enforcer, even for a pope. "I am afraid the humour of the situation escapes me." He said dryly.

"I am sorry. A reference to a television series in England. Sir Humphrey was a senior civil servant who saw his main role in life as preventing his master, the minister, from taking any action on any issue. Forgive me, I do not mean to ridicule the objections you raise. It is just that I think we tend to treat both our priests and laity as though they are ignorant peasants who can only be permitted to contribute to the Church as infantry while we, the generals, take the strategic decisions. Well there is nothing like reading military history to convince you that the view from the trench is markedly different to the view from Corps Headquarters. Generals who suffer the least casualties are invariably those who listen to their troops. I don't think we want any more casualties, religious or lay. I look forward to further discussions on the subject. There will be no decision until I feel better prepared."

"Yes, Holiness." Peroni left the apartment wondering what had caused the Pope even greater amusement.

Carterton marvelled at his own about-face. It was as though he had stood outside of himself and watched this confident man wield power over the most powerful cardinal in Christendom while the observer remained the frightened novice. Somehow the anticipation of Pat's common sense and support had enabled him to find a strength he did not know existed. It was a heady experience but not one to be repeated for its own sake. He must always remember that he was the servant of the Faithful and that included the Cardinal Secretary of State. Lord Acton, himself a staunch Catholic, had made his famous observation in regard to the very office he now held. He wrote the words into the front of his Breviary. "Power tends to corrupt and absolute power to corrupt absolutely." He would incorporate it into his Office.

Whatever immediate results Carterton's elevation achieved, consensus was not one of them. The Curia itself was divided though few expressed their opinions other than in ambiguous language and even then only to those whom they felt shared their views. As word spread that Westminster was to be filled on the basis of a popularity poll several allegedly open minds closed quickly. Franelli quietly observed and listened and chortled to himself. His treatment by Peroni had enabled him to discover his own anarchic streak and the new Pope was inadvertently feeding it.

Peroni instructed him to make himself available to the Holy Father and to provide him with a detailed appraisal of the workings of the Vatican. In so doing he emphasised the need for a 'molecular' approach: a broad brush treatment would be insufficient to enable the Pope and the Curia to function to maximum efficiency. Franelli de-coded the instruction to read; 'Smother him in minutiae so that he has no time for interfering in the real process of government'.

"I understand, Eminence. I will ensure that the Holy Father is provided with all the knowledge that I have acquired in your service."

"And you will, of course, report to me any issues which his Holiness finds of particular interest so that I may further guide him. I'd also like you to keep an eye on the one he has imported from England. He looks an odd fellow, more like a gardener than a priest."

CHAPTER 11

Franelli entered the papal apartment , knelt and made to kiss the Pope's ring. The Pope waved him up and shook hands.

"Now we are in the twenty first century I think we should behave accordingly. I'd like you to spread the word, Monsignor."

Mentally Franelli contrasted this unassuming man with Peroni. Gloomily he saw the Secretary of State running the Church and the Pope doing what he was told.

"Holiness, as you know, Cardinal Peroni wants me to assist you in familiarising yourself with the Curia and the Vatican. I will try my best but I have only been here for three years and my knowledge is limited."

"Good. If you had been here much longer you would have become an apologist. I don't want a justification for every nuance, just an objective introduction. So where shall we begin."

"Perhaps the Curia, Holiness. Or maybe the Vatican City?"

"Let's start with the City. I know the history but little more."

"Well this is the main building, the Apostolic Palace. I still get lost in it. There are well over a thousand rooms and almost as many staircases. There are numerous courtyards, beautiful gardens and even a small wood. Then there is the magnificent Galleon Fountain with its battery of water cannon, that is my favourite. Of course, you have your own private garden on the roof."

"Yes. I have found it already. I'm told it is very secure."

"It is, Holiness. You may walk there in the knowledge that no sniper can ever assassinate you."

"I feel safer already."

"That is not the only security measure. We have, of course, some 100 Swiss Guard and other security personnel. In the event of a siege, we have our own reservoir and, if supplies run low, we can always have the pope removed to safety via the helipad."

The Pope smiled. "What about the rest of the population?"

Franelli laughed. "I would dread to contemplate it. Over 3000 people work here and about 1000 actually live here. Then there are the tourists. On some days we could have as many as 100000 visiting the Basilica. I suppose, at a pinch, we could use the railway line, courtesy of Mussolini's government, but only if the present government could provide the trains."

"Quite an enterprise."

"Oh! There is much more. We have a fire brigade, a curfew at 11.30pm when the gates are locked, a supermarket and various other amenities. Yet you can stroll round the perimeter in less than an hour."

"And you, Monsignor? What shall I call you?"

"Carlo, Holiness." Franelli shook his head. "But it will seem strange. Cardinal Peroni has never once called me Carlo in the three years I have served him."

"Carlo it shall be. I am beginning to think that a relaxed attitude and a Vatican appointment are strangely incompatible."

"Not just incompatible, Holiness. They are mutually exclusive."

The high command of the Organisation was in some disarray. Pius's papacy had seen an unprecedented rise in its importance. Recruitment was up. Recognition was secure. The more dismal predictions as to the effect of Vatican II had been averted. Avant garde theologians had been disciplined or silenced. Liberalism was in retreat on both the religious and the political fronts. Even those pioneers of unfettered experimentation, the Dutch, were finally awakening from their false-reality and expressing their yearning for stability at the ballot box. It could only be a matter of time before the Faithful in Holland returned to sanity. Furthermore, the jewel in the crown, which had seemed so far away, was suddenly within grasp. Their founder was on the brink of sainthood. Pius had advanced his case at "indecent speed" to quote one hostile commentator. Now the timetable lay in the hands of the new Pope.

Carterton's views, as derived from his recent publicised sermons, suggested that he would be unsympathetic to the Organisation. At least that was the prevailing belief. If this was the case then momentum would be lost and, once that happened, other issues could obscure the claim of even the most worthy candidates for canonisation. In what amounted to a panic, a plan was devised. If the Pope could not be relied upon to support the cause, the next most powerful man was Peroni. Therefore, it was reasoned, Peroni must be conscripted to ensure a speedy and satisfactory decision.

This decision failed to take account of Peroni's dislike of anything that suggested a 'church within a church' but, since he had always disguised this attitude while doing his best to promote it, no one could be blamed for the oversight. A second and less excusable oversight was the choice of Archbishop Stanford as the delegate to the Secretary of State. Stanford, not a man to underestimate his own influence, had often referred to his conversations with Peroni and implied, with considerable modesty, that he regularly shaped Vatican policy.

As things turned out this unfortunate strategy postponed for the foreseeable future, and possibly forever, the canonisation of Monsignor Estoria while, in an unintended symmetry, it added an unlikely strengthening to the bonds between the Pope and his chief bureaucrat.

Stanford's request for a personal interview with Peroni was received with mixed feelings. Peroni shared many of Stanford's conservative opinions but disliked his presumptuous manner. In particular, he resented Stanford's overt treatment of Peroni as an equal in both rank and intellect. The very suggestion that a mere archbishop was in the same league as a Cardinal Secretary of State displayed both ignorance and stupidity. But, in the dangerous post-conclave situation, he needed to secure allies no matter how distasteful.

"My dear Cardinal Stephano." Peroni winced as this intimate greeting. "It is so good of you to see me at this critical time for our Church. I'm sure you and I are as one in our anxiety for the future."

"And what anxiety would that be, Archbishop?"

Stanford continued unabashed. "Why coming to terms with a new papacy and the radical change of direction which it implies."

"Go on."

"Well take this curious business of the appointment of the new Archbishop of Westminister. Rumour has it that it may be subject to some sort of popularity poll amongst the ordinary clergy perhaps, even, the laity. Full blown election campaigns can be seen on the horizon." Stanford shuddered dramatically.

Peroni was about to point out that he had the matter in hand but decided that such a statement could undermine his position if the Pope went ahead with the idea of wide consultation. Instead he replied cryptically. "A new papacy, a new approach. It is not uncommon especially when the new Holy Father lacks Curial experience."

Stanford interrupted. "That is exactly my point. The man.... the Holy Father is an academic, a theologian. He was only briefly an archbishop. He needs strong guidance." This time he noted Peroni's displeasure. "And how lucky he is....we are...to have you in a position to provide such guidance. Of course, if I can in my humble way assist, I shall be flattered to do so."

"Did you have a particular way in mind?"

"I am open to anything you suggest but I do have some ideas."

Peroni nodded.

"As you know only too well the Organisation has become a powerful force under the patronage of our late Holy Father. Though relatively weak in numbers, something less than 100,000 Catholics, it is strong in influence. It has contacts with leaders from the secular world as well as those in positions within the Church. In my own case I have assumed what one might describe as a sympathetic role, providing support and encouragement."

"Curious that you have never actually joined a body you so clearly admire."

Stanford smiled enigmatically. "Not everyone admires the Organisation and it has received its own share of unfavourable publicity. By remaining outside but supportive I am in a position to deny membership while defending it against the loony left of the Catholic Church and other critics."

'A position which enables you to jump either way when the wind blows.' Peroni reasoned but he replied neutrally. "The late Holy Father saw the Organisation as a bulwark against reformist abandon. As a balancing mechanism against those who interpreted Vatican II as proscribing origin sin."

"Exactly! One has only to look at the abandonment of the Sacrament of Penance to see the evidence of that heresy. Why even the pious forgive themselves and the rest don't believe that there is ever anything to forgive. One of my own priests had the audacity to tell me that 'to understand all is to forgive all'. I believe he was quoting a Frenchman. I told him he had better stick to quoting the Ten Commandments if he wanted to continue preaching."

"A robust response. Did he accept the warning?"

"No. He left soon afterwards and married a divorcee with a string of children." Stanford laughed. "He may have lost his belief in sin but I wager he now knows all about penance."

"I do not believe you have come all the way to Rome simply to give me your rather pessimistic view of the current situation."

"Quite so. I came to offer my assistance should you see it as useful but also to seek yours. The Organisation was looking forward to the early canonisation of its blessed founder. Such an act would not only raise the morale of its members but be a sign to the whole Church that conservative Catholicism is an option worth considering. If the Church is due for a turbulent voyage what better ballast than a well-connected, doctrinally reliable cadre willing to make sacrifices far beyond the average Mass goer. With the new Holy Father on a very steep learning curve, the canonisation could proceed without him having to divert valuable energy."

"I can promise nothing beyond raising the matter with the Pope."

"I ask for nothing more." Stanford replied happily while misreading the Cardinal.

"Anything else?"

"There is one other matter which I am loath to raise since it may appear self-serving. However, I have been pressured by many to convey their opinion directly to you. It concerns the See of Westminster. As you know I was considered as a possible candidate prior to Archbishop Carterton's appointment. Now such support has become overt in the light of the democratisation of the process. I have even been reliably informed that the Prime Minister favours my appointment."

"And what do you favour?" Peroni asked, barely concealing his annoyance.

"I favour the best choice for our Church in troubled times but, regardless of whether I am that choice, I am quite certain that trying to explain away harsh reality, and sin is a harsh reality, in the language of therapy rather than the traditional language of the Church is a short cut to irrelevance. We want a man who will stand up and be counted."

"But, hopefully, not counted out." And with this cryptic remark Peroni ended the interview.

CHAPTER 12

Despite the arrival of Fr Nolan, the early weeks of the papacy of John XXIV gave the impression of a holy man overawed by the office, one who would spend much time in prayer and little in Church governance. As the days passed Peroni became more optimistic as did Cardinal Kirst. As the Cardinals' foreboding abated, Franelli's rose. He had hoped for a reformist pope not a contemplative. His only consolation was that his reports to Peroni could be both true and innocuous.

"He shows little interest in the organisation of the Curia and prefers to spend time in his chapel. He celebrates Mass with the Irish priest and they often breakfast together. I think he is in a state of shock from which, I fear, he may never recover."

Peroni was beginning to see himself as the de facto pope. The Pope's brief assertiveness must have evaporated as quickly as it had arisen. He thanked Franelli with unusual warmth and visited Kirst. "Helmut, I believe we are in for an easier run than we feared. The Holy Spirit works in a mysterious way and confounds us mortals time and again. Elect a radical as Pope and far from being interventionist he leaves us with a virtual free hand to continue in the footsteps of our late Holy Father."

The German remained sanguine. "It is still early days. Maybe we were alarmist but, on the other hand, we may be experiencing the calm before the storm."

"I admire your caution but I cannot help feeling that optimism is justified. However, I have arranged to see His Holiness this afternoon and I will report back on my impressions."

John XXIV greeted Peroni with greater calm than is normal in a man traumatised by a major life event. He began with a further apology for his withdrawn behaviour.

"Only too understandable, Holiness. You scarcely had time to adjust to Westminster before you were thrust into the papacy. The speed of events, together with your lack of Vatican experience, would be enough to unsettle any priest."

"Thank you for your understanding however I do not intend to allow my lack of experience to excuse me from carrying out the role I have been assigned. I admired my predecessor for his strength of purpose and the astonishing achievements of his pontificate. If I can achieve one quarter as much I shall be well pleased. But we cannot, any of us, entirely escape from our background. Indeed, I believe that providence has a hand in shaping that background. Pius was, in some ways, a Cold War warrior. Now, thank God, the Cold War is behind us and Pius' huge contribution to its ending is universally acknowledged. I, we, have now to discard some of the siege mentality which the cold war and other situations hostile to Catholicism engendered."

The Pope's manner impressed Peroni. There was a quiet confidence about the man. Kirst's reservations were proving only too accurate. "Holiness, I can see that you have spent these past days to good effect and I am flattered that you are sharing your vision with me. I will, of course, be only too happy to help you translate it into practical terms."

John nodded his appreciation. "The spiritual exercise I have been conducting with the invaluable help of Father Nolan may sound arrogant but it seems to me the only way to go about setting myself some priorities. I have imagined that our saviour returned to earth at this moment in time and examined his Church in the light of his Gospel. I fear that he would not be well pleased with our efforts."

"In what way, Holiness?"

"He might well point to the secrecy with which we conduct so much our business and would remind us that men commit deeds in the dark because they do not want them exposed to the light. I believe he would call us to account for our negligence in regard to the abuse of children and remind us that a mill stone is the reward for such a heinous sin. I suspect he would ask us why so many of our senior clerics live in such luxury when he lived so frugally. Perhaps he would recall how he attacked the Jewish priestly class for laying so many burdens on the backs of their flock when he only asked that we love God and our neighbour. He might wonder whether we have not repeated history in this regard. Finally, and most damningly, he would accuse us of hypocrisy for continuing to say one thing and do the reverse."

"A serious charge which would require strong evidence."

"Take our much heralded principle of subsidiarity. We claim that decisions should be made at the lowest possible level yet seek to overrule them if they don't meet with the approval of a group of Curial bureaucrats. To give you a specific example. On what doctrinal grounds were the Sisters of Charity forbidden to operate a safe injecting room in Sydney, Australia?"

Peroni tried to stifle his anger. "Injecting rooms are a highly controversial issue which could potentially cause much harm to the reputation of the Church."

"A pity we haven't been so diligent over child abuse." The Pope threw up his hands. "I am sorry. That was not helpful. Controversial I agree, yet Jesus was also controversial. But that is not the heart of the matter. The Australian Church was taking an important initiative which, in no way, went against Catholic teaching. Many would argue quite the reverse and the Curia overruled what was essentially a local issue best dealt with locally through local knowledge." The Pope noted Peroni's discomfort. "I am sorry to be so blunt and I am sure the Curia acts in good faith in such matters but can you imagine the effect it has on thinking Catholics when they are treated as naughty children, caught trying to put one over on their betters. No wonder there are empty pews and empty presbyteries."

Peroni felt ill. The conclave had not just elected an unknown, it had elected a mad man. In a rare moment of self-doubt he wondered if he had the strength to control a Pope who was clearly set on destroying the Church. With an enormous act of the will he concentrated on salvaging the situation.

"But, Holiness, while sharing your wish to bring the Church closer to the Gospel we must beware that our enemies will be only too pleased to seize and amplify any public criticism which flows from the Church leadership. By all means let us put our house in order but let us do so discretely and slowly." Peroni laughed as though sharing a joke with the Pope. "As a footballer of some repute, I'm sure you don't want to give the opposition a free kick."

The Pope remained silent for a moment. Then he, too, laughed. "Let me continue with your football analogy. As you know my home town fields two Premier League sides. Both fanatically supported by laity and clergy alike. I recall a period when I was a boy and would go to the 'match' with my father each Saturday. Most often our team played badly but such was the loyalty of the fans that they turned out week after week and rarely criticised. At last, when relegation was starring us in the face, a new manager was appointed. He was interviewed by the Echo and voiced the disillusionment which we all felt but kept hidden. It didn't make him popular. In fact, if I remember correctly, his car was vandalised soon afterwards. However, within two seasons we were watching first class soccer and focused on League Championship rather than relegation."

"An interesting story, Holiness but the analogy escapes me."

"It is simply that sometimes one has to be openly self-critical and to accept the flack which may follow in order to achieve a thorough renewal. Pretending that the Emperor is dressed when he is patently naked is, in my view, the truly high risk strategy."

"And how is this aggiornomento to be achieved?"

"I am not entirely sure but I hope it will be with your help and that of all the Curia. Believe me, I do not want to belittle or undermine anyone but I do believe that the Holy Spirit was as aware of my attitudes as he/she was of my unworthiness. So I must conclude, Cardinal Secretary, that I was chosen because of the direction in which my papacy is intended take the Church. Bill Carterton, the Pope, is the same Bill Carterton who was briefly Archbishop of Westminster and, before that, Archbishop of Liverpool. To suddenly change my position because I am now Pope would be like a politician reneging on pre-election promises. Do not misunderstanding me. I have spent days paralysed by fear. I am not by nature someone who enjoys conflict and disturbance. However, I have prayed earnestly and sought wisdom from Pat Nolan. I know I will be given the grace and courage which I will most certainly need."

Peroni retreated down the corridor. The English were notorious for fostering eccentrics, one reason why there had only been one English Pope prior to John XXIV. The Irish were notorious for hard drinking and writing impenetrable prose. An oddity for a Pope with a bog trotter as his guru. An obsession with Poland seemed little short of perfection.

"I don't think the Secretary of State is too amused by the workings of the Holy Spirit." The Pope joked to Pat Nolan.

" I don't think he's too amused by too many things, Holiness. I suppose it's a penalty of high office."

"Well don't let me become overwhelmed by mine. Your job, Pat, is to keep me from taking myself too seriously......and anyone else who tries to convince me that 'the man who laughs has not yet been told the terrible news'. And, Pat, please call me Bill."

"Holiness. I couldn't. You are the Pope."

"Of that I am only too well aware and my request is not for your sake but for mine. If you keep calling me Holiness we both may come to believe it. Not fully perhaps, but sufficient for you to censor what you say to me and for me to assume that I am somehow superior to other men. I want you honest with me, Pat, and I believe that calling me Bill will aid that process and bring me back to earth."

Fr Nolan laughed. "Very well, Bill, but I'll be more formal when we not alone. You know, my old mother told me on the day of my ordination that I was destined for the Vatican. I think she had a red hat in mind and not a man treating the Pope as an equal. I wonder what she makes of all this." He nodded upwards.

"Let me give her even greater cause for concern. I want her son to tell me exactly what he would do if he were in my shoes?"

Nolan thought for a moment. "It's not original, Bill, but I'd call another council and this time I wouldn't just open the windows to let in the breeze. I'd open the bloody doors as well and really put our trust in the Spirit."

"You've been reading my mind. While I was paralysed with fear, I keep worrying about what my agenda should be as Pope. I'd already spelt out some ideas in Liverpool and Westminster, as you know. In fact some of them were your ideas. But were these appropriate as head of the whole Church or was I abusing the power of office. How do I know what is needed in Central America or China? I could claim some firsthand experience of Britain but not of elsewhere. Then it came to me. My principal role was to listen and to make sure that everyone gets heard, not just those considered safe by the bureaucracy. A council it will be."

"Bravo, Il Papa. And a word of advice if I may. Just announce it. Don't tell Peroni in advance."

"But common courtesy."

"Courtesy be buggered. If you tell him he will exhaust you with an irrefutable argument as to why it is impossible or, if not impossible, that it cannot be organised this side of the next millennium. That even if could be organised it would resuscitate world interest in Vatican finances, predatory priests, women's' ordination, married clergy and a host of other hot topics beloved by the tabloids." Nolan was now apoplectic. "Tell him nothing and just to be belt and braces, set a timetable so there can be no death by procrastination."

Pat, you are an inspiration. I just hope you will stay in Rome."

"And miss the greatest show on earth. Not likely. When will you announce your decision?"

"I'll do it at my weekly audience, this Friday."

"You mean to the run of the mill Faithful...your nuns, priests on holiday, Children of Mary and sundry others. Hardly the College of Cardinals."

"Exactly. The College of Cardinals already has its privileges and it's about time the rank and file had theirs'"

The Herald typified one section of opinion regarding John XXIV's unexpected announcement.

NEW POPE BREAKS THE MOULD
FIREWORKS TO FOLLOW

The election of Cardinal William Carterton, only recently appointed Archbishop of Westminster, to that of Pope caused tremors within Vatican City and beyond. The elevation of this relatively little known Archbishop of Liverpool, England, was the last cryptic act of Pius XIII. Carterton had recently begun to preach a sort of Social Catholicism which seemed not wholly in keeping with his conservative benefactor. Did this curious act mean that the old Pope had begun to view his own papacy as too illiberal and was he trying to signal this change of heart to the outside world? Did he believe that his conservative appointments had grown too self-satisfied and confident that they alone could shape Church policy? Or was it simply the gesture of a man whose faculties had deserted him?

Whatever the reason, he has done more than throw a pebble into the pond. More likely he has created a tidal wave. In the days immediately following John XXIV's election it seemed that the new Pope was to be an invisible man, dealing with the world through his Curia and especially Cardinal Peroni, the powerful and conservative Secretary of State. Then, to everyone's surprise, he demonstrated that not only was he calling the shots, but that he was calling them fast and furious and, not necessarily, to those who saw themselves as his legitimate confidants.

At last Friday's weekly audience, a normally quiet and low key affair, attended by the hoi polloi of the Catholic Church, he made his astonishing announcement. Not only was the medium unusual but so was the means of delivery. This is what he said as recorded by one of the very few journalists present.

"My dear friends, I thank you for coming to this gathering and I particularly welcome those who have come great distances or who may represent other Faiths. This is my first audience, though I prefer the

word meeting, with the ordinary people and I use the term advisedly for it was the ordinary people to whom Jesus directed his ministry. It is, therefore, a term of deep respect. Sometimes men or women in high office lose respect for the ordinary people and, when that happens, I believe that they have proved themselves unfit for their office. I pray that I shall never be guilty of that sin. So I do greet you as dear friends, People of God and my brothers and sisters, no matter what your religion, colour or gender.

Today I ask your prayers for me in this awesome office which is both honour and responsibility. During my first days as Pope I was so burdened by the whole idea that I was virtually a prisoner of my own fear. Then it was made clear to me that the burden of bringing Christ's message to the world is not mine but shared by all Christians and the weight began to lessen. I hope to make my pontificate one which acknowledges that fact in practical ways. That the People of God have a real say in the future spiritual direction of the Church and are not simply confined to supplying its practical needs. That we should be a Church which listens more than it instructs and which tries to avoid placing unnecessary burdens on mankind.

Today I want to announce a modest start in listening, not just to Catholics but to all people of goodwill. There is to be another council." Here there was an audible gasp from the crowd. *"It will commence within three years and will have participating laity and members of other Christian faiths, not just as observers but as full participants. I hope it will, and we must all pray hard for this grace, become a channel for the Spirit and the dawn of another Pentecost.*

Fittingly you, the ordinary people, the People of God are the first to hear this news. Together I know we can ensure that it is the Good News which Jesus promised and which we sometimes fail to deliver.

May God bless you all, the Father, Son and Holy Spirit. Thank you for being with me."

Reaction from within the Catholic Church has been interesting. For those disappointed by the seeming failure of Vatican II to usher in a more liberal interpretation of the Gospel, the Pope's message has been greeted with wild enthusiasm. For those who viewed Vatican II as a dangerous experiment to be terminated as quickly as possible, the announcement is seen as threatening to undo decades of revisionism. Of course, this latter group is far less strident in its reaction out of respect for the office of pope. Its adherents are reluctant to allow attributable comment or to use language which fully expresses their horror at what the Pope has proposed. Phrases such as "a decision which the Holy Father may wish to reconsider when he has examined all the implications" or "more of symbolic gesture than a firm statement of intent and subject to further clarification" are about as strong a reaction as the conservative forces are prepared to issue at present. However, the code is quite clear to anyone with a nodding acquaintance with Catholicism.

The real question is whether the Pope will back down in face of the enormously powerful conservative forces within the Church including those of the Organisation or whether he will risk what could amount to a schism. This newspaper has been a consistent critic of the way in which the US Hierarchy has failed to handle cases of sexual abuse by clergy. In particular, it has taken exception to the secrecy in which the American Church has conducted itself, a clear message that the reputation of the Church was more important than the rehabilitation of the victim. In order to avoid any charge of a double standard, The Herald applauds the openness of Pope John XXIV and will support him in his call for a new Council.

CHAPTER 13

Monsignor Franelli had never seen his master so angry nor so indiscrete. Anticipating a strong reaction he had tried to keep well away from the Secretariat but Peroni had summoned him back.

"Monsignor Franelli, tell me something. Do you have any ambition? Do you, for example, hope one day to become a bishop, an archbishop perhaps, or even a cardinal?"

"I think your assessment of my competence, Eminence, has long since removed any such ambition."

"I see. Then perhaps a simple parish priest?"

"Yes, Eminence. I believe that I could still aspire to that position."

Peroni's face blackened. "Well Monsignor, let me disabuse you of even such a lowly ambition, at least if the present Holy Father has his way. If he continues to make policy decisions on a whim, there will simply be no Church in which to serve. It is as though the Conclave willingly established a Fifth Column and is about to reap the consequences. I am scarcely able to sleep and when I do I awake believing that I have just experienced a nightmare and that, as consciousness returns, I will re-enter a world which has not gone insane. Unfortunately it is no nightmare but a terrible reality."

"But, Eminence, perhaps good will flow from the Pope's initiative and the negative reactions are simply adjusting to what is a very different management style."

"The Catholic Church does not cater for 'different management styles'." Peroni spat out the words. "The Catholic Church does not even talk or think in terms of management styles. The Catholic Church has existed, for two millennia, by gradually subjugating individual idiosyncrasy through the medium of the Curia or, when that proved impossible, by dispensing with the idiosyncratic person or persons. The Curia is the essential filter through which all information must pass in order to be purified. To by-pass this filter is to allow contamination to enter the Mystical Body and poison it, possibly beyond repair. It seems as though the present Holy Father believes in an immune system which can tolerate any toxin. Certainly he does not seem to need a Secretary of State to guide him in his inexperience. Well so be it, he shall have my resignation and have it today."

Franelli was shocked. He had never expected such a direct attack on the Pope or that Peroni would ever consider resigning. He wasn't even sure if cardinals could resign other than for age or some very public disgrace. "But, Eminence, surely you won't want to create a precedent. What if other cardinals follow your lead. Where will that leave us?"

"A precedent! A precedent, Monsignor! The new Holy Father is a living advertisement for precedents. Why, amongst other innovations, he has made a cosy arrangement with Archbishop Kowalski to meet with Sebastian Hart. Not a word to his Secretary of State. Not a consideration as to the message this will convey to the world. The new Pope's first personal audience is with a man who has done more to debase the standards of public morality than a legion of barbarians. If my resignation is a precedent then I am simply following the example of my Pontiff. Surely that cannot be unworthy?"

"That, Eminence, is too difficult a question for a humble monsignor. Perhaps Cardinal Kirst would provide a second opinion."

Again Peroni shook his head and wandered off down the corridor. Head shaking was becoming his trade mark since the

Conclave. However, Franelli's comment did cause him to think again. Kirst was certainly not a man to rush into a decision and it could do no harm to speak with him before seeing the Pope. He stopped and breathed deeply to calm himself. Kirst might be an ally but he had no wish to reveal any personal weakness to the Prefect. He set off for the Palazzo de Sant 'Uffizio.

"Stephano I must caution you against any precipitate action." Kirst made a rare use of his Christian name. "I appreciate that your close contact with the Holy Father has left you more vulnerable to depression than others like myself though even I have a deep sense of foreboding. I have always admired the skilful way in which you circumvented the more lunatic aspirations which followed Vatican II."

Peroni interrupted. "Not alone, Helmut. Your role and that of half a dozen others was highly significant."

Kirst waved the praise aside. "Some small part, perhaps, but you were our inspiration. Without your example, we would have lacked that inspiration and probably the courage. Surely that leadership is now even more vital. If Vatican II threatened to create a climate which substituted 'life style' for 'vocation', Vatican III threatens to replace 'sanctity' with 'socialism'. We will no longer be a Church but a branch of the Christian Democrats." Kirst drew himself up to his full height and raised his right arm like a Napoleon pointing to still unconquered lands. "Just imagine what will happen if you do resign. Life in a remote convent somewhere, hearing the confessions of worthy nuns and going quietly mad. While back in Rome the Pope appoints ......some.... some...maverick...Fr whatever his name is...as the Secretary of State. Did you know that he had a special prostitute's Mass in England....why stop at that, let's turn Vatican City into a huge bordello." Kirst paused. "I know, I am getting carried away. But we really don't know what excesses could occur if there is no one to apply the brakes. You cannot resign."

Despite his depression, Peroni was rather flattered. He felt that Kirst had more than repaid his own disclosures concerning the new Pope: he had not made himself a hostage. That he had been considered an inspiration in the dismantling of the Second Vatican Council's programme of reform was an entirely new concept for, whatever his faults, Peroni had never tried to use power for personal kudos. He had opposed many of the reforms because he believed that they were bad for the Church, not because he wished to establish a fan club. None the less to be complimented on your performance, in a role in which you had never cast yourself, was a heady experience and there is no better antidote to depression than an unexpected bouquet from an unexpected quarter.

"Thank you, Helmut. You have given me wise advice. I will not resign, at least not while there is a chance I can do something to save the Church. I will, however, inform the Holy Father than I fear the consequences of his actions. If he chooses to dispense with my services, so be it."

"Holiness I requested this audience in order to be honest with you about some matters which concern me."

"I hope you will never be less than honest with me."

"I hope that what I say will not be taken as arrogance or impertinence."

The Pope smiled. "I assume you are going to take me to task for un-pope like behaviour. You have the floor, be as brutally honest as you see fit......and please, sit down."

"I would prefer to stand." Peroni shook his head inadvertently. "Holiness, I accept that you are the head of the Church. I accept that the Holy Spirit had a part in your election. I accept that you are a good man and wish only to elaborate a vision of the Church in which you believe sincerely. I do not accept, however, that any one man is able to guide such a large and complex organisation as the Catholic Church without relying on experienced advisors and that, with respect, appears to be the way in which you plan to govern. If that is correct, then there will be a heavy price to pay and, as your Secretary of State, I have a duty so to warn you."

Peroni looked hard at the Pope who indicated that he should continue.

"To take the most recent example. You announce another council when we have scarcely got over the shock waves from the last one. Do you have any idea how much work was involved in ensuring that the unrealistic expectations of Vatican II were put to rest?"

"Not in detail but I would like to hear you out on the matter."

"The Second Vatican Council was, in hindsight, a dangerous experiment in Catholic democracy. Meaningless phrases like 'the People of God' were coined and gave the impression that the Catholic Church was subservient to vox populi. Nuns exchanged their centuries old habits for miniskirts. Priests wore the latest Levi's. The laity consulted their own consciences rather than the confessional. As one cardinal noted: 'They don't need confession, they forgive themselves.' The scriptures were considered in the same light as self-help books, to be ignored if reading them didn't produce a warm after-glow. Everyone, even some priests, demanded sex as a necessary adjunct to mental health and, for most of them, that meant sex without offspring. It was a descent into chaos. Fortunately the influence of the Holy Spirit was sufficient to ensure that the last Conclave elected a Pope who was strong enough to stride the world proclaiming the true Magisterium, undoing years of vacillation."

Peroni had gone quite red. He paused for breath. "Yet you know how this crusade to re-assert traditional teaching was lampooned? The Empire Strikes Back! Pius gave his long pontificate to the restoration of power in the successor of Peter and, as his delegates, the Curia. We all hoped and prayed that the next Conclave would elect a successor of similar mould to consolidate his work. However, his last act, the act which made you, a self-professed radical a cardinal, seemed to contradict symbolically much of his pontificate. Without that act many of the cardinals might have cast their votes elsewhere, elected another traditionalist, but they did not. My task, therefore, is to limit the potential discordance between two very different papacies. Whatever the late Holy Father's intentions in making you a cardinal I do not believe that he saw you as his successor and he, unquestionably, would not have ordered a new council, virtually before the corpse of the last one was cold, and without consulting with your most senior advisor seems...I have to say it...nothing short of madness." Peroni stopped again, aghast at his own words. The Pope remained calm.

"Holiness. I am truly sorry. Forgive me. Perhaps being bypassed was more hurtful than I had realised."

"Stephano, you have nothing for which to apologise. I know that I should have consulted you and I knew that if I did consult you I would be presented with an unanswerable case as to why the council could not and should not take place. You would have tied me in more knots than a fishing net. So I apologise for any offence I may have caused and I realise that, in opposing me, you would have had the best interests of the Church at heart. Indeed, I would have respected you less had I informed you prior to the announcement and received anything short of a most forceful objection."

Peroni appeared confused. Clearly he was dealing with a very different type of man. There was no anger only, it seemed, understanding. "Holiness, you are very generous."

"I hope that I am but, far more importantly, I hope that I am open to all shades of opinion within the Church. Yours just as much as the opinion of those who share ideas closer to me. And that, Stephano, is why I could not consult you. If I am to hear the true voice of faith, in all its flats and sharps, with all its harmony and its discord then I need to have a council which is receptive and not just expressive and, above all, which is not stage managed. And now that you know what I want I hope you will help me bring it to fruition, knowing that conservatives will be as influential as liberals and that neither group will conduct the orchestra."

"Holiness! It will be chaotic. It is a well-established principle of governance in all organisations that you do not call an open forum unless you can predict the outcome. Unless you are able to write the minutes before you have distributed the agenda. Such events are to showcase decisions already made and to present the audience, be they shareholders, or electors, or the Faithful that the organisation is a model of consensus. Thus the outside world, which inevitably contains enemies, is too circumspect to attack in the face of such cohesion. And the inside world, which inevitably contains doubters, exerts a form of peer pressure which ensures their silence. In essence that was the failure of Vatican II. The minutes could only be written the event"

This time the Pope laughed. "Cardinal Machiavelli! What you have just explained to me is so close to reality that I have no rational way of refuting the argument. However, it fails to take account of just one factor and that alone gives me the courage to reject what I cannot refute."

"And that factor?"

"The Spirit, of course. We have to trust him...her...it. The Spirit will not let us down if we act in good faith."

He looked at Peroni. "Oh I know. It's a bit like jumping from a plane with a parachute. Most people believe that it is safe but few actually choose to jump. Those who do are exhilarated. I want you to jump with me, Stephano."

"Holiness, with great respect, I must emphasise that I have absolutely no head for heights. Furthermore, if my memory of war films is correct, parachutes have a tendency to form a Roman candle. I wonder if that terrifyingly apt phrase may not also be prophetic."

"May I suggest then Stephano, that you give me the benefit of the doubt. I am still a very junior Pope and I know that I have much to learn but I would like you to get to know me a little better before you classify me a incurably mad. Promise me one thing, that you will pray before you reach a final decision."

"Of course, of course. But there is one other matter. The English priest, Fr Nolan, what exactly is his status? "

"He is my minder and, actually, he's Irish."

"Your minder?" Peroni again shook his head. "It is not a phrase I have encountered in Canon Law."

"No! Another reference to a BBC series, I'm afraid." The Pope could scarcely contain his amusement. "It was a long running series. A minder is someone who keeps his master from getting into trouble and, when that fails, is there to drag him back out."

Peroni's eyes rolled. The Pope continued. "I don't mean literally. At least not where I am concerned. Pat Nolan is here to keep me grounded.....in touch with reality. At least reality as seen through the eyes of a parish priest and not, with respect, solely through eyes of the Curia, no matters how 20/20 its vision."

"I see. And is your minder to be exalted in rank. A monsignor perhaps, even a bishop."

"I'm afraid not. I asked him if he would accept a promotion but he refused outright. He said his girls would think he had sold out when he visit's Liverpool. No Pat will remain a humble father."

"Well, Holiness, it has been a most instructive meeting. It seems that we are in for a remarkable papacy."

Pat Nolan entered as soon as Peroni had departed. "How did it go? What's he like under pressure? Did he resign? Did you sack him?"

"To answer you in reverse order. No! I did not sack him though I feared that he might resign. What's he like? I am taking to him. I think he has courage and possibly the making of an open mind. How did it go? As well as could be expected. If he gives me a little time to get more comfortable on the Throne of Peter, I think we may even have an ally.....at least a man who will deal honestly with me."

Nolan was about to leave when the Pope stopped him. "Tell me, Pat, how have you found celibacy? We never talked about it when I was living in your presbytery."

Nolan scratched his head. "It depended. I'm almost sixty now so it isn't too great a problem but as a young priest it could be difficult. There were temptations and I once asked to be moved to forsake that which I wanted to embrace. I've been lucky in that I've always had friends. I sometimes think it's the loneliness which causes the problem and not the libido. But if what you are really asking is do I agree with a celibate clergy then the answer is that I think it should be voluntary and my guess is that a large majority of priests feel the same way." He gave the Pope a cheeky look. "How about you, Bill? Have you ever fancied a dalliance?"

"No! So I can claim no virtue for resisting a temptation which I never experienced. I think my excitement has been too cerebral. If I'd had to take a vow never to read a book then I'd have been a spectacular apostate. But if I substitute my lust for books with a more normal lust for sexual gratification, I can only believe that we ask too much of our religious, nuns, priests and brothers. I want a commission to examine the whole issue of religious sexuality and report to the council."

"And if we are to review practice in regard to religious sexuality then I believe that we should re-examine other aspects of sexuality, notably contraception, pre-marital sex, homosexuality and abortion. Not because I believe that we've got it all wrong but because I think we have shown an inflexibility in relation to these matters when we have been prepared to do some pretty amazing volte face on other issues. Jesus was spot on when he nailed the Scribes and Pharisees for hypocrisy. If we can accept change in some areas in the light of new knowledge and experience, then we must surely subject all doctrine to the same analysis. As a cynical friend of mine once remarked, 'With the Catholics everything is forbidden until it becomes compulsory'. I don't believe that all, or perhaps any, doctrine will require change. In fact, we may arrive at the same conclusions on a more robust basis but let us remain open to the possibility of change and of the Spirit to guide us in our efforts."

"Such an examination is also to be part of the pre-council agenda and we won't stop there. However, it is not my council and we must canvas the whole Church as to what is seen as vital to a thorough stock take. I agree with you that most priests favour voluntary celibacy. Perhaps you could look a little further into celibacy and let me know what you find."

"If you do open up these issues, you're going to have to face the big one."

The Pope nodded. "I am only too conscious of that."

CHAPTER 14

"Well, Pat, what have you got for me?"

Fr Nolan seated his ever increasing frame into his favourite chair. Though by no means haute cuisine, Vatican fare was an improvement on his own cooking and he was taking full advantage. With no Kyrie to walk and the oppressive heat of Rome, he had abandoned any pretence of weight control.

"Sure you could spend months on the research but I don't think the picture would be much different however long you looked. The fact is that there is absolutely no reason why we shouldn't have married priests. No reason why you shouldn't have a married pope, the Church has already had about 40 of them or about fifteen per cent of the total of 265. Even the last Pope said as much though he didn't go so far as to make any changes. Mind you I think he only had Mrs Priest in mind and not Mrs Cardinal."

"Perhaps he would have changed things had he lived."

Pat was not one to speculate so he returned to his brief. "Take the United States, for example. There are about twenty thousand married priests no longer employed in the priesthood. Many of them would love to return to their vocation if the rules were relaxed. To add to their discomfort, we have been ordaining married refugees from the Episcopalian Church who fled from the ordination of women. The situation in Britain would be similar though the numbers would vary and you'd have to read Church of England for Episcopalian."

"I hadn't realised the numbers were so great."

"It seems both unfair and wasteful. Maybe a hundred thousand worldwide have left the priesthood to marry in the past twenty five years. So far as I can tell, and I'm no scholar, the ban on married priests, which didn't come into force until the fourth century with the Romanisation of the Church, was aimed at consolidating power and property. Essentially two classes of priest emerged, the lower class, family based priest, and the higher class celibates. With the passage of time, the celibates achieved domination aided by an increasing streak of misogamy, the one feeding off the other. Augustine, hardly an impartial commentator, declared that, 'Nothing is so powerful in drawing the spirit of a man downwards than the caresses of a woman'. Sorry about that, Bill, I know you're a bit of a fan."

"Then why didn't Pius make celibacy optional? He had declared it inessential back in 1993?"

Nolan laughed. "I don't think the arguments have changed too much since the fourth century. Power, wealth and scandal. Priests having wives, officially recognised wives that is, would allow women to have greater influence on the priesthood and, ultimately, within the Church and we all know how unstable women are." Pat said mockingly. "Priests with families might establish rights to Church property and would certainly require higher salaries than do single men. Finally, mistresses of priests currently active could demand marriage possibly to the accompaniment of several offspring. And what if married priests didn't have large families or divorced or had affairs? The Faithful might prove only too faithful as followers."

The Pope put his head in his hands. "It is all too difficult. You have answered my question about Pius not changing the rules. What would you do?"

"Look at me. I'm celibate. I'm overweight. I have atrocious table manners. I'm not exactly looking at a rosy future. Maybe, just maybe, with a good woman to care for me and sharpen me up from time to time, I'd be in better shape. Getting out of a warm bed on a cold night would be harder but getting back in would be easier. Kyrie was a great companion but I think I'd prefer a little conversation to the sound of my own opinions. Change the rule and bugger the consequences. Jesus chose married men and he wasn't afraid of women. They weren't the ones who deserted him."

Fr Bernard Pryor had returned from the cemetery. It had been his third funeral in ten days and unquestionably his most distressing. Not only had he attended school with John Adams but he had married his old friend, baptised his children and celebrated his silver wedding in August. Now John was dead leaving a widow and four children, one severely handicapped. He recalled how long they had hoped for a family and how, when hope seemed exhausted, it had all happened. He had rejoiced with them and now he grieved with them. More than that, he questioned the point of it all. What did God hope to achieve by short changing Liz? No doubt she could cope with three adolescents but little Kevin was another matter. Blind, incontinent and epileptic: there was no way. Did the poor in spirit really inherit the earth? There was not much evidence that they did and, as he felt now, not much to support his own faith in a benevolent creator.

He had tried his best to comfort Liz but his own despair intruded. In the end it was she who had comforted him. "If your faith was even as this mustard seed you could move mountains." If he had any left it must be in the sub-atomic particle range.

All that was two years previous and for a year after the funeral people had noted a difference. He carried out his duties but in a robotic way. He was indecisive and forgot appointments. His old approachability was absent and his relations with parishioners became increasingly formal. On one occasion he had lost his temper at Mass and screamed at a woman whose mobile phones rang during the consecration. Bad enough but, to add to the fiasco, he chose the wrong culprit. He slept badly and woke exhausted. He knew he was depressed but the venom of depression paralysed his will to do anything about it. So he staggered on from baptism, to reconciliation, to marriage at a minimum level of engagement. As he raised the host at the consecration, he wondered if the congregation really believed any more or were merely going through a well-rehearsed and mildly comforting drill. He wondered if he believed any more.

Despite his detachment the one duty he did not neglect was that of Liz and the children. Curiously he actually gained strength from being with them. At first Kevin frightened him but, gradually, he began to relate to the little boy. As is so often the case, he assumed the severely physically handicapped lack normal intelligence. It was a revelation to him that Kevin enjoyed stories and conversation and was just as curious as any other seven year old and just as egotistical. His school reports described him as both impulsive and opinionated with a wicked sense of humour. It was all a revelation.

It was another revelation when he had to help Kevin to change when he baby sat while Liz took the other children to the cinema. He did not enjoy the experience but, with Kevin's cheerful and amused guidance, he managed. Liz was highly impressed and offered him the contract. When the children were all safely in bed they laughed together about the incident.

"It is the first time you've laughed since John's funeral." Liz observed.

Bernard was astounded that she could be so aware of something so small. "I think you may be right but however did you know?"

"It's been obvious. Even the kids noticed it. It's good to see you back to normal."

"Do you think I am back to normal?"

She took his hand gently. "Bernard you are a lovely man and a dear friend. Seeing you go downhill since John died has been almost as bad as watching John die. You two were so good for each other but when you love someone, and we both loved him, part of you goes with him."

"But it's been worse for you. He was your husband and...and...."

"And he left me with the kids and Kevin." She finished for him. "And that made it easier for me."

Bernard shook his head.

"You don't understand that do you? But it's true. I may fall into bed exhausted at night but I have held each of them, kissed them and, yes, changed Kevin and given him his medication and he has given me back

that amazing smile which he will never see for himself. Who holds you and kisses you good night in the silence of the presbytery?"

Bernard was deeply touched by her ability to feel beyond self. "You know, when I held Kevin to-night as I changed him I felt, somehow, more of a priest than when I lift the host in these same hands." He was shocked by the admission. "Does that sounds like blasphemy?"

"No it does not!. It's exactly what we believe. Both are the body of Christ, a broken man and a broken boy."

All that had been a year ago and it had been the turning point in more ways than one. His depression began to lift and his perception of the episode with the mobile phone changed from one of tragedy to one of black comedy. He now laughed as he reflected on it and hoped he had provided amusement for others. The old informality returned and he slept better. If imperfect, life still had its attractions. Contact with Liz and her children was a major focus: he had become the regular baby sitter. This made him feel useful and gave the rest of the family a necessary break. He loved the way Kevin referred to him as 'my special friend, Bernie'.

He looked forward to his visit to-night. To his surprise the children seemed settled for the evening.

"I thought you were off to the movies. Where's your mother?"

Anna giggled and pointed at the ceiling. "She's got a date." Kate whispered. Peter gave him a knowing look. "His name's Brett and he's up himself." Kevin added.

"Bernard's not very happy." Anna added.

"Of course I'm happy if it's what Liz wants. She's entitled to some fun in her life."

Liz entered the room and sensed the atmosphere. "I'm sorry, Bernard. I should have warned you but it was all last minute and you had agreed to come anyway,"

"Not a problem." Bernard noted Liz's slight changes of appearance. Nothing too obvious but enough to suggest that she wanted to impress. "How long have you known him?" He tried to make the question casual.

"Not long. Just a few weeks. That's the door. I must fly. Be good you lot and thanks again Bernard. Oh! And could you give Kevin a bath, please"

"I don't like him. He's an idiot."

"That's not fair. If you get to know him better he may be a decent sort after all."

"I am not going to like him and the others don't either."

"Kevin. I know it's hard when you've all had your mother to yourselves but she has to have some life of her own and maybe Brett is going to be part of that life."

"Anna says she might marry him."

"I suppose she might but not just yet."

"I want you to marry her then you can be my dad."

"Kevin, I can't. I am a priest and they can't get married."

"Well it's stupid."

"Life is sometimes stupid."

"Mum loves you. She told me."

"She loves me like a friend. That's a different sort of love."

"I don't think so."

"How did it go?"

"Oh! OK. When you get to 49 and you come with all my baggage, even if it's baggage I personally love, if anyone asks you out and they're not obviously psychopathic, then you're deeply flattered."

"That's ridiculous. You're a very attractive and intelligent woman. Don't sell yourself short."

"Thanks. I'll use you as a referee."

"I've got one, too! Kevin! He told me that I should marry you and be his dad."

Liz laughed. *"Good for Kevin. The others just expressed their silent disapproval. Kevin is already planning the counter attack."* She shook her head. *'So, what did you tell him?"*

"That I was a priest and priests can't marry and, in any case, that you loved me as a friend."

"And?'

"He said he thought otherwise."

"The little matchmaker."

"If priests could marry. Would you really consider me?"

"Like a shot. We know each other so well, the kids all love you, especially Kevin and….and….I love you too….. in the way Kevin means."

"Bernard, the Church cannot afford to lose a priest of your calibre but my hands are tied. If you were a drunk, a chronic gambler, an occasional adulterer or a raving lunatic I would have a place for you. But a mere bishop cannot grant a dispensation to marry or retain a priest once married."

"I realise this but I want you to know that it is my connection with this woman and her family which brought my priesthood alive again. She would make a wonderful priest's wife and be a shining example of courage under duress. It is all such terrible waste."

"I have no doubt the day will come when priests will have the option to marry or remain celibate. Unfortunately it has not yet happened and you are caught in the hiatus. I wish I could do more than simply ask for an expeditious handling of your case but, do not hold your breath, the Vatican deals in eternity rather than reality."

As Bernard was leaving the bishop called out. "Remember that priests who leave the priesthood have a strong obligation to avoid giving scandal. It is a debatable point as to whether the greater scandal follows from a priest who lives with a woman while awaiting permission to marry in the Church or one who marries outside of the Church as an interim measure. Theologians can employ themselves for centuries over such niceties but for humble men, such as ourselves, decisions have to be made rather more rapidly. May God bless you whatever you decide."

CHAPTER 15

"Monsignor Gomez has asked for a personal audience, Holiness. Will you see him."

"Of course."

"Perhaps I should warn you. He represents the Organisation."

"Thank you but I know.'

"And as such represents a sort of church within Church. I do not believe that this is healthy."

"Neither do I, Stephano, though I suspect that you may share similar views to those promoted by the Organisation."

"Some but by no means all. But that is a side issue. Our late Holy Father saw the Organisation as a bulwark against the excessive liberalism which threatened to dilute doctrine. That was why he decide on a personal prelature. I believe he saw the Organisation as taking on the role fulfilled by the Jesuit's in the Counter Reformation. His intentions were of the highest but, as I said, the result has been influence without accountability."

The Pope laughed. "Isn't that what we enjoy? To whom is the Vatican accountable?"

Peroni was not amused. "We are accountable to God."

"I would like to think that we are accountable to the humblest Catholic in the poorest country and if we have that as our yard-stick then I believe we are truly accountable to God."

Sometimes it is not irrefutable logic or deep catharsis which changes entrenched attitudes but a throwaway line or a passing image.

Days later Peroni mentioned the conversation to Kirst. "I think it is possible that we have a real pope in the making. Very different from Pius but maybe, just maybe, he is the man for the season. You and I Helmut will still need all our experience to guide him, along with a little of his humility."

"He has converted you, Cardinal Secretary. I am yet to be convinced. However, he has the tricky question of Fr Pereira to consider. Let us see how he approaches that tantalising problem. Pereira has taken little heed of our previous warnings and continues to undermine the Magisterium."

The high drama of the past weeks had caused Peroni to forget all about Fr Pereira and his taste for controversy. The death of a pope and a Conclave rather eclipsed the ravings of a fringe theologian. Still, as Prefect of the Congregation for the Doctrine of the Faith, it was Kirst's problem. For once he rather enjoyed not being at the centre of things.

"I am sure he can rely of your wise counsel, Cardinal Prefect."

"To rely, definitely. To accept, questionably."

"And that counsel?"

"The man has to be silenced. Warnings do not work with him. Our late Holy Father forbad the very discussion of women priests and, in direct abrogation of his vow of obedience, Pereira states publicly that there is absolutely no theological justification for the Pope's attitude towards women priests nor for his autocratic attempt to stifle discussion of that or any other subject."

"So I recall. But he has been quiet since. Perhaps he has taken notice."

Kirst laughed without humour. "Calm before the storm. He is writing another tract. This time on infallibility."

Peroni winced. "Couldn't he take on something simple like the ordination of extra-terrestrial beings, should any ever materialise.? Pius IX left too many skeletons in the cupboard. Our late Holy Father was wise enough never to speak 'ex cathedra'."

Peroni was encroaching on Kirst's territory and, not for the first time, had showed that whatever his other talents, theology was not one of them.

"It is a common error to assume that only 'ex cathedra' proclamations are infallible."

Peroni was angered. "Yes! Yes! I know that the bishops speaking in unison have the same prerogative."

Kirst gave him a patronising look. "Current theological scholarship would suggest that a great many papal pronouncements carry infallible status. It has sometimes been the task of my Congregation to issue a supplementary statement to that effect. It is a myth that the pope must preface all infallible dogma with 'ex cathedra'. A second myth makes infallibility dependent upon the personality and state of mind of the pope. Not so, infallibility is a charism, independent of personality, sanity or even intention: it is a function of the office and not of the incumbent."

Peroni gave silent thanks that his office was not that of the CDF. Dealing in such abstractions must distort normal judgement. His own thinking was probably closer to Pereira's than Kirst's and Pereira's probably closer to the Pope's. The Cardinal Prefect was in for a testing audience.

The Pope met with Monsignor Franelli as part of his continuing initiation into the workings of the Vatican. They had developed a relaxed relationship, much facilitated by Franelli's command of English. How much easier to deal with the Holy Father than his own demanding master.

"Carlo." The Pope began. "I have been thinking about sins of omission. I've always had a bit of an interest in what we don't do rather than what we do do. I used to preach a half decent sermon on the subject."

Franelli was unsure where the Pope was heading and slipped back into his Peroni defence posture. "To be sure, Holiness." A sound neutral response.

"Perhaps our thinking stems from the ten commandments. Eight of them tell us what not to do and only two tell what we should do. However, at a personal level, I think it is salutary to look to our omissions as well as to our commissions. If that is true, we should apply the same process to how we operate in the Vatican. And that, Carlo, is where I need your help."

Still uncertain, Franelli smiled. "Of course, Holiness. Anything I can do."

"You have worked for Cardinal Peroni for three years. You know on a day to day basis which matters were referred to the Pope and which were not. Who gained access and who was refused." John gave Franelli a conspiratorial look. "Where are the sins of omission?"

Months, even weeks earlier, Fanelli would have jibbed, denied the knowledge or referred the matter for Peroni's attention, but different forces were now operating in his life.

"There has been a tendency for the Pope to see important people from the secular world and, indeed, those of other religious persuasions but to largely ignore some within the Church."

The Pope sighed. "And in seeing Sebastian Hart I am proclaiming 'business as usual'?"

Franelli nodded. "It could appear that way."

"Specifically then, Carlo, whom should I be seeing?"

"The Superiors General of Congregations feel excluded... have been excluded"

"For any particular reason?"

"A humble monsignor could only speculate."

"Go ahead. Speculate as wildly as you wish."

Franelli felt his courage slipping away. Where did his loyalty now lie? To Peroni? To the late Pope? To this new and very different Pope?

John sensed what was happening. "Carlo, be honest with me. You are entitled to hold an opinion which differs from Cardinal Peroni, from the late Pope and especially from myself. I don't want the Church to be an organisation, like so many, in which uniformity rather than robust debate is seen as the criterion of good health."

Franelli's shock was evident. He was changing but not, it seemed, at a speed which kept up with John XXIV. The Pope sensed his confusion.

"A brief history lesson if I may. The British Labour Party used to have a strong tradition of robust debate, not infrequently verging on the self-destructive. On one celebrated occasion, Churchill, the Prime Minister at the time, brought jeers from the Tory benches when he ridiculed the Opposition by pronouncing gravely that, "There are no differences in the Conservative Party". Aneurin Bevan, a prominent Labour Minister, rose from his seat, looked coldly at Churchill and his supporters and retorted, "Neither are there in the graveyard". The Pope smiled at Franelli. "Our task, Carlo, is to avoid the graveyard whether by self-destruction or by excessive conformity."

Franelli breathed deeply. "It seemed to me a matter of control. The Congregations do not fit quite so neatly into the chain of command. Their structure is more nebulous and, quite often, there is a tradition of eccentric behaviour and lax discipline. The Congregations are perceived as being more likely to express views not in conformity with official thinking. Better sidelined than included. At least that is my reading of the situation." Franelli paused and reflected on his surprising openness. "The Organisation, on the other hand, was granted much greater access and seen as a model of papal loyalty. No question of aberrant behaviour in that quarter."

"Perhaps that depends upon one's viewpoint but thank you, Carlo, I really don't want to sideline anyone. I want to remain open to contrary opinions but I know the danger of good intentions being shelved through practical expediency. I rely on people like yourself and Pat Nolan not to let me regress."

"I am excited, Holiness, excited and frightened."

"So am I but only when I rely upon my own strength."

Franelli looked at his watch. He had spent an hour with the Pope and they had barely touched on the organisation of the Vatican. Peroni would not be impressed. "Holiness, you have an appointment now. I must leave."

"Of course but would you ask Cardinal Peroni to arrange for me to begin meeting with the Superiors of Congregations as soon as possible."

Franelli was leaving when the Pope called after him. "Carlo! Whom would you recommend that I see first of all."

Franelli stopped and thought. Then his face lit up. "Sister Catherine of the Congregation of Hope."

"Perfect." Said the Pope.

"Sister Catherine."

"Holiness."

John XXIV was surprised by the seeming youth of his visitor. He had rather expected a venerable lady in late middle age. Instead he was confronted by a woman in her forties and, he had to admit, an attractive woman who did not look remotely nun-like.

"Welcome to the Vatican." He held out his hand, uncomfortable as always that the ring kissing was traditional. He need not have feared as Sister Catherine shook hands vigorously and, in what sounded like an Australian accent, announced: "The invitation has been a long time coming".

Peroni retreated, confirmed in the belief that the congregations were anarchic.

"I am sorry about that…about the absence of direct contact between the pope and the congregations but today is the start of making amends. But, please." He motioned to a seat. "I have much to learn but I am hoping that the advice I receive from people such as yourself will at least ensure that I learn something. So today's meeting is for you to help me see things from your perspective and from that of your sisters throughout the world."

Catherine was impressed. She had arrived somewhat defensive, expecting a lecture of how nuns should behave and how women had a distinctly different vocation from men. She began to change direction mentally.

"I appreciate that chance, Holy Father. I suppose that the congregations are not so different from the Church in general. We have fewer vocations, at least from the developed world. Many of our sisters are well into old age and their care is an increasing concern. We began as a teaching and nursing order but increasingly have moved into what might be considered a social welfare role. The shanty towns of the third world appeared more needy than the daughters of the middle class. Our sisters are often trapped between a doctrinaire belief system and the extreme hardship of the very poor. It can be a damned if you do and damned if you don't situation. Sometimes it is hard to reconcile the teaching of the Church and Christ's compassion."

The Pope nodded in encouragement. "Go on, Sister. I want to hear this."

"To be more specific. What do I tell a woman in a Rio favela who by age twenty three has five children and whose husband is unemployed? That she must use only the rhythm method of birth control. Either that or abstain. That the one small pleasure left to them is the well-named Vatican Roulette. That, if she refuses sex, her husband may go with a prostitute and contract AIDS. I, we, try to envisage Jesus going into the same shack and telling them life wasn't meant to be easy. They bloody well know that, they have always known that. We're doing our best to make their lives that bit harder. That's the Good News we bring to them." Sister Catherine stopped and bit her lip. "You know, an old friend of mine, a priest, told me that the moment priests are allowed to marry the issue of contraception will be swept under the carpet. I would hate to think he is right but, if he is, where does that leave us? With the Scribes and Pharisees, no less."

Catherine was uneasy at the Pope's silence. "You don't want to hear all this do you? You must have enough troubles without crazy nuns running off at the mouth. I'm sorry but I visit my sisters and often feel that I have nothing to offer them. One, an old Indian sister, once asked me, 'When the pope travels the world what does he actually see?' I had no answer for her. I think we have got it all wrong. We're a bunch of sinners pretending that we are a bunch of saints. We exclude people from the sacraments for what we define as serious sin. In other words we deny grace to those most in need. What did Jesus say when he was accused of mixing with sinners? 'It is the sick who need the doctor, not the well'. It is like denying a man penicillin because he may responsible for his own bacterial infection. We regard life as a state rather than as a journey. You are in a state of sin or a state of grace when most people, clerical or secular, are trying to behave better in an environment which is not entirely of their choosing. Nor, for that matter, is their heredity. Better to regard them as in a state of evolving, hopefully with the grace and support of their religion, whatever it might be." Catherine breathed a great sigh of relief. "Well that may not have been beneficial for the Pope but it did me a lot of good and I didn't even know half of it was there."

The Pope clapped gently. "Well done, Sister. I had heard you Australians could be blunt. Don't ever become too civilised. We need a few catalysts around the place.

Catherine was leaving. The Pope held both of her arms and, symbolically, kissed her on both cheeks. "I intend to establish a commission to re-examine the whole question of birth control. The previous one had recommended in favour of a doctrinal change before the Curia took a hand in the matter. I would like you, if you can spare the time, to lead that commission. It will be a genuine commission composed of a cross section of Catholics but with minimum Curial representation. In the meantime I intend to issue a preliminary statement that contraception used in circumstance where the physical, financial or mental health of the family is in danger and where natural methods are impractical is no impediment to receiving the sacraments."

Catherine gasped. "Holiness, I would like you to bless me."

CHAPTER 16

"You sent for me, Holiness?"

"Thank you Stephano. I know you are busy and I will try not to detain you. I would like your views on a sensitive topic and one which, I fear, we have exacerbated by our reluctance to concede guilt. I am referring to the sexual abuse of children in our care."

"A terrible scar on the Church which only time will heal."

"A terrible scar on the victims which time may never heal."

Peroni's bearing signalled his unease. "Holiness, I know that the Church, even its most senior leaders, did not act as decisively as they should. Perhaps from ignorance, perhaps even from complacency. However, I believe that most dioceses now have systems in place which will ensure, to the extent that it is humanly possible, that there is no recurrence."

"Please sit down, Stephano. Let me put the situation, as I see it, in the context of reconciliation or confession, to use an old fashioned word. When dealing with the Faithful, the Church has traditionally demanded an admission of guilt, a promise not to re-offend, restitution if appropriate and completion of a prescribed penance. In dealing with its institutional self the Church has been significantly more lenient. Only with reluctance and often after a great deal of external pressure, did it confess it's sin. To some extent it has made reparation by way of financial compensation or counselling or both. As you rightly say, it has established procedures which suggest a firm purpose of amendment. However, one element remains absent and that is my concern."

The Pope looked quizzically at his Secretary of State. "I presume that you refer to the penance which is normally placed on the penitent." The Pope nodded encouragingly.

"But giving an individual a penance is only practical when the confession is voluntary and, in this case, we are dealing with religious who have not voluntarily admitted guilt but who have simply been exposed. I do not believe that they are seeking a penance." Peroni smiled. "In any case, the Courts will impose a penance much harsher than anything the Church could apply."

"I am not referring to the perpetrators. I am referring to the Church leadership. Those who should have been more vigilant, less protective of the Church and more protective of children, less prone to denial and more prone to action."

Peroni was increasingly uncomfortable, uncertain of exactly where the Pope was heading but certain that the journey was going to be unpleasant. "I think that being hounded by the media and various other groups might constitute penance enough."

"Perhaps but that is not really my point. I believe that the Church should make a public and symbolic act of penance so that an understandably cynical world and, indeed, many of the Faithful can begin to see us as less hypocritical."

"And what form would such an act take?"

"I am open to suggestions but I thought that if I, as Pope, were to kneel in St Peter's Square for 24 hours, fasting and in pray, and if other Church leaders throughout the world were to carry out a similar act in similar public places, that might be an appropriate gesture. I have amused you, Stephano?"

"Holiness." Peroni could scarcely speak. "Holiness, you amaze me. You have taken me so far out of my comfort zone that I don't think I shall ever sleep again."

"I did not really expect you to approve and, as I said, I am open to alternatives."

"Forgive me. I have spent most of my priestly life in the Vatican and many years as Secretary of State. It is not a background which

encourages radical thinking still less radical action. It goes without saying that you frighten me. You import a personal advisor
to keep you honest. You preach sermons which anger powerful
politicians. You prefer to persuade gently rather than to direct.
But, Holiness, a small part of me, a very small part, thinks that
you may be right. With that proviso, I believe that you should
go ahead with you penitential project and I will try to ensure that
you are joined by many volunteers."

"Thank you, Stephano. Thank you very much. But volunteers only. No pressed men. Oh! And by the way, would you
care to join me? As a volunteer, of course."

"As a volunteer, Holiness! You leave me no other choice."
He was about to exit when he turned to the Pope. "Perhaps we
should see the results of your initiative as a navigational guide Is
the papal compass functional or dysfunctional?"

On Ash Wednesday, Pope John XXIV together with 57 cardinals, 180 archbishops, 1059 bishops, numerous priests, brothers, sisters and many thousands of the laity assembled in St
Peter's Square and in numerous other venues. The paramedics
were kept busy but, miraculously, there were no deaths.

On Thursday when the fast ended, the Pope addressed the
multitude.

*"I cannot adequately express my gratitude to all of you for being here
with me and especially those who have travelled so far to be part of this
collective act of penance. Not only here, but in so many sites throughout
the world, we have joined together to express our contrition for the terrible
scourge of child sexual abuse in the Catholic Church. We do so with deep
humility and the hope that this acknowledgement will bring some small
comfort to all who have suffered at the hands of the Church. But today is,
I pray, only the beginning of a more humble Church. One which is not
afraid to admit imperfection. One which does not see itself as superior to
other religions. One which has absorbed, in its very heart, the command
of our saviour to serve rather than to be served. I cannot make this happen but you, the People of God, can make it happen. Jesus tells us that
if we have faith the size of a mustard seed we can move mountains. We
must take him at his word and seek to move mountains. When we look*

at our world we see mountains of poverty, of disease, of oppression, of injustice, of despair, of greed. It is tempting to blame God for these evils. To ask why does he not intervene? As Christians our answer must be that he has intervened. He has created us with that sublime gift of free will. Our coming together in this penitential act is a symbol that we accept the challenge of the Gospel. You could have said, 'I have never molested any child therefore I will not participate'. But you chose not to take that path. Instead your presence declares that, to misquote John Donne, 'We are involved in mankind'. Be true to that involvement. We must see ourselves as trustees not as owners. Whatever gifts we possess were freely given to us, be they physical strength, intellectual power, financial wealth, robust health. One day we must account for our trusteeship. Whatever talents we possess must be used in furtherance of the Kingdom. Let us leave St Peter's Square, and all other meetings today, strengthened in our resolve to purify ourselves first so that we make our contribution to world in need for purification. May God bless you all."

"It was a great success, Holiness. As you well know I was rather cynical but you were right and I was wrong."

"That is very gracious of you, Stephano, but I'm sure there will be occasions when the reverse is true. I think I am learning to be more trustful of the Spirit. I just pray that I don't start to confuse my own ego with a higher authority. But that is not why I asked to see you. There are two matters which concern me, one large, one small. I need your guidance on both."

Peroni took the proffered seat.

"To begin with the small issue. I am concerned at the use of the term 'Holiness'. You and I appreciate that it is used out of respect for the office rather than as a description of the office holder. So, I'm sure, do most thinking Catholics but many, especially those not of our Faith, must find it somewhat presumptuous that a mere man should be designated as holy. Holiness is an aspiration rather than a description and, in my case, a description which is far from accurate. Historically there have been times when it was manifestly an oxymoron. I would like to dispense with the title. What do you think?"

Peroni lowered his gaze and scratched his left ear. "Logically you are right but then logic does not always apply to our use of language. We call priests 'Father' when, hopefully, in most cases they are not, biologically speaking. Bishops get 'My Lord', cardinals 'Eminence' and so on. Do you intend to do away with all such......courtesy titles?"

The Pope laughed. "Of course not and I agree with you, language is not always logical. But my particular title implies a saintliness which I do not wish to claim, the other forms of address make no such claim."

"Do you have an alternative in mind?"

"With close colleagues such as yourself I'd be quite happy with Bill."

Peroni scratched furiously. "Out of the question, Holiness. Sorry! Sorry on both counts."

"Then why not just Pope. That has been conferred on me legitimately by the Conclave guided, I like to think, by the Spirit and implies nothing more metaphysical than a specific job. Could the Curia live with that?"

"We have lived with worse. Whether the Faithful can cope is another matter. But it will sound so odd."

"Not once you get used to it."

"Well, Pope, if we have dispensed with the minor issue what, then, is the major item?"

"Not quite! Allied to the salutation is the matter of kissing of the ring. I find is positively medieval. I would like it to cease with immediate effect."

"And in the case of cardinals and others?"

"Many have already discouraged the practice. I suspect others will follow the Pope and, if they don't, I expect the Faithful will eventually discontinue it for them."

The Pope noted the briefest of smiles before the Secretary asked again. "The major item?"

"It is the question of the canonisation. I think you know which one I have in mind?"

"There is quite a background to the matter. Are you familiar?"

"Not really except that the process, thus far, has been remarkably rapid. To be canonised within three decades of one's death might cause some to cry 'indecent haste'."

Peroni shrugged and looked heavenwards. "It already has."

"But before you educate me, would you say that there has been much change in the composition of the communion of saints over the centuries?" The Pope grinned.

Peroni shared his amusement. "Being male and celibate certainly gives you an edge on the competition."

"I thought so. Now, the background."

"The late Holy Father believed that the modern Church had been too timid in its creation of saints and that, amongst other problems, this acted as a disincentive to the Faithful to try to lead saintly lives. He created, as we all know, more saints than any previous pope. I think the final figure was about 470 which exceeded the total of the previous four hundred years. In his eagerness to facilitate the process he abolished the office of the Promotor Fidei or Devil's Advocate, as enacted in Canon Law since 1917, and replaced it with a less draconian office of Postulator. Unlike the Devil's Advocate, who was responsible for stating the case against canonisation, the Postulator is responsible for presenting the case both for and against sanctity, a less clear cut role. Not only that, but he is actually appointed by the Petitioner."

"I thought that a Promotor of Justice is also established to ensure fairness?"

"Indeed he is but there is no obligation for him to be physically present during the canonisation process."

The Pope whistled quietly. "You know, Stephano, I am dredging my mind, so correct me if I am confused, but did not an earlier pope state that without the Devil's Advocate a canonisation would be invalid?"

"Urban VII in 1631."

"Oh dear. Rather puts my mode of address in the context of the real world. Do you have any suggestions?"

"I am not being disloyal to Pope Pius when I say that I tried very hard to dissuade him from changing the rules in 1982/3. More accurately from ignoring the Canon Law. But to announce that all canonisations since 1982 are invalid would have an horrendous impact on both the reputation of an exceptional Pope and the faith of many simple Catholics. It is not a course which I could recommend."

"I see that and, besides, the majority of cases, perhaps all, are probably valid despite the procedural changes. None the less, I would like an unobtrusive examination of the case histories and notification of any which may require review."

"I think that is the better course. And as to cases currently in hand?"

"We must return immediately to the requirements of Canon Law and appoint a Devil's Advocate."

"Excellent, Pope but it will win you no friends with powerful forces."

The Pope shrugged. "Somehow I don't think the Organisation approves of me anyway and I know this will increase my disapproval rating. It is a pity because I believe that I am to be a Pope for all Catholics not just the fuzzy liberals like myself. I must try to engage with the Organisation but perhaps after the dust has settled on the interrupted canonisation."

"I appreciate your sentiments, that you must be a Pope for the whole Church, but I am not sure that engagement with the Organisation, other than on their terms, is realistic. Pius and the Organisation had a similar perspective on many matters though by no means all. I find it hard to believe that you would find much common ground."

"I don't disagree but I feel that I must try to do so. Especially as the delay of beatification will cause such hurt."

"Holiness. Sorry! Pope. I was wrong in the matter of the public penance but I do not believe that I am wrong in this instance. The Organisation has already canonised it's founder. Indeed, some would say that it has deified him. What influence can a mere pope exert on such people? We have effectively a church within the Church. One which is secretive, extremely rich, influential, not answerable to any diocesan bishop and which sees itself as the guardian of dogmatic purity. My guess is that it will fight a rear guard action against you over the Devil's

Advocate, in the pious belief that the end really does justify the means."

The Organisation has its own intelligence network and this includes the Vatican. Within days of the Pope's decision on the process of canonisation, the bad news was being digested. The leader and his top aides made a series of phone calls, many of which were to bishops in the developing world. Subtly and, if necessary, quite crudely they were told that the financial support upon which they relied came with a price tag. Within weeks the Congregation for the Causes of Saints was inundated with requests that the Pope reconsider. Had the Holy Father taken into account the effect on the reputation of Pius XIII so soon after his death? Might not a more discrete interval be in order? The inevitable delays would impact on the faith of the local Church, now accustomed to a rapid transit from blessedness to sainthood.

"The Holy Father is not afraid of controversy, Eminence." Franelli ventured.

"And is that a virtue or a vice in your humble opinion, Monsignor?" Was the acerbic reply.

The Franelli of old would have retreated from such a response, had he even dared to pose the question. Not so the current version. "I was not seeking a moral judgement, simply expressing an opinion, knowing that you, Eminence, have always favoured a cautiousness in Church management."

"I do not think that the Holy Father is the only inhabitant of the Vatican who can provoke strong feelings. Even monsignors have been known to enter dangerous waters."

Once it appeared that the Pope was not going to acquiesce to the pleas of third world bishops, the Organisation decided to open a second front. Well cultivated media contacts were used when this proved necessary but, often, an idle hack would cooperate simply by being given an article ready for publication. Imitating a particular style of journalism was a easy technique to master and paid generous dividends. The United Kingdom tab-loids were a much favoured outlet for such 'press releases'. The Planet published one article without altering even a comma.

WHEN THE SAINTS GO MARCHING - OUT!!!

The Red Pope is not going to be content with placing the Catholic Church to the left of New Labour. No! He has more plans for upsetting the Faithful. Pius XIII created more saints than any other pope and, to this end, did away with the archaic method of assessing sanctity - the Devil's Advocate. The late Pope reasoned that even the truly saintly had human failures but that it was their very sanctity which enabled them to operate beyond these faults. In other words, saints are ordinary mortals, with ordinary vices, who do extraordinary things in the service of God. The Faithful identified with this view and it probably inspired many to see themselves, despite their human weakness, as potential saints. But no longer!

John XXIV has re-instituted the Devil's Advocate. Now good men and women who struggled hard with their humanity and rose above it will be subject to a nit picking examination of their whole life. Every little foible will be scrutinised, each blemish exposed. The Catholic Church claims to be the direct descendant of the Apostles and the heir of Jesus Christ. And what did Christ say when confronted with a judgemental crowd about to stone a woman for adultery. "Let him who is without sin cast the first stone." No one took up the challenge and nor should they have done. None of us is perfect but some, Mother Teresa for example, are clearly outstanding role mod-els. Being an outstanding role model is another way of defining sainthood.

There is an old saying that saints make difficult companions. They can be impatient, demanding and focused on a different agenda than lesser mortals. They can present an easy target for muck raking. Some might even say that there is a sadistic pleas-ure in trying to destroy the reputation of someone really good.

In some ways it mirrors the adversarial system of British Law, a system foreign to many cultures and subject to considerable criticism. John XXIV may feel more comfortable with adversarial justice but he should remember that he is no longer an English bishop but Pope to the whole Church.

Already there are reports from several countries, notably from those with a local candidate for canonisation, of discontent and falling church attendance associated with the Pope's action. This is almost certainly the tip of the iceberg. With the exception of some of the Pentecostal and Evangelical churches, Christianity is in retreat throughout the world. The resulting gap may well be filled by religions which have their fanatical elements. As we enter a new and frightening period of international terrorism, Christianity as currently constituted, offers a bulwark of moderation. Any action which weakens this bulwark is to be decried not just by Christians but by all civilised men and women. It may well be that the Pope has not appreciated the global implications of his decision. If not, now is the time to do so. The Planet urges him to reconsider this retrograde and dangerous step.

Of the greatest concern to devout Catholics is the possibility that, at the eleventh hour, the canonisation of Monsignor Estoria, founder of the deeply religious group known as the Organisation, will be delayed. Dissenting voices within the Church have campaigned vigorously for such a delay, motivated by jealously and fear that the elevation of such a strong advocate of traditional Catholic practice would act as a rallying point for others who lament the loss of discipline. One of the reasons Pope Pius XIII was so supportive of his cause was this need for a symbol of obedience to the Magisterium. The support for the cause has been international and massive, approximating to canonisation 'vox polulii' as it existed in the early Church. To resist such an outpouring of emotion would be both an insult to Pius's memory and, quite possibly, result in an exodus of disillusioned Catholics.

Now is not the time to change the rules. Indeed the rules have already been changed to reflect a more human approach to sanctity. Let the people have their Saint Javier Estoria. Not only

will Spain rejoice in the recognition of one of its finest sons: the whole Catholic world will join in the celebration.

Pat Nolan read the article to the Pope. "I don't think they like you, Bill."

"It's an expanding club, I'm afraid. I'll be even less popular with the conservatives if Cardinal Kirst resigns as I think he may well do. It's a depressing thought. I don't want to be the polarising Pope but I don't want to regress into the Carterton the Cautious."

Nolan looked at his watch. "We'll make it a three Guinness night to-night and things will look better in the morning."

CHAPTER 17

Though Peroni had disseminated the Pope's wish to abandon the term Holiness, it had failed to impact on Cardinal Kirst or most others. The Pope was beginning to think it was not such a good idea.

"You wished to see me, Holiness?"

"I did and thank you for coming so promptly." John XXIV had decided to ignore the issue of address. "As Prefect of the Congregation for the Doctrine of the Faith, I want to have your reaction to some thoughts."

Kirst nodded but said nothing. He had a strong sense of what was to follow.

"I am concerned that the Church's doctrine on sexuality needs re-examination in the light of new knowledge. On the question of artificial birth control I believe that Cardinal Ottaviani prevented, if not a complete abandonment of the doctrine then, at least a major revision. I do not have to spell out the consequences for so many of the Faithful trying to live in accordance with Church teaching, sometimes to the detriment of their health, their marriages and their children. Now the AIDS pandemic has raised the matter to one of great urgency. That is my first concern and I would like your views."

"My view is that the Faithful have already decided, Holiness. Where are the large Catholic families of the past? It is an issue which has become a non-issue."

"I am afraid that I do not agree. It may be an issue which has ceased to affect most Catholics in the developed world in their personal behaviour but there are still those who maintain an allegiance to a doctrine which is very likely flawed. What is, perhaps, more important is the official stance of the Church in blocking or attempting to block international approaches to contraception. It also impacts on the operating effectiveness of the Catholic Development Agencies."

"As I am sure you are aware the commission which Pope John XXIII established to examine the issue and which was further authorised by Pope Paul VI, did favour an acceptance of artificial birth control. The 1966 report was never officially published though it did appear in the Sentinel and National Catholic Reporter of Kansas City. Subsequently Cardinal Ottaviani established his own commission. Two years later the encyclical Humanae Vitae was published which re-stated that artificial contraception was intrinsically evil. That remains the official position."

"I recall that Ottaviani's commission consisted only of priests, whereas the previous one had many lay Catholics, including a range of experts and a married couple. Somehow the People of God, so important to the spirit of Vatican II, were proving too independent and had to be silenced. Not a happy epitaph."

Kirst cleared his throat. "I can only agree but, faced with such a difficult choice, Pope Paul clearly opted to defend the reputation of the Church. If he had reversed the teaching on contraception, what next? If the Church could be wrong on such an important issue, it might be wrong on a whole variety of issues. Once the dyke was pierced the resulting flood might submerge everything. I am relieved that I did not have to bear Ottaviani's burden."

"I think you illustrate the point well, Helmut. May I call you that? Thank you. Are we a Church which can never be wrong? Can never say sorry? Or are we a human organisation, which will be wrong from time to time and which must be humble enough to admit error when it is revealed?" It seems to me that the answer to this question is fundamental to all our discussions."

"Holiness, we rely on the promise of our Saviour, that the Spirit would guide the Church. That is why we have not been prepared to admit error."

"If that is our position, then we ignore free will. The Spirit may guide but the Spirit does not compel. The Church, through its human agents, you and me, can remain closed to the guidance, perhaps out of the very highest of surface motives but below that surface? Who knows?."

"What of those heroic couples who have abided by the teaching? How will they feel if they are told that years of abstinence or of the rhythm method have been in vain? Betrayed I would imagine."

"I am sure you are correct. We can only attempt to put any change in its broader context, ask their forbearance for our past failure, and hope that God will give them the grace to forgive. What I cannot accept is that we let that consideration, tragic though it is, nor the office of pope or any other Church leader stand in the way of what we believe to be true."

"Then you will be asking the Faithful to drastically revise their image of Church. To downgrade it in fact."

"Revise? Yes! Downgrade? No! Failure to deal with reality, whether by denial or rationalisation or by any other means, is simply a way or mortgaging tomorrow to pay for today. I do not have great ambitions for my papacy but I do not intend to leave my successor with a vast moral overdraft and I need your help to avoid that failure."

"As you wish, Holiness. Did you have other issues? Er, related to sexual behaviour?"

"Indeed, I do. I believe we need to re-examine our doctrine on clerical celibacy, on homosexuality, on women priests and on abortion."

"Four quite distinct issues."

"I am not suggesting otherwise and they can wait their turn and the outcome of the council" The Pope suddenly looked old. "Believe me, Helmut, I am not an iconoclast nor am I a hero. It may well turn out that Church teaching is strengthened by such an examination. In the meantime let us not be diverted by imaginary fears."

Mary Henry looked up from the ironing and admonished her youngest child. Lucy was three and, already, showing signs of precocity. Having six older siblings had given her two assets: significant imitative learning and a determination to fight for her place in an over-crowded family. Now she was exercising this second asset on John, her senior by 11 months.

"Wet the bed! Wet the bed! Baby! Baby!" She chanted. John obligingly burst into tears.

"Go to your room, now!" Her mother yelled. Lucy pretended not to hear and began to demolish John's Lego, causing further discord. Mary advanced round the ironing board. Lucy fled down the hall. Eight months pregnant, Mary had no energy for the chase. John continued to bawl in the hope of a more drastic treatment of his sister.

The door burst open and the three older children charged in all shouting their news and demanding food. In a semi trance, Mary tried to recall a time, not ten years ago when she danced, sang in the choir, played net ball, taught third grade and was shaking life by the throat. Now life was taking it's revenge.

"Not bread and jam again." Complained Matthew. "Josh gets cake for tea every night."

"So does Alice and her mother lets her watch Simpson's."

"Well Josh's mother doesn't have to feed seven children and Alice doesn't have brothers and sisters to play with."

"I don't want brothers and sisters. They're horrid. I want to be an only child."

"Too late now and you're going to have another sibling soon. So better make the most of it."

"Alice's mother says It's disgusting."

"What does 'gusting mean."

"It means yucky."

"Her mother said that to you?"

"No! She said it to Alice and she told me." Rebecca blushed. "She said it was a secret so don't say I told."

"What's yucky?"

"He doesn't know what yucky is." The others laughed. "It's what you are."

"Yucky! Yucky! Yucky!" John burst into tears again.

"You wait till your father comes home. He's told you about teasing each other. You'll be in big trouble."

"We'll all be asleep. It's one of his special nights."

Mary felt like joining John. She wasn't coping. She was tired, depressed, her life was out of control. She was like a battery hen: incarcerated and used for breeding, feeding, cleaning and ironing. Other husbands came home and took over but not Peter. He was busy saving the Church from dark forces and promoting the Organisation. At first she had tried to reason with him, compromise, but as his commitment to his new allegiance grew so his commitment to his old one faltered. Not just time but money, too. A chartered accountant was well paid but when it came to a choice between a cleaning lady and the Organisation, there could only be one winner.

That had caused a major row. She had accused him of being unfaithful to his family and to her in particular. He had told her that she was privileged to serve as the wife of a sub-associate. She had told him that she would sooner be the equal wife of a man who didn't have the pathological need of a father figure. He told her that by marrying her he had deprived himself of becoming an associate.

The verbal violence frightened them both so much that, in trying to make up, they had broken the rhythm cycle and now number eight was imminent.

At nine o'clock Mary staggered to bed, read for five minutes and fell asleep. At half past nine Rebecca woke her. "He's wet the bed again."

"I've made you a coffee, Mum." She held the tears back. "Thanks, 'Becky. I'm sorry I lost it."

She hugged her child and, in mistaken gratitude, drank the coffee. It tasted like mud. An hour later she feigned sleep when Peter arrived home. Now wide awake and seething, she tried to pray but all she could think of was: "Fuck Peter, fuck the Organisation, fuck the Pope, fuck the Church".

Next morning proved even more stressful. Peter was demanding a clean shirt. Matthew wanted money for an excursion. Lucy was remind-

ing John that he was still a baby who wet the bed. Someone had turned the TV up to maximum volume. Suddenly she screamed. Except for the TV there was a silence followed by Peter asking, in his most patronising voice.

"What's the matter this time?"

"The whole fucking lot of you, that's what's the matter."

"How dare you use such language in front of my children."

"My children! My children! Are they your children when they have to be fed? Are they your children when they fight? How can they be your children when you're never here. Too busy kissing the arses of a bunch of fascist priests and other lunatics."

Peter went even paler that his normal, washed out look. He advanced towards her, seeming to raise his hand.

Mary lost all control. "That's it, you cowardly little prick. Not content with self-flagellation, am I to be put on the list? Does that earn you extra brownie points?"

"You have no idea, do you? So drowning in self-pity that you can't see the big picture. You have your head in the 'ain't it awful bin' while we're fighting for the future of the Church. Instead of support I get ridicule. You should be proud but you can only be selfish. At least be thankful that I believe in marriage for life....otherwise..." He left, ignoring the children.

"She's asleep. Let's put the video on." Lucy wanted John implicated in case they were caught. The conspirators shut the door, turned down the sound and hugged each other with glee. It was an ill wind.

Mary struggled back to reality and the phone ringing. "It's me, Poppet. Just catching up." It was June, Peter's mother. "You sound dreadful. Are you all right?"

"Yes. I'm OK. Just a bit tired." She realised that she was perpetuating the myth, as she always did for outside consumption.

"Of course you're tired. How could you not be. Anyway I'll be over later to take the monsters off your hands. What is it? Are you crying?"

"Yes! I am crying!" No more pretence.

"Poppet!" More sobs. "I'm coming over now."

"I can't pretend anymore. My life is shit. You son is a selfish bastard. The Organisation is a heartless, sanctimonious collection of dysfunc-

tional Catholics who feel they can mitigate their own misery by spreading it about. I don't have hope anymore. You know I rather like the idea of dying in childbirth and leaving Holy Peter to sort out the mess." She burst into tears again.

June held her. "Let it all out. I knew this would happen." She felt the tears splash on her neck and the she, too, began to cry.

"You mean you don't hate me? You don't think it's all my fault?"

"No! Poppet. I think it's a miracle that you've lasted so long. No woman should have to put up with your life. Yes!" She held up her hand. "I know he's my son but I've seen him grow away from us both. It's been hard for me but, for you, it's been catastrophic and God knows what effect it is having on the children. Poor little blighters."

"I don't know what to do. It's as though we've become a great mill stone holding him back from some modern version of the crusades. The plain truth is that he loves the Organisation and he doesn't love us anymore."

"As you know, his father died when he was seven and I never re-married. I think he always needed a father figure but there just wasn't one around. When you came along he admired your strength and vital-ity. June smiled. "So did I. I thought here's a girl who can put some steel into Peter. Make him seize life instead of waiting for it to come to him and, for a time, that's exactly what you did do."

"Me strong?" Mary shook her head.

"You were…you are. You're just tired and demoralised. I don't think you realise how strong you really are. Sometimes we only see our own best features through the eyes of a friend."

"Then what went wrong?"

"Babies basically. Your strength had to flow in more than one direc-tion and Peter needed one hundred per cent of it. He'd become used to it and, like an addict, he couldn't make do on less. I don't think he had enough insight to work it out. He just felt different, scared probably, and the Organisation was there to provide the sort of certainty which is so attractive to the weak. You know, Poppet, I don't think you can be truly adult and not be prepared to live in a sea of ambiguity."

"Well I certainly qualify on that criterion. I have ambiguity in spades." Mary laughed, for what seemed the first time in months. "I am the queen of ambiguity. I love my children and I hate them, in about equal measure. I want to be a Faithful wife and mother and I want to be a sexually active single. I want things to be right between Peter and *myself and I want him to drop dead, preferable a long way from here. I want to be a good Catholic and I think the Church is a seething mass of hypocrisies to which only the mentally challenged could possibly belong. I believe in a loving God but He serves me shit three times a day so He must be a sadistic old fraud. There! I may have missed some but that's a start."*

"What about me? Don't I qualify too?"

"Here goes. I think you are a decent woman who has been far too soft with her son. So much so that he believes women are there to serve him. I think you embraced widowhood when you should have screwed around a bit even if you never met Mr Right. It would have given you a better perspective on life. You are right about Peter seeking a father figure but he also wants a permanent mother. " Mary laughed again. *"We might have the best part of eight kids but he's too Madonna fixated to see me naked. To do so would, I suspect, seem incestuous. I often wonder if he confesses having sex with his wife. Maybe not as a mortal sin but as a sign of imperfection. I fancy the Organisation does little to dispel such aberrations."*

"I admit it, I am responsible for the way he is and I am so very sorry that you are paying the price."

"Rubbish. Peter is responsible for the way he is. He's got greater freedom of choice than most people and plenty of objective advice if he had but the courage to seek it. But he is too frightened of the temporary confusion which that would involve. You hit the nail on the head, Peter cannot cope with ambiguity."

Kirst went straight to Peroni and repeated what the Pope had just told him. It was the first time they had spoken in some weeks.

"It pains me to say it but I think the Conclave made a terrible mistake. This man will turn us into an amorphous mass. A Church devoid of solid teaching where today's doctrine is tomorrow's topic for debate. We already have a membership which makes up its own mind on birth control and divorce and, if surveys are anything to go by, half the priesthood is in the same camp."

Peroni, whose English was better than Kirst's, raised an eyebrow at the word 'camp' but gave no further indication of the paraprax. "Today was, I think, your first meeting with the Holy Father?"

Kirst nodded.

"I have had a better chance to get to know him. Like you, my first impression was one of discomfort and apprehension. On further acquaintance I feel less disquiet. Certainly he is of a different calibre than Pope Pius and, in some ways, more radical. However, we should remember that Pius' early pontificate was seen by many as being too publicly interventionist and too obsessed with communism. After Paul VI and Pius XII it seemed like having a pop star follow two bashful academics. Increasingly I think the Conclave may have made the right decision and, as I said once before, he is the man for this particular season."

"I am surprised. No! Shocked. I had expected you to be even more pessimistic than myself since you undoubtedly have more information as to his plans. Remember, too, Stephano that what may invite a judgement of 'openness' in Western Europe may be viewed as 'sacrilege' in Africa and east of the Danube. I, for one, do not wish to contribute to a schism."

"You may be too far ahead of the Holy Father himself. He is proposing no more than a series of commissions on some important aspects of doctrine. The results of such enquiries may only enhance existing positions in the light of new knowledge. If, however, they demonstrate that we have been wrong, is it better to proceed in error or admit fallibility and proceed honestly?"

"You use the same argument he used to me. Our conversations increasingly tell me that you have been converted."

"Not converted, Helmut. I think he has caused me to stick a toe outside of my comfort zone. You are being invited to do no more."

Kirst left saying that he would pray for guidance. "As do I." Peroni called after him.

"How did it go?" Pat Nolan asked for the second time, poking his head round the door.

Carterton beckoned him in and motioned to close the door. "Not too well, I fear. It is asking a lot of a man who has been faithfully doing his duty for sixteen years to suggest that he may have been defending the indefensible. I felt like an assassin. I am increasingly convinced that he may resign."

"Probably for the best. I thought you'd have to sack Peroni but you won him over. Too much to expect Kirst as well."

The Pope looked sad. "Pat, I'm not cut out for the ruthless bit and, in any case, I may be quite wrong. Perhaps I am tilting at windmills when I should be simply trying to shore up the Faithful by following in Pius' footsteps and traipsing the world."

Nolan shook his head. "As I see it, you're trying to kick start a jumbo. It is exhausting work but what use is a plane that isn't flying any more. When we're tired we easily fall into depression. If Kirst stays on board, well and good. If not, choose another pilot." He laughed. "You know, when I first started my monthly Mass for the girls, I lost a quarter of my holiest parishioners. I can laugh now but, at the time, I was sure I had acted stupidly and out of bravado: Pat Nolan, saviour of the working girl! Some drifted back. One couple even apologised and said they'd come to realise just how judgemental they had become. New people turned up because they believed in a compassionate God and the Girls' Mass somehow made that idea concrete. What you are trying to do is show that compassion on a global scale and, God knows, the world needs a spot of compassion."

"Thanks, Pat." Nolan left and the Pope went into his small, private chapel and wept at his own lack of faith.

CHAPTER 18

The news that commissions were to examine a number of controversial topics provided a rich source of speculation and a torrent of advice. Both the speculation and the advice varied from the bedrock conservative to the anarchic radical. The Herald took the opportunity for a spot of self-congratulation.

POPE HEEDS OUR CAMPAIGN

The radical announcement that the Vatican is to re-open question of birth control and the even more radical news that celibacy, homosexuality, abortion and women priests are, for the first time, to be subject to a rational analysis is to be applauded. This newspaper takes pride in the fact that it was instrumental in providing the wake up call to Rome after it's complacent handling of the sexual abuse of children by Catholic priests and religious. It takes no pleasure in the subsequent resignation of a cardinal and the imprisonment of the perpetrators, though this was a necessary element in justice to the victims.

However, the matter is far from closed. There remains the question of compensation and the establishment of standards which prevent any recurrence of such abuses of power. The American bishops have moved a long way in the direction of prevention though their work remains incomplete. But their task is essentially one of dealing with effect rather than cause. The Vatican's announcement provides some hope that cause is also on the reform agenda.

This is not to say that allowing priests to marry will eliminate clerical paedophilia though it may, through the legitimate channelling of sexual energy, reduce the temptation. This is not to say that a recognition of a homosexual orientation will prevent men seeking sexual gratification with children who fall within their power. It does, at least, create a climate of openness in which the deployment of such priests and their access to treatment can be better managed. Furthermore, the balance of heterosexual men becoming candidates for the priesthood is likely to increase if the option of subsequent marriage remains open. Currently, as is well documented, the number of homosexual candidates far exceeds their relative strength in the general population.

The ordination of women priests has already caused a dilemma for the Episcopalian Church in America and the Anglican Church in the United Kingdom and in Australia. For some it necessitated a decision to leave the church and seek more conservative pastures, not infrequently the Roman Catholic Church. While the Episcopalians have an untidy situation whereby individual bishops make their own decisions and the remaining flock shift allegiance accordingly, they have at least a toe hold in the twenty first century. In another generation, it is safe to predict that women priests and bishops will seem so every day that all controversy will have died away. For the Roman Catholic Church life is not so straightforward.

Ordaining women priests would alienate a considerable number of the Faithful, notably those who support, actively or passively, the secretive Organisation. Since the Organisation is powerful both in influence and wealth it is a dangerous antagonist. Pius saw it as a bulwark against excessive liberalism. It seems unlikely that John XXIV regards it in quite the same light. Beyond the Organisation, there are many older Catholics and those in the developing world who could not easily accept such radical change. While the churches may claim a remit from God they are essentially rooted in a particular culture at a particular point in history.

Then there is the question of the Eastern Churches. Pius was fond of talking about the Church breathing with both lungs, East and West. To continue this analogy, women priests would probably amount to a case of institutional pneumonia. Women priests in a culture where gender equality is, at least, a theoretic norm is one thing. In a culture where it is not even a concept is quite another. In the latter it may simply be a synonym for schism.

Artificial birth control or contraception is a less emotionally charged subject. It should never have survived as an agenda item if previous popes had not put the concept of an errorless Church above the concept of simple truth. Fortunately the Faithful did not show the same reluctance and Catholic families in the developed world now match their non-Catholic contemporaries in the number of children. This has resulted in a form of collective denial by Church authorities and, almost certainly, accounts for the decline in attendance at confession (reconciliation as it is now called). Brought up on a diet, constructed by a celibate and probably sexually frustrated clergy, on which sexual sin was about the only whopper (mortal sin in the catechism), once the Faithful had decided that contraception was OK there wasn't too much left to confess. Fraud, drunkenness and wife beating had never been seriously censured whereas the genitals had been a rich and permanent source of damnation. Even those older Catholics, who had heroically raised children by the cartload, probably feel more relief than anger that their own children are less obedient and notably less fruitful. The prospect of legions of grandchildren is a sobering thought, even for the most devout.

Finally, there is the question of abortion and associated matters such a stem cell utilisation. Like contraception, the majority of Catholic laity in this country seem to have made their own decision though opinion is polarised to a degree which leads to periodic violence. Whether science or ethics or both can reach a conclusion as to when a soul becomes part of a human or potential human is the essential element which will determine if abortion is morally neutral, or murder, or manslaughter. It is hard to believe that a resolution is imminent.

John XXIV has begun his papacy by showing real courage and a determination to deal with important and controversial issues in the public arena. The Herald applauds his determination but cautions that his actions are in direct opposition to the secretive and defensive culture of his own Curia. In the past that same Curia has shown itself to be adept at managing or diverting change in order to retain its own intransigent position. Having laid down his blueprint for change, the world will anxiously await the victor of the inevitable power struggle. The Second Vatican Council spoke wisely of 'People of God' implying that the Church was not an unequal dichotomy consisting of the officers and the 'grunts'. The phrase was seen a seditious by the conservatives and is now largely erased for the lexicon. John XXIV seems determined to re-instate it.

An email addressed to the Organisation leadership worldwide expressed a very different view.

Subject: ***Proposed Pontifical Commissions***
Recent pronouncements by the Holy Father suggest a lack of appreciation of the nature of our mission. The Church is here to assert the word of God and not pander to the weaknesses of mankind. Concern for falling church attendances, the regular and flagrant disregard for the commandments, the hedonism of modern man cannot be accepted as an excuse for undermining existing doctrine. Better a church of a ten true believers than of one billion nominal Catholics. But do not be dismayed, our loyalty to the true Church is unquestionable and this loyalty transcends that to any individual, even if that individual be the Pope himself.

The revision of the process for canonisation and re-instatement of the Devil's Advocate is seen as a direct attack on our beloved founder. It is an assault which must not be ignored. Our duty is clear, we must uphold the Magisterium by whatever means. I know that I can rely on you all to prepare for action.

Peroni anticipated a strong reaction to the announcement of the commissions and he was not disappointed. Cardinal Murengo was his first assailant and the most opinionated.

"Does he wish to alienate the entire Catholic Church in Africa? Africans do not share the liberalism of the Europeans and Americans when it comes to men who have sex with each other. For us it remains the unnatural act as depicted in the Bible. Why only yesterday it was being described as objectively disordered, not just the act but the orientation. Today it may be embraced as akin to sex within marriage. What is this madness? I can tell you that we have enough problems here without the Pope adding to them. Our people attend church and then the witchdoctor. They worship God but also their ancestors. They are more likely to attribute ill fortune to a spell than to the collective result of sin. But on at least one issue they are four square behind existing Church doctrine, namely that intercourse between members of the same sex is a grave sin and contrary to the way in which God created mankind."

"I understand your concerns as does the Holy Father. He is not changing Church doctrine merely asking an expert panel to examine the issues. This reflects his openness to change but not his unfettered desire to reverse all teaching which may be out of step with the secular world."

"That is exactly my point. He is too open to change when change is out of the question. Did you know that he is being described as the Poofters' Pope? Even if the exercise is simply cosmetic and designed to convince the world that Catholicism is a dynamic religion, it will achieve that only by undermining the already committed. I say our first loyalty is to the existing Faithful and not to the tabloid press."

Peroni could tell that he was in for a long day and many an encore of the present performance. "Cardinal Murengo, you are the senior African cardinal and, as such, it is your duty to communicate to your brother bishops and through them to the Faithful that the Holy Father is simply ensuring that Church doctrine is consistent with all available knowledge. In so doing he is strengthening our position when criticism is levelled not weakening it as you have presumed. You and I may have chosen to act differently were we in the Pope's position but the fact remains that the Conclave chose William Carterton and not you or me. We both took a vow of obedience and I respectfully suggest that we both keep it."

Murengo made another phone call. He expressed similar sentiments but, this time, the recipient was wholly receptive. "Do not believe that you are a lone voice on this issue or, indeed, on the way in which the Pope is approaching his pontificate. But the Church has withstood bigger storms than a cavalier Pope without capsizing and his resolve has yet to be fully tested. There are forces both within and outside of the Church which are being deployed as we speak. Let us be patient but also active. May God bless you, Africa is in good hands."

The first shots were fired in the editorial of a small circulation, conservative journal known to be read in the Vatican.

THE MAGISTERIUM AND FASHION

Pope John XXIV was an unlikely candidate for the throne of St Peter but his actions since ascending have increasingly labelled him as an unsuitable occupant. It is a tragedy that, so early in the pontificate, the good will which accompanies a new Pope is being rapidly dissipated. Why has this occurred?

First, the background of the new Pope is essentially academic and most certainly not diplomatic. Academics are commissioned to critically examine received wisdom. To contradict that which appears to be false and to suggest new explanations when old ones prove inadequate. Diplomats are required to assess the timeliness of interventions and the manner in which they should occur. They deal far more in perceptions than in naked realities. Good diplomats are inclusive rather than exclusive. They manage to promote consensus and avoid division. It goes without saying that a diplomatic pope is more likely to unite than to disperse. The same claim cannot, regrettably, be said for an academic pope.

The Roman Catholic Church is over two thousand years old and while it has changed over the centuries, change has almost always been gradual and incremental. This very slowness to embrace new ideas has, generally, been a strength in that it recognises that people adapt to change gradually. Too much change, too many challenges to orthodoxy, create confusion and, not infrequently, the confused seek out places of greater certainty or simply abandon all allegiance to previously held beliefs.

The modern world, especially the lay world, has experienced change of ever increasing momentum. Initially such change was greeted as progress. Now we are beginning to experience the negative side of change. Children are born to temporary unions and virtually abandoned when such unions fall apart. Men and women are no longer certain of their gender roles and, in their confusion, adopt behaviours which are contrary to their God given natures. Employment opportunities are shifted around the globe in the pursuit of cost savings and in denial of the rights of retrenched workers. The spiritual hunger present in all humans is fed not by the word of God but by the peddlers of drugs and pornography. Change which outstrips the capacity of the human spirit is change for the worse. That the Church should follow this modern mindless charge into an unpredictable future is surely the greatest folly.

We implore the Holy Father to turn back before it is too late. By all means let him tackle an area of Church governance with patience as well as with zeal but not overwhelm the Faithful with an apparent assault on virtually all received doctrine.

Pat Nolan read the editorial as requested.

"What do you think, Pat? Am I causing confusion and driving people away from the Church?"

"Probably yes on both counts." He scratched his head. "I don't agree with all of it but they do make a point."

The Pope nodded. "So what am I to do? I believe that we need to examine so many aspects of our teaching that to tackle one at a time would merely scratch the surface."

"I can see that and so can many of the Faithful. Don't think this represents all opinion but you are a Pope who is going to cause division or, rather, cause existing divisions to be more marked. But don't forget the conservatives are better organised and are far better at promoting their agenda. Under your predecessor they established a dominant position and left many within the Church feeling sidelined. In that sense you are only restoring the balance."

"I hope you are right and that people will come to accept the fact. I want it to be an inclusive Church but I don't want the price of inclusion to be an inability to seek truth in the light of modern knowledge. Perhaps we have failed in the past by nurturing too much dependence on what Rome decrees rather than encouraging individual Catholics to be fully adult and to rely on their Church for guidance and their conscience for decision making."

Pat laughed. "Well statements like that will earn you a few enemies. Why I've heard more than one bishop claim that our greatest mistake was to let conscience out of the bag instead of just demanding obedience."

"That's what I mean. Perhaps, and only perhaps, such attitudes were suited to an ill- educated, illiterate flock struggling simply to survive. But today's Catholics are no longer ignorant and denied knowledge. We have to assume that they are trying just as hard as any cleric to live honestly, to educate their consciences and to make moral decisions in good faith. You know what Newman once said? 'I will raise my glass first to my conscience and then to the Pope.' I believe that he was absolutely right. Power is too seductive an experience to allow those who wield it to intrude too deeply into men's lives. In fact to do so will eventually incapacitate the individual conscience."

Nolan laughed again. "Well you've convinced me. All you have to do now is to convince a billion other Catholics and I think I know how. You must communicate with them via the web. Carry them along with your thinking. A weekly or monthly chat with the Pope."

"Rather a radical way of reaching the Faithful."

"It's a radical agenda."

Peroni pondered. "I suppose it is very modern. Not the idea of a website, per se, we already have a comprehensive one but the idea of a pope speaking directly to individual Catholics. That is something I had not considered. Indeed, I am not sure that it is a practice adopted even by secular leaders. Do presidents or prime ministers communicate in like manner? I think not. Perhaps that suggests that there are pitfalls which are not immediately obvious."

The Pope laughed. "Perhaps it suggests that presidents and prime ministers have to face an electorate at regular intervals, an ordeal which popes are spared."

"It may also suggest that the hierarchy has become redundant. Why have bishops to mediate between pope and people when the pope is bypassing them?"

"But that precedent already exists. Papal encyclicals are not distributed solely to bishops. They are readily available to anyone."

"Theoretically yes, but the language is such that the average Catholic is more likely to read Chaucer than an encyclical. It has always been the bishops and clergy who have explained the message thus maintaining the chain of command."

"Stephano, it seems that whatever issue we tackle, we find evidence of support for a power structure overriding the dissemination of the Good News. If I were an examiner marking a first year undergraduates assignment and it read like an encyclical, I would fail him or her for obscurity. Both as priest and bishop I felt I needed a code book to understand every nuance and always ended up with the sneaking suspicion that a clever decoder could produce diametrically opposed positions based on the same text. In other words, if we ever needed to change our mind we could do so on the basis of a previous misinterpretation. Bit reminiscent of Big Brother's Ministry of Truth, don't you think?"

"It is not the first time I have listened to such sentiments. However, my long time in the Curia has taught me that our methods are not all dishonest or designed to confuse. The very language of an encyclical can allow some degree of latitude when a local bishop is explaining the implications or when theologians are considering context. The effect is similar to the priest in confession who has to administer justice to a sinner but in the context of God's mercy. "

"Let me approach it from another and personal angle. My greatest regret as Archbishop of Liverpool was that I was insufficiently courageous. I won applause for being a 'steady hand on the tiller' and similar platitudes but I failed miserably to take risks and God knows that is exactly what he did and he paid a high price for so doing. I don't really care if I am buried as the 'stupid Pope' but I do care if I am buried as the 'cowardly Pope'. Opening a direct channel to the People of God may prove to be a mistake but at least I hope it will not result in the loud yawn which currently greets papal encyclicals."

"If you are determined then I would most strongly suggest that you first explain your intentions to the hierarchy. That way you may carry most of them with you otherwise you may well strengthen the conservative element."

With the Pope's agreement, Peroni informed the various prefects and other departmental heads within the Curia. The news was not universally well received. In fact, Peroni found himself in the unusual position of trying to explain why a radical departure from received practice might have some benefits. In a further ironical twist, it was the American Prefect for the Congregation of the Clergy who seemed most at odds with this 'descent into modernity' as he described it. In so doing, he quoted Marshall McLuhan's axiom: "The medium is the message".

"I suppose the next innovation will be the issue of roller blades so that we can career down the Vatican corridors thus symbolising our emergency from the Dark Ages. Consider for a moment the demographics of our clergy in the Western world. The majority are past middle age. They are overworked. Some service two or more parishes. By and large their congregations are aging. Some may have been young radicals thirty years ago but we all know that yesterday's radical is today's conservative, revolution gives way to evolution. Now, to add to their burden, they will have to deal with an onslaught of questions and criticisms arising out of the Pope's weekly, monthly, whatever fireside chat. Who is going to edit these communications? Is there going to be a right of reply? Will the Pope and Mrs Terminally Confused of Grand Rapids enter into a public conversation as to the relevance of blue in statues of the Virgin? Am I to become Prefect for the Congregation of the Suddenly Retiring Clergy?"

Peroni nodded inscrutably. "Cardinal Truong."

"I respect Cardinal Morrison's concern for his priests and he is right to place the Holy Father's intentions in that context. However, I think there is merit in seeking new ways in which to reach the people. Asians, as I am sure you all know, love technology, some would say they are obsessed by it. The mobile phone is considered more necessary to life than a decent meal. I believe that, potentially, the Pope will be speaking not just to Catholics but to a whole generation of young Asians and they, like most young people, experience a spiritual hunger. I cannot see many of them buying an encyclical or, indeed, the Lives of the Saints, but to log on to a web site is a distinct possibility. However, being Asian myself, I am also cautious. Could not the Holy Father explain that what he intends is a trial rather than a new institution. That way we can monitor the results and make a final decision on the hard data."

No vote was taken but Peroni promised to convey their sentiments to the Pope and to urge a trial rather than a fait accompli.

Cardinal Morrison was not a happy man. He phoned Cardinal Duffy in Chicago. Duffy immediately saw the proposal as an erosion of his power. He made a phone call to New York followed by several others including two to South America. Time zone differences made teleconferencing awkward but with such important issues at stake Duffy was prepared to rise at 3.00am. By 4.15am strategy had been agreed and the Organisation would coordinate a response to the Pope's first message to the Faithful.

"Thank you for seeing me, Holiness."

"I'm sorry to have kept you waiting, José. What have we got?"

José Samosa cleared his throat and took the seat offered. "I have to raise a delicate matter. Two delicate matters, in fact. The one concerns the web site, the other my own status."

The Pope motioned him to continue.

"As your senior adviser on media matters I think the idea is a serious mistake. Furthermore, I feel that I should have been consulted prior to any public announcement. I know that sounds presumptuous but it is my true belief."

"Not presumptuous at all. I am very slow learner where Vatican protocol is concerned. Indeed, if I am honest, I think we have far too much protocol. Granted that some is necessary but when it clogs up decision making and, more importantly, impedes the implementation of agreed decisions, the tail really is wagging the dog. That said, I am sorry that you have been a victim of my unorthodox approach."

"I appreciate your graciousness, Holiness, but where exactly does that leave me?"

The Pope laughed. "I don't think you do appreciate my graciousness. Nor, I suspect, do you approve of my method of conducting papal communications. That is not a criticism simply my impression of your relationship with Pius. We are different beasts and I do not expect people who served him with such dedication to necessarily be able, in conscience, to do the same for me."

"A gracious way of telling me that I should seek alternative employment?"

"As I said, not necessarily. But I would like you to make a decision in conscience as to whether you can remain in post and help execute an agenda with which you may not agree."

"And that agenda, Holiness?"

"It is somewhat in the evolutionary stage but, as a generalisation, I am trying to give the Church back to the People of God. Not to abolish all central control, because a core of values and procedures must be retained if we are to remain a recognisable institution, but not to be so detached from ordinary lives that the Good News we are supposed to convey is submerged in a plethora of regulations and protocols which bear little relevance to salvation. This may sound radical but it merely recognises what many parish priests have been doing since Vatican II. What saddens me is that this approach may, itself, lead to divisions within the Church. I hope, that by communicating directly with the Faithful, I may avert such divisions. If you can help me achieve this goal I shall be delighted but, if you cannot, I would not wish you to remain in an intolerable position."

"Then, with regret Holiness, you shall have my resignation and I fear it will not be the last."

The elegant prelate was admitted to the office and Maier waved his personal assistant away: this had been agreed as a meeting without a written record. Maier almost laughed, as he concurred to the request and glanced up at the video camera. The tape would be a useful reference when he wrote his best seller in years to come. It might even be needed sooner.

"Welcome Monsignor. May I get you a drink?" Maier motioned to a chair.

"A soda water. No ice."

"I must say I am both flattered and surprised. I don't believe I have even had the pleasure of a direct contact with a senior officer...if that is the right description...of the Organisation. Nor, to be honest, have I seen our interests as being similar. However, I am always open to new partnerships." He gave the Monsignor a quizzical look.

"Quite so. I too, would not have anticipated such a meeting but we live in interesting times."

"You more so than me, I fear. Your new Pope is causing a few anxiety attacks so I am told and not only in relation to the Vatican Press Office affair."

"You are very well informed, and that is still something of an understatement. Our new Holy Father is a radical with a new broom but, without doubting his good intentions, he is producing much more dust than enlightenment. However, I do not propose to lecture you on the internal problems of the Catholic Church, your interests lie elsewhere. My purpose today is to suggest that our problems may, indirectly, result in problems for your interests or rather those of Sebastian Hart."

"I am intrigued. Please explain."

"As I am sure you are aware, the Pope has begun an experiment in communication. He has bypassed the usual channels and now speaks directly to the Faithful. In fact, not just to the Faithful but to anyone who cares to access his personal web site. For us, those who seek to retain and return to tradition, this is a serious matter. The normal filtering process is redundant and the whole rank structure of the Church is undermined. Even when he does communicate directly with the hierarchy, what he has to say causes even greater disquiet. It is as though Mr Hart was replaced by a new chief executive who ignored the corporate structure and dictated the editorial comment directly."

Maier tried not to smile since the Monsignor was describing exactly how Hart usually chose to operate.

"So how does that affect us? I can see you are wondering. The Pope has a number of .....let us say interests...some might say hobby horses....one of those is the corrosive influence of the media and particularly the monopolistic position of some media owners. Clearly Consol fits that description. Presently the Pope is more concerned with examining matters of Church doctrine and communicating on these issues. Ultimately he will turn his attention to the media and, if he is successful, who knows what will result. A boycott of certain publications or television channels? Media ownership becoming a more prominent election issue? Spawning a single issue party, similar to the Greens, which aims to curtail the power of the media. From your position you can probably envisage additional, unwelcome scenarios."

Maier remained inscrutable. "You paint an interesting picture, maybe a disturbing one. Though, I must admit, I cannot see why the Organisation should be so concerned over the future of Consol. Does it have significant share holdings?"

The priest shook his head. "The Organisation holds no shares in Consol. What limited funds are available we like to use for the benefit of our brothers and sisters in the developing world and in leadership education . Our major concern is the future of the Catholic Church under Pope John XXIV and that future looks exceedingly troubled, as might the future for Consol when he returns his attention to the media. So we have a common cause in convincing the Pope that a adopting a more conservative modus operandi is in the interests of everyone. We shall be using our not inconsiderable influence to achieve this end and we hope that you might be persuaded to do the same."

"You are suggesting that we carry out a joint campaign?"

"Let us say that a worldwide campaign by Consol together with our efforts, and the Organisation is by no means a single voice within the Church on this matter, could save us both from a very costly haemorrhaging. A haemorrhaging of revenue in your case and of believers in ours. Based on some existing articles in the Consol press, you are not unaware of this clash of interests. My visit today is to encourage you to extend that critique in both duration and intensity."

"So Consol would be out in the open fighting while the Organisation was comfortably in the background, allegedly contributing but without any public exposure. A comfortable arrangement for the Organisation, providing the ammunition for us to fire."

"We all have constraints. You can scarcely run a secret media but what you can do is provide the most commendable reasons for pursuing your own interests. A technique which Consol appears to have perfected. The Organisation, on the other hand, has found that covert pressure is best suited to achieving results. Parallel methods suited to our respective operations. You provide the publicity, we provide the intelligence"

The Monsignor passed a document across the desk. "It is the draft of the next web site polemic. Consol isn't the only target but it is clearly recognisable as is another media baron turned politician, one a little closer to the Vatican."

Maier read quickly and chortled. "I think the Holy Father should learn to choose his enemies with greater care and, perhaps, read David Yallop's book. Pius had a narrow escape and we live in a dangerous world. That aside, Monsignor, you make a convincing argument. I will certainly give it some thought after I have seen the quality of the intelligence. One question though. Why did you bring this proposal to me rather than Mr Hart or some other board member?"

"Mr Hart is not an easy man to access and, in any case, we are aware that he values your opinions beyond any others. If you are convinced, we are sure that Consol will side with us and, if it does, may I presume to leave you with these initial suggestions for tactics." Maier accepted the folder and ushered the Monsignor into the outer office.

José Samosa's resignation received little publicity and then only in the more serious media, however it caused further disquiet within the Organisation. Samosa had been an associate for many years and his influence and ability to manipulate information had been invaluable. Gradually he had been replacing his staff with other associates so that the Vatican Press Office had virtually become a branch of the Organisation. Internal Organisation discipline required that he first discuss his intentions with the leadership but in, acting unilaterally, he was in breach of the Code. Today he appeared before the tribunal to account for his actions.

"Associate Samosa this tribunal is tasked to enquire into the matter of your resignation as Senior Media Officer and further into the lack of consultation with the Organisation. As an associate you are aware that our Code requires all significant individual decisions to be approved. Your decision was neither discussed nor approved. We should now like to hear your explanation."

Samosa, who had confronted an often aggressive media for over a decade, was surprisingly unsettled in front of these three seemingly innocuous men. He coughed nervously.

"I was taken by surprise. I was hoping to achieve some influence with the Holy Father. Instead he virtually told me that I would be required to support a radical agenda and one which ran contrary to that of Pope Pius. He framed the question as one of loyalty to my conscience rather than to the Pope. I believe that I had no option. I could not, in conscience, promote ideas which I felt were detrimental to the Church so I resigned."

"Associate Samosa, let me remind you that on your investiture as an associate you took a vow to respect the authority of the Organisation's leadership. Do you contend that you have kept that vow?"

Samosa squirmed. "I can only say that I acted out of conscience."

"I repeat the question. Have you kept that vow?"

"No. But....."

"No qualifications if you please. You plead the excuse of conscience as do so many sinners. I do not recall our Blessed Lord or, indeed, our own Holy Founder telling their followers to consult with their consciences. What do recall is an emphasis on obedience. Jesus did not say to the fishermen, 'Come follow me but only if after due reflection your consciences allow you to do so'. God did not ask Isaac to consult his conscience before being prepared to sacrifice his own son. The Organisation did not admit you with the caveat that you should be obedient only when it accorded with your conscience."

Samosa had turned very pale and was trying to say something when he was silenced. "Please wait outside while we consider the matter."

"José Samosa, this tribunal finds you guilty of breaking your vow of association. Such an act, by definition, renders you ineligible for continuing as an associate and would normally result in your expulsion from the Organisation. However, in mitigation we have considered your previously faithful service over many years and your achievements in promoting our cause. We have decided, therefore, not to impose the penalty of expulsion but to offer you the option of a period of penance and counselling which may lead to your re-instatement. Your nominated counsellor will report monthly on your progress and a final decision will be made based on his reports. Do you accept the option or do you accept expulsion?"

Samosa was shaking and had begun to weep. The Organisation was everything to him: family, friends, safe haven, and his very purpose in life. Expelled he would be nothing. "I am most grateful. I accept the option. I accept."

The Pope's first web site message was generally well received though, as one commentator observed, "It is hard to quarrel with a quasi-philosophical monologue described as 'thinking aloud'. When the thinking becomes concrete, views may be less tolerant."

COMMUNICATIONS IN THE ELECTRONIC ERA

My dear people, like many ancient institutions the Roman Catholic Church is often cautious in embracing new ideas. While this caution has its place and prevents the Church from being swayed by every fashion as it arises, it also has its drawbacks. It can prevent the Church seizing new opportunities to present the Good News and communicating the Good News is our essential role as Christians. Like most of you, I have no background in the electronic media so I am, perhaps, well placed to reflect what might be loosely termed the 'layman's thinking' on the subject. Thoughts as to how new developments in communications technology should or should not cause us to re-shape the way in which the Vatican speaks to the Universal Church and how the Universal Church speaks to the Vatican. It is my belief that all the Faithful should be a part of this process and so I invite you to reflect with me in order that we may make the optimum use of this new opportunity.

Jesus was a magnificent if sometimes cryptic communicator. We have only to re-read the Sermon on the Mount, or consider how he dealt with the crowd waiting to stone the adulteress, to marvel at how much he was able to convey with such economy of words. If only we could emulate his skill, think how the world might digest his message with far greater enthusiasm.

As I see it, we are called upon to be ever better communicators and, through this web site, I hope to provide both an example and an opportunity. To achieve this aim, I will attempt to use simple language and to avoid the rather portentous style of past Vatican documents. I will aim to speak directly to the individual and not through the medium of the local hierarchy, not because I wish to undermine the authority of bishops but because I believe there is something patronising in the presumption that the Faithful represent the kindergarten of the Church and, therefore, need teacher's guidance on every issue.

I am not unaware that I am venturing into uncharted waters and that, as with every novel enterprise, failure is as least as likely as success. Therefore, I see this initiative as a trial rather than as a new institution. *Two rather obvious criticisms have already been expressed. The one concerns the authority of bishops. I can only repeat that I fully support that authority but support does not mean now, nor has it ever meant, that the Pope cannot address the Church directly. The other concerns the possible deluge of responses to the web site and the difficulty of processing. That is being examined by a small committee of experts and they believe that an electronic filtering system can be developed which will, over time, enable all incoming email to be catalogued. While individual emails are unlikely to be acknowledged, the general issues raised will certainly receive a response via the web site.*

Personally, I am excited by the prospect of this trial and its implications. I hope you will also be enthused rather than overly cautious. Institutions which resist all change are destined to decline or, at worst, to disintegrate. We talk often of the need to reach out to our young people. As a priest and bishop I would often hear parents lament the fact that their teenagers had lost all interest in religion and worshiped their computer rather than their God. Perhaps the web site may be a way of re-engaging our lost but electronically-minded youth. I am put in mind of Berthold Brecht, when he observed, "That man will succeed who is in league with the future". As a Church we may have been guilty of looking too much to the past, too ready to quote tradition and too insecure to embrace the opportunities of change. Perhaps we have forgotten that the Holy Spirit descended on the frightened apostles and breathed fire into their souls. May the Spirit re-kindle our fire.

May God bless you all and, if it is His will, this initiative.
John XXIV.

CHAPTER 19

"The questions of celibacy and women priests are relatively easy to address." The Pope said, picking up on their earlier conversation. "There is no direct scriptural impediment to either though they still require delicate handling. Homosexuality is a different matter but to describe as 'objectively disordered' a condition which in many, if not all, cases is involuntary and therefore God given, seems both excessive and devoid of compassion."

Kirst's lips tightened. He was the author of this very phrase and was about to reply when the Pope held up his hand. "Forgive me, Helmut. However, a Congregation such as yours tends to foster a culture of defence. The very title suggests something static and its traditions have hardly encouraged radicalism. This is understandable when the elimination of heresy rather than the evolution of doctrine has been its rationale. But the fact that a man is homosexual does not make him a heretic and yet, somehow, the same attitude seems to be applied to this case and others like it. Perhaps a deliberate cultural change is now timely."

"A reversal of previous doctrine?"

"I didn't say that, but I do want to engage with you more actively and explore new ways of dealing with such matters as sexual orientation. What I emphatically do not want is to provide some doctrinal justification for treating homosexuals or other minorities as inhuman. I have no psychological qualifications but my brother, Stephen, does. He introduced me to the concept of defence mechanisms, in particular, reaction formation. Are you familiar with the idea?"

"I find psychology inherently anti-religious, exchanging the sacred for the profane."

"Curiously, I am beginning to think that it simply expresses religious concepts in a different language. However, reaction formation occurs when one defends against a personal desire by claiming the absolute opposite. For example, a bigot may defend against bigotry by claiming universal tolerance. I now wonder whether the most ardent despisers of homosexuals are not defending against the same interior urge. If that is the case, it could well lead to extreme language."

Kirst remained non-committal in the face of such arrant nonsense. If the Pope was adding psycho-babble, to his already long list of eccentricities, the future was indeed bleak.

"Even leaving such theories aside we know, for example, that the Church has a disproportionate number of homosexual priests. A disproportion which may well be increasing. Are we saying, in effect, 'St Patrick's! Welcome your new parish priest who just happens to be objectively disordered?' But I am not simply concerned about priests but about all marginalised people. Could homosexuals now be the tax collectors of the twenty first century? A despised minority with whom Jesus chose to associate. Remember Newman's advice that, if we are to observe the tradition of our ancestors, we may well need to use language apparently different from theirs'."

Kirst winced visibly at the mention of Newman, whom he considered an Anglican double agent. His new master increasingly relied on pseudo-science and pseudo theologians "Holiness, you seem set to abandon the traditional teaching of birth control. It is likely that married priests, who may or may not happen to be female, are only just round the corner. Are you now about to square the circle by declaring active homosexual relationships to be on a par with heterosexual relationships? If so, my services would appear to be virtually redundant for, following your reforms, there will be little left to police."

"On the contrary, I would welcome your partnership in establishing a new rationale and that is not an idle statement. But I do
want to be clear that a re-examination is on the agenda and give
you time to reflect on your place in that process. I pray that you
will wish to be involved but I accept that you have as much right
to a decision in conscience as anyone else."

"With respect, holiness, you seem to have already made up
your mind on so many of these matters."

The Pope nodded. "I have a view ." Then he smiled. "But
not an infallible view! What I really want is an unbiased review
of doctrine for a variety of reasons. What I emphatically do not
want is the commissions to operate under the limitation that the
reputation of the Church is the highest priority. The highest priority is that we deliver the truth as best we can discern it and that
we do so in a way which, to quote John XXIII, 'makes use of the
medicine of mercy rather than of severity'. As Lumen Gentium
tells us, the Church embraces sinners and, while holy, is always
in need of being purified through penance and renewal. I do
not believe that describing someone as 'objectively disordered'
has much in common with embracing them. In fact, since modern scholarship seems increasingly to suggest that sexual orientation is involuntary, are we not being arrogant in describing a
creation of God as 'objectively disordered'?"

Kirst found it hard to breathe. He wanted only to be away
from this madman. "Are there other controversial issues concerning my Congregation?" He asked, in a tone which reflected
this desire.

"There are but they need another forum."

*Martin Jenkins had grown up in rural Minnesota. As a child he had
been unusually quiet and compliant. Perhaps a function of having four
noisy older brothers. His father was a taciturn farmer who worked long
hours to provide for a wife and five children. He died when Martin was
seven. Jane Jenkins was a formidable woman with a philosophy which
she was determined to impart to her children. It was a simple philosophy:
tell the truth, work hard, go to Mass, say your prayers and obey the ten
commandments. Like most authoritarian parents, her system worked*

well until the older boys became teenagers. Then a combination of an increasingly rebellious brood and breast cancer undermined her ability to impose her will. Martin remained loyal to Jane's code of conduct while the older boys set about having fun.

As his brothers departed, the farm became untenable and had to be sold. Jane, now in very poor health, bought a modest house in St Cloud and moved there with Martin. Her Faith sustained her though a slow and painful death and Martin marvelled at the power of religion. When Jane died it seemed a natural progression that he should enter a seminary.

From the first Martin felt completely at home. The daily routines were soothing after the unpredictable demands of Jane's illness. Sometimes he felt that Jane was watching over him, now free from all pain and suffering. He wondered whether he should pray to her as he felt sure she was a saint, but his confessor suggested that he should direct his prayers to the already canonised.

Four years passed with only one small problem. Martin found socialising difficult. Many of the other seminarians reminded him of his brothers, being insufficiently serious for his tastes. What is more, some vague premonition told him that too close an intimacy could be dangerous. Not long after he received his deaconate he realised why he had isolated himself.

Karl Freyer was a year or two older than Martin and a mirror image of himself. Outgoing and gregarious, overtly cheerful and with an ability to engage with everyone. It was rumoured that he had homosexual tendencies and may have exercised these with other students but Martin's detachment protected him from rumours. So it was that his first close encounter with Karl was both frightening and exciting for reasons he did not comprehend. Putting aside his anxiety, he was flattered by the attention of this popular man. Karl began to inhabit his dreams and, one night, he woke in panic as he ejaculated involuntarily.

He carefully scripted his confession, choosing words which were as innocent as he could make them.

"Martin, I can't help you if I don't know what you are talking about. Just spit it out. You can't shock an old fellow like me."

"I ejaculated." He whispered.

"You'll have to speak up. There are no bugs in the confessional."

"I ejaculated."

"On your own?"

"Yes. In bed. Asleep."

"You mean you had a wet dream. Perfectly normal. You'd be odd if you didn't from time to time and It's not a sin, not even a venial one."

"But, but I was dreaming of someone when it happened."

"Martin you're suffering from scruples. You can't commit a sin if you don't intend to commit a sin. You know that already or, if you don't, we've done a bad job in preparing you."

"Is there anything else? Then say an act of contrition."

Fr Martin Jenkins was assigned as assistant priest to St Timothy's Parish in Duluth. The parish priest was an elderly man of Irish extraction. He had two notable obsessions, raising money and horse racing.

"I've no time for all this modern stuff." He told Martin at their first meeting. "Our job is to get them to Mass. Get them to dig deep in their pockets. Hear their confessions, baptise their kids, marry and bury them. We're not social workers, we are not anarchists, and we are not theologians. We are not here to confuse them with wishy washy sermons and the like. Bear that in mind and we'll get on fine." He looked at his watch. "Now I have to go. I'll see you at supper. And by the way, you call me Monsignor."

Martin's training had not equipped him for dealing with Monsignor O'Mara. Suddenly he felt very alone, a feeling not helped by the Monsignor's manner at supper. An unsuccessful day at the races had left him ill disposed towards humanity. He looked across the table at Martin and decided that he didn't like the look of this soft young man. You had to be tough to survive in St Timothy's. Let your guard down and you would be overwhelmed by the social problems and the capriciousness of the Faithful.

"What placements did you have?" He asked aggressively.

"St Mary's in St Paul and St Pat's in Hinckley."

"Well it's a bit different here. We don't have too many people who eat cucumber sandwiches and drink tea out of china."

Martin felt as though he should apologise. "I think it will be good for me to be in a working class parish."

"Working class! Working class! It would be nice to think that they are working class. Working class enough to have jobs. We have unemployment rates here in double figures. See if you feel the same way in a month."

*O'Mara's words seemed to haunt him. Poverty might be attractive
in the abstract but it was only too ugly in the reality. He visited families
who existed on welfare and had done so for several generations. He saw
examples of domestic violence brought on by frustration. He tried to provide hope for people who had none. He found, too, courage among the
disadvantaged and occasionally felt he had made some small difference to
broken lives. He needed to de-brief himself at night but the Monsignor's
attitude precluded any such indulgence. The isolation which he had previously enjoyed had become a burden under the pressure of poverty.*

*One bleak January day he escaped from the weather into a bar. He
rarely drank alcohol but, cold and dispirited, he ordered a whisky. The
effect was magical. He felt the liquor burning down his chest like liquid
optimism. He ordered another. A man sitting in one of the booths joined
him at the bar.*

"I haven't seen you here before." He said pleasantly.

"No. I haven't been here before."

"My name is Teddy. What's yours?"

*They shook hands. Teddy held his hand for what seemed an age.
Martin wasn't sure how to behave. He was enjoying the physical contact
but remained uneasy.*

*"Would you like a drink?' He asked as an excuse to break contact
without offence.*

"I'll have what you're having."

*The barman poured them both a whisky before Martin could object.
No sooner had Teddy downed his than their glasses were refilled. By now
Martin was only half conscious. He knew he must leave. Teddy tried to
make him stay. Martin declined.*

*As he staggered out into the cold his head started to spin. He reach
out an arm, missed the wall and began to fall. Teddy caught him from
behind with considerable strength. Minutes later they were in a taxi and
then in Teddy's apartment. Teddy helped him to a bed and Martin collapsed. When he woke he was naked and Teddy was lying next to him
stroking his penis.*

*Martin returned to St Timothy's and sneaked into his room to avoid
O'Mara. His confusion was extreme. He recalled Karl Freyer from the
seminary. Now there was Teddy. He could not remain in denial any*

longer. What was to become of his priesthood? He slept little and was afraid as to where his dreams might take him. At breakfast his appearance gave away his distress. O'Mara looked at him as though his worst fears were being confirmed.

"You look awful. Can't you take it here?"

"I need your advice. I am seeing this man who thinks he may be homosexual. In fact he's sure he is and he wants to know where that leaves him with the Church."

"Didn't they teach you that sort of thing in the seminary?" O'Mara barked.

"Yes but I thought there might be a more gentle approach out in the real world."

The Monsignor laughed without humour. "A more gentle approach! There is sin and there is sin. Homosexuals are objectively disordered, the Church says so. The scriptures say so and, if it's any help, I say so. Maybe he can't help what he is but he can help what he does. You tell him that and don't mince words. He probably thinks you'll tell him it's all right provided he doesn't hurt anyone. Well it isn't and that's all there is to be said on the subject."

The fact that Martin should have known better than to consult the Monsignor did little to comfort him. 'Objectively disordered.' He felt as the lepers of the scriptures must have felt. He should buy a bell and call out "unclean" wherever he went.

Martin went to confession in a church on the other side of the city. The priest was sympathetic and told him that the only sin he had committed, if it was a sin, was drinking too much so that his judgement was impaired. Martin's spirit's rose. The man was being so kind to him, like a father he had scarcely known. He was reluctant to leave the sanctuary of the confessional.

"Is there something else?" His confessor asked, aware that Martin had remained after absolution.

"Can I be cured?" Martin blurted out in his naivety.

"I'm sorry, my son, but It's not something you can cure. I'm afraid It's something you will have to live with but God's grace will support you. Keep coming to the sacraments. I will pray for you."

Out in the cold night air the Monsignor's words kept coming back to him. 'Objectively disordered, objectively disordered.' That's what he was, not really a priest, not really human.

After two weeks, his brothers agreed that the life support system should be switched off. The police enquiry had exonerated the driver. Three witnesses all said that Martin had walked out into the path of the truck as though in a trance. Accidental death was recorded. No one thought to inscribe 'objectively disordered' on his headstone.

CHAPTER 20

The Pope entered the Palazzo del Sant'Uffizio, a building rendered even less impressive by its proximity to St Peter's Basilica but it's architectural mediocrity is inconsequential when compared with its historical importance. Originally it housed, under the first of its labels, the Sacred Congregation of the Roman and Universal Inquisition, founded to repel the tide of the Protestant Reformation which threatening to engulf Italy in the sixteenth century. Over the subsequent centuries the significance of the institution has waxed and waned. It was even abolished briefly when Napoleon controlled the Papal States. However, it was not until the beginning of the twentieth century that the title Inquisition was dropped and it was renamed the Sacred Congregation of the Holy Office. Now, courtesy of the Second Vatican Council, it had further evolved into the Congregation for the Doctrine of the Faith or the CDF, as it is now known to both admirers and critics.

To put events in their historical context, it is necessary to distinguish between the Inquisition as it operated in Italy and as it operated in Spain. It was in Spain where the worst excesses occurred, more as a method of maintaining political cohesion than of eliminating heresy. Ferdinand and Isabella needed a means of creating national unity in a country which had evolved as a mixture of Catholics, Muslims, Protestants and Jews. Catholicism became the chosen vehicle and the Pope agreed to the strategy. Later attempts by the Vatican to halt the resultant persecutions failed since the political agenda was now paramount. It has been estimated, that between the sixteenth and eighteenth centuries, the Roman version was responsible for less than two hundred deaths while the Spanish counterpart, initially under Tomas de Torquemada, was responsible for thousands.

That is not to justify the one by contrast with the excesses of the other. But, in the context of the times, the Roman/Italian version was relatively benign and its influence exerted more in the banning of books than the burning of heretics. The majority of cases resulted in penances which might equally well have been handed out in confession, harsh by today's standards, but not terminal.

Of course, certain famous decisions have been shown to be at complete variance with the truth and have resulted in a much delayed and rare admission that the Church might just conceivably have made a mistake. The house arrest of Galileo, for the last decade of his life, being the most famous. Here, the admission of error took a mere four centuries. To those who fall foul of the CDF, a long delayed posthumous acquittal is about the best they can expect.

To an outside observer, especially to the vast majority with no background in theology, the cases dealt with by the CDF must seem as distant from their lives as alchemy. In part this is because the CDF takes a top down approach to theology. Traditionally the Vatican has dictated the dogma or Magisterium and instructed the hierarchy to implement it down to parish level. Increasingly this process is honoured more in the breach than the observance, as the closer one comes to the actual impact on ordinary people's lives, the harder it becomes to pass on instructions which appear to take scant account of reality and, not infrequently, are of dubious provenance. Thus a situation has arisen similar to that of the declining years of the Roman Empire. At that time, Rome issued edicts which never actually permeated the whole Empire or, if they did, were blithely ignored. Thus the illusion of governance was maintained but only by ignoring the reality.

Similarly the Catholic Church's teaching on artificial birth control has not changed, yet Catholic families have shrunk to the size of their non-Catholic peers and it would be a rare event to hear a priest or even a bishop berate his congregation for not observing the Magisterium on this and many other prohibitions. Ignoring the lesson of the Roman Empire may prove a serious neglect.

Pope John XXIV is well aware of these portents. Not having been shielded by a long isolation in the Curia, he is also aware of the reality of ordinary Catholic's lives, at least in the developed world. He is unhappy with the word 'defend'. Jesus was pro-active. He came to "fulfil the law". Not to abolish nor to defend it. Though no mean theologian himself, he has asked Cardinal Kirst and the progressive, the CDF would say heretical, Franciscan Friar, Fr Pereira, to debate their very different views of the operations of the CDF as a means of broadening his own knowledge. Kirst, though clearly unenthusiastic, has agreed to the Pope's request and today is the day.

"Gentlemen, I thank you both for agreeing to provide me with two differing views on the workings of the Congregation. In so doing I am conscious that Jesus promised to be with his Church to the end of the world, so we do not need to fear a little controversy. So may I suggest that we take St Augustine for our guide. 'In essentials, unity. In inessentials, liberty. In all things, charity'. Cardinal, perhaps you would like to begin."

"Holiness, Father Pereira. The Catholic Church is an unique institution. Founded by Jesus Christ as the channel by which his saving grace is to be delivered to mankind. It has existed for two millennia and will continue to exist until the Last Judgement. This task of salvation has to transcend all other considerations, whether they be of a political, social or individual nature. Often discharging this overriding duty can cause us to place burdens on men and women in this life in order that they may achieve that goal which God wills for all of us in the next."

"We are guided in this task by the scriptures, the natural law and the tradition of the Church as laid down in the Magisterium. It is the duty of the CDF to ensure that dogma is not corrupted by Catholics, clerical or lay, who may, even with the best of intentions, stray from the true teaching of the Church. No other church has the doctrinal purity of the Catholic Church. Most do not have even the mechanisms for maintaining purity. Islam has no central authority. Nor does Hinduism. Nor does Buddhism. The Anglican Church most clearly lacks such an authority. As to the majority of the other Protestant churches, preachers preach what they feel like preaching. I see my role as Prefect to safeguard our unique heritage, uncontaminated by either fashion or expediency "

"Holiness, Cardinal Prefect." The Friar began in his strong Portuguese accent. "Essentially I have two issues with the operations of the CDF. Issues which I believe are common to all human organisations." The Friar detected a hint of annoyance from Kirst at this unflattering comparison. "While the Church has a divine founder it is staffed by mere human beings with all their frailties. The issue of power is fundamental. Does power emanate from Rome or is it conferred by the people, the ordinary men and women who come to Mass, raise children, lose their tempers, watch too much television, prefer science fiction to theology and, generally, try to live good lives? Do we belong to a top down or bottom up Church? To put it crudely, who pays the bills? Jesus chose to associate with the poor, the uneducated, and the downtrodden. He could have signed up for the Sanhedrin. I believe that, if we follow his example, we will develop our theology bottom up."

Kirst responded. "With respect, Father Friar, what you have said is largely a re-run of the debate on liberation theology. In Christ's own words, 'The poor are always with us'. Doesn't that tell us something? No matter how idealistic the views of those who preach a form of proletarian renewal, the fact remains that we are not going to eliminate poverty. We have his word for it. Our focus must be salvation through Jesus, not revolution through misguided priests. As our late Holy Father indicated, to take the path of liberation theology is to adopt a form of Catholic communism which is, itself, a contradiction. That is why my Congregation has been so diligent in tackling this particular form of error."

"I can personally testify to diligence, of your office Cardinal, though I cannot say the same for its justice. This is my second issue. The Church has often championed the right to a fair trial of those accused under civil law. Pope Pius was a strong defender of such rights. However, when it comes to the treatment of priests or nuns who are considered dissident, no such rights exist. Accusations are levied without the accuser even being named. Why! Sometimes the accusations themselves remain secret. If the Church really wishes to disassociate itself from communism it should abandon methods which are closer to the show trials of Stalin than the Universal Declaration of Human Rights. Surely one has to be cynical about an organisation which claims that Church teaching 'has a validity beyond its argumentation'. Humpty Dumpty said something similar when he claimed that, 'Words mean what I mean them to mean'."

"I will ignore that tortuous analogy. What you claim as injustice is simply that the Church does not launder it's dirty clothes in public. In any event, your own South American bishops have largely concluded that liberation theology was an aberration whose time has passed."

"If you appoint conservative bishops, in particular those with connections to the ruling classes, you can hardly expect a radical voice. Mice do not bark. But regardless of whether the crime is the promotion of liberation theology or the questioning of papal infallibility, the processes of the CDF are both secretive and flawed. What democracy would accept as fair, a judicial process where the accused is not allowed to see the documentary evidence against him; nor know his accuser; where his defence council is not of his choosing and where his access is restricted; where judge and jury are one and the same and there is no right of appeal?"

Kirst smiled. "But the good father knew when he was ordained that the Catholic Church is not a democracy. The Church is not answerable to the electorate, only to God."

"I might even be able to accept that if the Vatican did not assume that it actually was God: humility is an attractive quality, especially in those who have power. But while the Church may not claim to be a democracy, it certainly claims to be a communion and a communion implies the sharing of thoughts, feelings and interests and not the habitual suppression of voices not in harmony with the leadership."

After about an hour of such point and counter point, the Pope held up his hand. "Thank you both for stimulating my thinking."

Fr Pereira had left and the Pope was alone with the Cardinal. "Helmut, I really do appreciate you agreeing to this meeting against your wishes. However, Father Pereira has raised some serious questions. Questions which are more often asked outside than inside of the Vatican. I think we need to take account of both perspectives."

"What would you have me do, Holiness? You are aware of my position. I have never hidden it."

"Essentially I would like to move the focus of the Congregation from 'defence' to 'development': to use your skills to increase the relevance of the Church to the twenty first century. To assume more of a pastoral role and less of a punitive one. To put it in the vernacular, to replace the bad cop with the good cop."

"I have been anticipating something like this. No! Fearing is a better word. With great respect, Holiness, you seem determined to undo all we have accomplished in eroding the unrealistic expectations stemming from the Second Vatican Council. I cannot, in conscience, serve you to that end."

"I, too, feared that this would be the case and I understand your position. Reflect on it and, if you see a change of emphasis as impossible, let me know how you would like to see your future."

"To me, Holiness, it is very simple. We have an infallible founder who relies on fallible men.....no disrespect to yourself... to bring his Good News to the world. Personally, and I have written as much, I believe that the doctrine of infallibility is a mistaken one, both practically and canonically. If it is correct, we have to believe some things which defy belief. If it is wrong, the result is the same. The Vatican seems to have a schizophrenic attitude towards the doctrine. Your predecessor, despite his strong convictions, chose never to issue an ex cathedra statement. Yet, his subordinates, notably the CDF, issue proclamations which imply an infallible status. It is like a form of theological coitus interruptus: we want the power but not the responsibility. You, of all people, do not need a history lesson but the whole circumstances surrounding the doctrine are educative. Pius IX adopted a 'back to the future' attitude, verging on the lunatic. Muddled thinking allowed support for a Pope, under anti-clerical pressure, to become confused with support for an indefensible doctrine. The pressure on the opposing bishops caused many to succumb in bad faith. Cardinal Newman was so affronted by the whole circus that he is reported to have prayed that Pius might die and the bizarre idea be interred with him. But, worse still, Pius erected a further barrier to the Church being able to say 'we were wrong'."

"As you say, you are not telling me anything I did not already know but it is helpful to be reminded. So please continue."

"In a sense I have said it all. We are in danger of becoming a rump of true believers. A billion Catholics may sound impressive, but how many attend church regularly. Of those who do, how many accept the teachings on married clergy, on women priests, on birth control.? The trouble is that, when so many teachings are seen as impractical, without a coherent scriptural/philosophical base and often downright cruel. What is worse is that core values can end up in the same category. Your earlier quote from St Augustine is just so relevant. 'In essentials unity, in inessentials liberty, in all things charity.' The CDF may have a role in the first but unfortunately it has expanded its remit into the second and, so far as I can see, ignores the third.

"I have a proposition for you, Fr Pereira. Cardinal Kirst has resigned as Prefect. I would like you to take his place."

The Friar looked stunned. Then he laughed. "As you English say, poacher turned gamekeeper."

"Exactly."

CHAPTER 21

POPE JOHN XXIV TELLS BISHOPS TO LIGHTEN UP

Not for the first time in his brief pontificate, John XXIV has caused alarm amongst leaders of the Catholic Church. His most recent website communication to the hierarchy is being interpreted by liberals as long overdue and by conservatives as verging on heresy. Pope John's rule has been controversial ever since the Conclave and, before that, he had established a reputation as an outspoken Cardinal and Archbishop. Often the assumption of high office has a sobering effect and turns yesterday's radicals into today's conservatives: not so with the new Pope. Whether at the macro or micro level, he seems determined to create a papacy unlike any other. One well informed source confided that he wished to do away with the title of Holiness since he considered himself unworthy. The same source said that he actually asked to be called 'Bill' but that the Curia could not cope with such a departure from custom. Another straw in the wind was the recent transfer of Cardinal Helmut Kirst from Prefect of the Congregation for the Doctrine of the Faith (previously the Inquisition) to be Cardinal Archbishop of Cologne. There is a rumour that it is to be re-named the Congregation for the Development of the Faith. If true, that is ominous news for conservative elements already talking of a schism.

Kirst's Vatican department had been responsible for the issue of many controversial edicts in recent years and for using the imaginative descriptors, 'definitive' and 'irreversible'. Thus laying a heavy burden of observance of the Faithful without raising the even more controversial issue of papal infallibility. Kirst's departure is being interpreted as a sign that some or all of these doctrinal edicts are under scrutiny.

If Cardinal Kirst's departure was seen as inevitable by many, the retention of the conservative Cardinal Peroni as Secretary of State (Vatican Prime Minister) has caused amazement. One rumour has it that Peroni was against the Pope's appointment as Archbishop of Westminster. Yet he remains in office with more power than any other member of the Curia.

In the light of these apparently contradictory actions, it is little wonder that John XXIV has become known as the Pope of Surprises. The cardinals now heading for Rome must be praying that the surprises will be palatable to their flocks back home. Some may even be praying that they are not on the Pope's transfer list.

"My dear brothers, I thank you for attending this unusual meeting at such short notice. I hope that your accommodation arrangements are satisfactory and that you are able to enjoy something of our magnificent Roman spring before your return journey."

"It is almost a year since you did me the great honour of electing me as head of the Catholic Church. In common with anyone so elevated, I felt intimidated by the responsibilities. I had hardly got used to being a cardinal before I was thrust onto the world stage. At first I was almost paralysed by fear and was unable to make a decision. Fortunately for me, Cardinal Peroni shielded me from my own cowardice and did so with considerable compassion."

"When I consider the pontificates of many of my predecessors I can only marvel at their achievement. If I could achieve a quarter of what Pius XIII achieved, I should be well satisfied. However, that does not

mean that I must never change the direction of the Church as set by such illustrious predecessors. My election was a surprise. Indeed, one paper has dubbed me the 'Pope of Surprises'. That very fact gives me a confidence that the Holy Spirit did influence you to elect a non-entity. Not because that non-entity possessed some eternal virtue but simply because God had been guiding him in a certain direction, patiently over decades, to be relevant at a particular point in time. We know from the scriptures that God often chooses the least likely of men, and women, and transforms their inadequacy into His grand design."

"When we look at organisations outside of the Church, especially authoritarian organisations, we often find that they operate in a state of denial, of unreality. They have to because not to do so would be to admit that they can be and have been wrong. The very nature of authoritarianism depends upon being right. If it is not always right there is no basis for legitimacy. Since this foundation is essentially flawed, the edifice can only be supported by a massive and growing fiction. Those who point out errors are certified insane or sent to re-education camps. U turns are proclaimed as being wholly consistent with dogma. History is re-written to accommodate actuality. As the organisation ages, more and more energy has to be devoted to maintaining the mythology until, at last, the only purpose of the organisation is the maintenance of the organisation. What started off, quite possibly, with the highest motives of service to the people has now to suppress the people in order to save guard the organisation. We have seen too many examples in the last century to be unaware of this progression."

"It is easy to see and mock such pretence when it occurs outside of ourselves. It is less easy to see when it has become the enemy within. My dear brothers, let us not assume that the Catholic Church is immune from this debilitating disease. Jesus told us that, 'The truth would set us free'. He also warned us, indirectly in his criticism of the Pharisees, about 'placing unnecessary burdens on men's lives'. Are we, as a Church, sometimes guilty of doing the latter because to proclaim the former would suggest that the organisation, the Church, can actually be wrong?"

"Our beliefs rely on three sources. The scriptures, tradition and the natural law. While we should be scrupulous in any attempt to reassess teaching based on these pillars, we should also be open to re-examine such teaching in the light of new knowledge or scholarship. Scriptural scholarship is a dynamic discipline, subject to input from associated fields,

archaeology and linguistics for example. Discoveries such as the Dead Sea Scrolls, when fully scrutinised, may enhance our understanding of scripture. The natural law will be more fully elaborated as the human genetic code is finally unravelled. Tradition is a particularly interesting and, perhaps, the most volatile concept.. Tradition has, by definition, it's genesis in a culture and we are all aware that cultures change. Jesus had to operate within his culture, we have to operate within ours'. Indeed, when he told us that he had come not to abolish but to fulfil the law he was implying that this was the exact moment when a fresh approach to an existing tradition should occur. A practical assertion that tradition could develop, be refined or, to use Newman's insight, to maintain a tradition may require us to use language which, superficially, appears contrary to that same tradition. As time passes we often come to abhor the cultural practices of the past. We no longer believe that burning heretics strengthens a religion or meets the requirement to love our neighbour. I believe that we should be more open minded in examining our traditions in the light of the cultures which spawned them."

"I put these thoughts to you as a precursor to the various commissions which I am in the process of establishing and, of course, in advance of the council which will follow. A reading of Church history shows us that this process has often occurred. We are not creating tradition, merely maintaining it."

There was unease amongst the cardinals and a degree of quiet comment. The Pope smiled at them and waved with both hands.

"I have almost finished and you will be given plenty of opportunity to take issue with me or raise other matters. My final observation is this. I think we have become too respectful towards authority, mine included. Why, in the past, popes and cardinals were treated with much less deference and for good reason. At various times, as you well know, they enjoyed mistresses, great wealth, secular power and were guilty of almost every sin you could name. Dante, in his Inferno, consigned a pope to hell for avarice and he was not the first creative artist to do so. The Church consists of fallible men and women and, despite the best efforts of the Spirit, some of our venality is bound to leak out where it may corrupt doctrine or simply place our claim to authority above the need for truth. I recognise the dilemma and its implications but, in my opinion, truth must prevail over the reputation of any organisation, be it church or state or pope."

CHAPTER 22

Franelli ushered Hart into the Pope's chambers. Maier had briefed his boss on the protocol but had uncharacteristically, perhaps deliberatively, omitted to incorporate recent changes. As a consequence Hart attempted to kneel and kiss the Pope's ring while the Pope attempted to shake hands. The Pope found the incident comical, Hart was less amused. Each sensed the other's different reaction and remained stoic.

"I appreciate your seeing me, Holiness. Running an organisation of one billion must be rather time consuming."

"I am flattered that a media mogul should take the trouble to call. You, too, must have time management problems."

Hart shrugged. "It is the modern plague. Each advance is supposed to save us time but ends up by filling our days even further. Time is our mistress and we serve her like slaves."

"A false goddess, perhaps?"

"I am not a religious man."

"But I trust you are a moral one, as you wield great power for good or evil."

"This is exactly what I wanted to discuss. I am aware of that power and how easy it is for the media to take the blame for all human folly. Even, for an atheist like me, that sits uneasily but for a business man it has far more practical implications, as I am sure you appreciate."

"And so you are seeking moral guidance?" The Pope asked with a hint of sarcasm.

"Not so much guidance but partnership, though I would be open to suggestions."

"I am intrigued. I can see what you have to offer the Church but I cannot quite imagine our contribution to Consol."

"Not so much a contribution but an absence of contribution. The media often gets a bad press, sometimes deservedly, sometimes undeservedly. You have, yourself, been an outspoken critic and periodically there are pressures for limiting or even reducing media ownership. Claims that unelected media owners are too powerful. These can be damaging and expensive to rebut. Church leaders have sometimes been the cheer leaders in anti-media campaigns. I would like to believe that the most powerful religious leader in the world has, at least, an open mind on the subject or, as a radical Pope, even a positive attitude to the good which the media can help to accomplish."

"An open mind I can promise you but that does not mean an uncritical mind."

"Nor should it, but my purpose today is to suggest some ways in which Consol might make a significant contribution for good and to listen to any ideas you may have on the subject."

"I am still intrigued."

"Well, I am aware of your compassion for the poor and of the good work which the Catholic Church does through organisations like Caritas and Cafod. You are no doubt aware of the UN commitment that developed countries set aside 0.7% of their GNP for overseas aid. A commitment which has rarely been met by any member of the UN with the Americans being amongst the least generous. Suppose Consol was to exert media pressure on governments to achieve the 0.7% target, surely that would accord with the Pope's wishes and promote a more positive acceptance of media."

"Unquestionably. But a more positive acceptance would not equate to a blank cheque."

"Of course not. All I am seeking is a more balanced view and an acceptance that we really can help mainstream religions, and others of good will, to bring their message of peace to the world. Take China for example, where you have in effect two Catholic Churches: the official Church which is virtually an arm of government and the true Church which has no status. The expansion of Consol into China could provide a channel for quietly supporting a more conciliatory attitude on the part of the government."

"It is a very attractive suggestion but, Mr Hart, please understand that I am not anti-media, quite the reverse. Without a free and truthful media to inform and, if necessary, expose corruption our very civilisation is under threat. It is when the media fails in that duty that criticism is appropriate. I recognise, too, that the media has sometimes done more to promote human rights and to expose corruption than either politicians or churchmen. The recent cases of sexual abuse of children by clergy has been largely media driven and, even though the motives may not always have been the highest, it was a necessary call to accountability. That the media can be a force for good is not in doubt but it is important to remember that acts derive their morality from their intention and not from their outcome. The most desirable outcome can result from the most heinous act and vice versa. There is a story in the New Testament where Jesus is taken to the top of a mountain and there the devil offers him dominion over the whole earth in exchange for an act of adoration. We are all subject to such temptation, myself included. I will follow your campaign for overseas development aid with great interest and do anything I can to support it and I will guarantee you an open mind. Beyond that I cannot promise."

Hart did not express his anger until he was back in New York. Two directors discovered that they were surplus to requirements and Maier was instructed to give top priority to a counter attack. In Europe and the Unites States, politicians at the highest level were to be informed that the support of the Consol media should never be taken for granted. Hart's personal lawyer was instructed to prepare for divorce proceedings. Even anger could be put to good use.

"I played the China card and the Third World card and failed to take a trick. The man is too honest for the job. He doesn't make deals which means that you can't negotiate with him. He might as well have come from another planet."

Maier was secretly amused, Hart's humiliation was worth his failed idea. It put the Pope in the same category as himself, impervious to Hart. "So we can't whisper that certain agenda topics might cause a significant portion of the media to become hostile. In the past that might have been sufficient but, alas, no longer."

"You seem to be enjoying the whole pantomime. I don't share your enthusiasm."

"I regard it as a challenge. How do we control the second most powerful man in the world? It's a cause worthy of our talents."

"Then you'd better come up with some good ideas." Hart snarled.

"Come now Sebastian, you know I always have a Plan B in reserve. First of all we need better intelligence. Are the web site attacks on media oligopolies to be advanced in the council?"

Hart shrugged. "So what! They can rant and rave in their funny clothes but the punters like big tits and celebrities making fools of themselves. How many topless models does the Pope have?"

Maier laughed. " Maybe not the Pope but there is at least one cardinal with a taste for the topless and bottomless and therein lies our opportunity."

"Go on."

"I heard about a tape made in a Hamburg bordello, for blackmail. So I bought it."

"How expensive?"

"$150,000 US."

"And what do I get for $150,000 US?"

"A high ranking Curial official enjoying a rather unchaste spot of titillation. What's known in the trade as an exhibition. An exhibition in case......"

Hart waved him on. "Of course I know."

"So we have our mole and all we have to do is to activate him. I thought it rather a bargain."

"Who is this high ranking Curial official?"

Maier whispered a name and Hart nodded happily. "A bargain indeed."

Maier continued. "Irony is that the old goat is a staunch conservative in everything except boudoir frolics. I can imagine his reaction when he learns that, if he doesn't do what he's told, he's going to be entertaining the public sans crook and crosier."

Hart digested the information. "Having a mole isn't going to stop the Pope creating problems. So how do you intend to use him?"

"That's easy. He's our eyes and ears during the council which is only eighteen months away. Not only that but you never know what other useful snippets he'll produce. It will be made very clear that concealing any information we might find of interest means that all bets are off."

Hart didn't seem convinced. "I thought these councils are supposed to deal with esoteric topics like virgin births and levitations and leave the real world to men like us."

"Historically that has been so but the business is under new management. Bad publicity on the Pope's website is one thing but it can be discounted by the fact that John Paul XXIV is seen as eccentric by many Catholics and probably most others. But an encyclical on the media carrying the weight of the world's bishops would be a far more potent weapon. That couldn't be dismissed as the ravings of a madman. If we know who is saying what inside the council we have a much better chance of influencing the outcome. We may not have video footage of every bishop but I'm sure I can find the odd skeleton if a little gentle persuasion becomes necessary. It is surprising how many temptations can be placed in front of a tired prelate in the Eternal City."

Hart relaxed somewhat. Maybe he could now concentrate on the divorce and the succession.

"Oh! And I had an approach from a rather odd little Monsignor, a representative of the Organisation. It seems they want to climb into bed with the devil, namely us."

Hart gave one of his rare and mirthless laughs. " Christianity in bed with naked capitalism. What an inversion."

"I rather enjoy the irony. Sebastian Hart saving the Catholic Church from itself. St Sebastian, perhaps."

"A little too clever, Karl. We know what happened to him."

Only days later Maier's forebodings were justified when he accessed the website.

TRUST AND TRUTH

The essential ingredients in any relationship, whether it is between two people, within a nation or even between nations, are those two fraternal twins trust and truth. With their presence it is possible to co-exist and cooperate even with those whom we dislike. Without them a relationship, even with someone we admire or love, is essentially dysfunctional, leading not to mutual advantage but lessening the humanity of all participants.

When Jesus told us that 'the truth will set us free' he was not offering a counsel of perfection. Rather he was telling us that to do otherwise is to live in a captivity which exists when we cannot trust our neighbour. To live in a society where truth has been corrupted into expediency is to live in a society which has ceased to trust. In such circumstances, individuals restrict their relationships to the shrinking group within which trust can be maintained. At Its most extreme the individual trust only themselves and, at that point, society has ceased to exist in any meaningful way.

To our shame, the Church has been guilty of placing expediency before truth. In dealing with child sexual abuse. In dealing with ideas which might be seen as inimical to Church interests. In drawing a sophisticated distinction between members of the Church who behave badly and the Church itself, for what else is the Church if it is not its members?

However, the Church does not stand alone at the bar of public opinion. Governments and corporations are equally guilty. The old saying that the first casualty of war is the truth has never been more descriptive of the action of governments in the early years of this century. What is more, in maintaining these fictions, powerful media interests have supported deceptions for corporate gain. In the business world, some senior managers have lied and defrauded in order to line their own pockets, while their workers and shareholders were left poverty stricken.

When the independent media or a whistle blower tries to expose such malpractice, they are subjected to various forms of intimidation in the expectation that power and wealth will prevail over courage and truth. My own Church has been guilty of crying persecution when its own unsavoury conduct has been exposed, while the Church controlled media has remained cravenly silent.

So the appeal I make today is made in great humility and without any sense of moral superiority. A free and impartial media is essential if clergy, politicians and business leaders are to be subject to scrutiny and scrutiny is essential if the people are to retain trust. Often it has been a courageous investigative reporter who has publicised a scandal or even brought home the true horror of war sufficient to bring about change. Often the media has done the job which priests, politicians or business leaders should have done themselves. Today this most necessary service is being undermined by two factors which interact with each other. One is the increased concentration of the media into vast international monopolies. The other is the need for government assistance or, at least, non-interference while these monopolies are created and maintained. Thus the media owners court the politicians and the politicians court the media owners, a cosy arrangement which excludes the public and, not infrequently, the truth.

If this in itself were not sufficient cause for alarm, there is the tendency for the media to entertain rather than to inform. A diet of celebrity and tragedy, junk food instead of protein. Not far removed from the bread and circuses which preceded the fall of the Roman Empire. Sadly, Italy is the most extreme and conspicuous example of the danger which occurs when politics and media become intertwined. The democracies were all founded on the doctrine of the Separation of Powers: that the Executive should not also be the Judiciary; that jus-

tice would be separate from the expediency of politics and vice versa. It seems that we now need an additional definition of the Separation of Powers, that the Executive cannot also be the Media or share the same bed. So that the media can be separate from the expediency of politics and vice versa. We have long recognised that the media is an arm of government in totalitarian states. Increasingly the same situation is developing in the 'so called' democracies. As Pope, I am concerned for the corrosive effect this has throughout the world. As Bishop of Rome I am concerned at the flagrant abuse of media ownership for political purposes in this country.

To governments, I say, be honest with the people even when this means admitting error. They have a capacity for forgiveness which might surprise you, provided you can retain their trust. They do not believe themselves to be infallible nor do they expect you to be infallible. No matter how attractive the short term advantage, do not allow media monopolies, their interest is self-interest, not truth.

To business leaders, I say, be satisfied with adequate rewards and be aware that you are trustees, effectively servants, of your workers and investors. Do not act as though they are pawns in a selfish pursuit of personal wealth and prestige.

To the media, I say, yours is a noble and responsible vocation. Honour it by always placing truth above convenience. Do not pander to the powerful at the expense of the weak. Wield your influence with responsibility. You have a mandate to tell the truth, not to manipulate opinion.

To the Catholic Church, I say, let us be humble enough to admit mistakes. Be brave enough to speak out against injustice. Be charitable enough to see all sinners, including ourselves, as individuals for whose salvation Jesus gave his life.

In this last connection, I exhort the bishops to ensure that the Church owned media is not the Church controlled media. Editors are not to be appointed on the basis of their obedience to Church authority but on their journalistic qualifications and their intellectual honesty. To our shame some laundry lists provide greater interest than the local Catholic press.

"Holiness, I have completed my preliminary researches into the Organisation, as you requested." Franelli offered a folder.

"Thank you, Carlo. I would prefer you talk me through the results."

"Forgive me if I cover familiar ground but I have tried to make it comprehensive and brief. The Organisation was founded by the late Monsignor Estoria in the 1920s in Spain and it's growth has been extremely rapid. It's secrecy makes it difficult to be exact, but it is estimated to have around 100,000 members worldwide including some 200 priests, of whom a number hold important Church offices. It is active throughout the world and recruits continuously. It has, for example, a presence on about 500 university campuses, numerous schools, a multitude of media outlets and very considerable wealth. It owns substantial properties in Rome, Manhattan and internationally.

"About twenty per cent of its non-clerical members are associates and live full celibate and segregated lives in Organisation owned houses. They turn over their income in return for an allowance and are forbidden credit cards. Others, usually married, are sub-associates and are expected to contribute generously in terms of both time and money. All are expected to evangelise."

The Pope interrupted. "Tell me about that. I know that Cardinal Fearns, Cardinal Harding's predecessor, issued a restriction on their recruiting practices."

"Yes. He limited it to those over 18 and demanded that spiritual direction outside of the Organisation should be permitted. That was in 1981, just a year before Pope Pius conferred prelature status putting the Organisation effectively beyond the reach of diocesan bishops. 'A church within a church as Cardinal Peroni describes it.' I think that what Cardinal Fearns objected to was the tactics by which recruitment is said to occur. Though I have had no direct experience, it appears to follow a similar pattern to that used by cults."

"Go on."

"Well, the initial approach is one of seeming friendship and admiration. Only later, often much later, does it become apparent that the Organisation is behind the proffered friendship. According to testimony of those who have left the Organisation, no easy task in itself, a spiritual crisis is engineered so that the aspirant is rushed into a decision to make a greater commitment to the Organisation and enter an early stage of full membership. Subsequent backsliding is implied to be synonymous with damnation."

"And Monsignor Estoria, whose case for beatification is under consideration. What manner of man was he?"

Franelli shrugged. "A mixed bag really, like all of us, but beyond that highly charismatic. He had great charm and huge commitment. He could be both stiff and unbending and highly emotional. Personally, I find some of the statements in his book, The Path, to be rather silly and very authoritarian. There has always been an allegedly strong connection between the Organisation and fascism especially in Spain and South America. As an Italian I may be in no strong position to comment but, despite Estoria's advocacy of a simple life style for his followers, he was not averse to the trapping of luxury himself. He is said to have furnished his house in exotic but questionable taste and, at the age of 68, petitioned for and was granted the title of Marques de Paella. However, any lack of humility did not result in any lack of veneration. His image adorns all Organisation premises and he is typically referred to as 'Our Father' a form of address not normally accorded to mere mortals."

"I have read some disturbing reports about his dealings with apostates."

"There are quite a number though, clearly, Monsignor Estoria is not able to give his version of events. To quote but one, a high ranking female associate with personal connections to Estoria was forced to resign, kept under house arrest and in the expulsion hearing accused of having sexual relations with two Organisation priests. 'Whore and sow' were the words he is alleged to have used in denouncing her."

"So why did Pius facilitate the beatification process in the face of such, to say the least, conflicting reports?"

"He had a strong wish to create saints, particularly recent ones with whom the Faithful might identify more easily. There was also a great deal of pressure from within the Church in general. Some genuine, some not unrelated to the Organisation's capacity to distribute largess."

"Thank you, Carlo. You've done well. So well, in fact, that I have another small job for you."

"Of course, Holiness."

" I am curious as to the average length of a Vatican appointment. I wonder if you could provide me with some statistics."

A day later Franelli had the information. "Holiness, I have only taken a sample but the average seems to be about seven years."

The Pope whistled. "Quite a long time to be away from parish life."

"Oh! It is actually much longer because one appointment can be followed by another different appointment, often with a promotion. It is quite possible to spend virtually one's whole career within the Vatican City. For many it is the supreme ambition."

"But not exactly conducive to a wide perspective."

Franelli's information alarmed the Pope. If the Organisation was a church within a church it would seem that the Curia was little different. He felt that he needed a second opinion, one detached from the Curia. Pat Nolan had returned to Liverpool to hand over his parish and complete his transfer to Rome. Then he recalled that his brother, Stephen, had done some work on organisational structures. Now that he was retired, a few days at Castel Gandolfo might provide just the right perspective.

CHAPTER 23

The Pope decided to confront the issue which he had been half avoiding, virtually since the Conclave. He opened the summary and began to read.

The nineteenth century witnessed a change in the conduct of scholarship and the beginnings of modern research methods. In part this was due to the availability of documents, a by-product of the revolutionary wars of Europe. Literacy was spreading and revivalist movements such as Methodism had taken root. At one level ecumenism began to thrive as Catholic and Protestant theologians sought common ground: there was a sense of progress in the air. When the young Pius IX was elected to the throne of St Peter at age 54, he appeared as a liberal, a modernist, almost a revolutionary who was extreme enough to believe that Protestants might actually be saved. His conversion to anti-modernism was rapid and total.

The struggle to retain the Papal States and their subsequent loss must have contributed to Pius's change of heart as it did to his support within the Church. The Pope under siege was an heroic figure, one who must be defended by all right thinking Catholics. So to disagree with the Pope within was to agree with the enemy without.

One of his first controversial actions was to initiate the infamous Syllabus of Errors. Religious freedom was unacceptable, only Catholicism should be permitted and other forms of worship denied.

Any separation of the Catholic Church from the state and vice versa was condemned. Attempts to remove the temporal power of the Holy See, and with it the obligation for obedience to that power, were likewise condemned. The encyclical Quanta Cura in 1864 asserted the supremacy of the Church over all forms of civil authority. The direction of Pius's papacy was becoming clearer by the edict. Within the Church, factions loyal to the Pope rejoiced while others tried to lessen the impact of such dictatorial behaviour.

At one extreme, the English Cardinal Manning was said to prefer a papal encyclical to the Times as his breakfast reading. At the other, his fellow countryman and fellow convert, Cardinal Newman, referred to Pius's pontificate as "a climax of tyranny". George Talbot, a confidante of Pius, called Newman the "most dangerous man in England". The Catholic historian, Lord Acton, coined his famous phrase on the corruptive nature of power as exemplified by Pius. So the battle raged in an atmosphere of 'take no prisoners'.

It was becoming increasingly obvious that Pius was heading down the road to have himself declared infallible. Indeed, Newman and others say the Declaration of the Doctrine of the Immaculate Conception on 8th December 1854 was a tactical move which made infallibility more difficult to reject, since it might shed doubts on the nature of the Virgin.

Not only was infallibility seen by many as a minefield, but as a minefield potentially without territorial limits. Would it be restricted to a few small areas, the Immaculate Conception being one? Or would it encompass anything and everything that Pius had ever produced and, quite possibly, all of his predecessors' legacy? If the Syllabus of Errors was to be included, there would follow division within and derision without, as Pius exorcised his paranoia.

Evidence of the latter can be seen in his treatment of the German bishops, some of whom wrote a confidential letter to Pius, simply suggesting that an imminent Declaration of Infallibility might be untimely. Pius responded like a medieval sovereign, compelling them to kiss his feet rather than the customary Ring of the Fisherman.

The further the Pope John read the more convinced he became that the whole question of Infallibility required a review. At the same time he questioned whether he might not be simply frightened of ever deciding anything for fear it became immutable. Too complex to be resolved by himself, too important to be shelved.

"What do you think, Pat?"

Nolan was uncharacteristically noncommittal. "It's such a big issue. If you get it wrong."

"But even a cursory reading of history shows that we have often been wrong. Take Galileo for example. Condemned in 1632 for promoting Copernicus' theory that the earth went round the sun. Poor old fellow repented but was still put under house arrest for the last nine years of his life. In 1835 the Vatican finally got round to withdrawing its denunciation of Copernicus but forgot about Galileo. A French priest, whose name escapes me, began an independent review of the original papers around 1960. Eventually in 1983, my predecessor announced that the Church had got it wrong. But even then it was explained away as a misunderstanding between science and faith. I'm sorry to say this, but what a mealy mouthed way of saying we hounded a decent man in his lifetime and never had the courage to restore his reputation when it became clear that he was right. Church history is littered with similar examples and I'm not even an historian. What about Peter thinking the gentiles couldn't be converted. Women's head coverings. From the sublime to the Gawd bli'me, as they say." The Pope laughed. "Just think what a fix we'd been in if the Church had opted for creationism. I reckon we had a narrow escape there. Yet we continue to maintain a dubious doctrine of infallibility with remarkably little public outcry."

Nolan laughed. "That's because your average Catholic prefers to watch the Premier League than indulge in an analysis of doctrinal gymnastics."

"It's no laughing matter." Said the Pope, himself sniggering. "If the Church was reluctant to admit error in the past, Pius IX made it even more difficult."

Pat felt his caution slipping away. "With great respect I have always thought he was a bit dotty."

"Dotty doesn't do him justice. Kidnapping a Jewish boy to have him brought up a Catholic. Baptising another without his parent's permission. Thirty two years when the Church was ruled by a man whom modern psychiatry would probably diagnose as paranoid narcissistic. Followed by a successor who has been described as a Catholic McCarthy. Pius IX was, in some ways, an anti-Catholic in his hatred of the modern world. Catholics have tended to embrace the world and believe that, for all its imperfections, it is basically good because it is God's creation. If they sometimes display too much exuberance with neon lit Madonnas and weeping statues, better that than a dour, sanitised creed that replaces thou shalt with thou shalt not."

"So are you going to declare yourself fallible?"

"The thought had occurred but I think I am learning a few tricks and not to fight a war on too many fronts. I thought that doing away with Holiness as a title was a suitable act of humility. In the event it just left people embarrassed and tongue tied so I have let it quietly re-emerge. I think the web site will begin to erode the concept of an infallible Pope and replace it with a consulting Pope. Then, in about five hundred years, John XXXV can do a Galileo and find for fallibility by which time it will no longer be an issue."

Nolan chortled. "My old Mum went to daily Mass and brought up eight children. She was as tough as a goat and would give away her last penny. If the pope had said that pigs could fly she would have asked the butcher for a wing of pig. I wonder what she would make of her son, the Pope and this conversation? Are you going to tell Peroni?"

"I have to and I think I may have the right tactic."

"I have been re-reading Augustine and his emphasis on truth. I don't think he would approve of us."

"Ah! Augustine!" Peroni answered, giving nothing away.

"He talks about telling lies as a way to spiritual death. Of course, I had read him before but never with quite the same impact."

"A great doctor of the Church, Holiness."

"You hold no opinion yourself?"

"As I said, Holiness, a great doctor of the Church."

"Which sounds to me like Curia-speak for non-approval. Damned with faint praise."

Peroni knew he would have to offer something more. "As I recall he preached a doctrine of perfection. Admirable in itself but impractical. I have always taken his views to be more of an academic exercise than of a blue print for everyday behaviour."

"Once I would have agreed with you but not any longer. I now see that he was placing truth at the centre of everything. Why he even wrote of the necessity avoiding a lie when the consequence would mean someone's death, as in telling a murderer that his victim was absent when he was hiding in the next room."

"Exactly my point. More of an intellectual game than a piece of practical advice."

"I am sorry, Stephano, but I believe it is more than that, much more. What he is telling us is that physical death is preferable to spiritual death. Nor is he being disingenuous. He freely admits that he had to wrestle with the temptation to lie in order to escape unpleasant consequences."

Peroni was losing patience. He had work to do and neither time nor taste for esoteric discussions, even with the Pope. The latter sensed his annoyance.

"Indulge me just a little more." Peroni bowed slightly. "There really is a point to all of this. You know that Augustine and Jerome had a heated correspondence regarding a dispute between Peter and Paul. The question of whether Gentiles could become Christians and the conditions under which this might occur."

With all this talk of telling the truth, Peroni felt compelled to admit only the vaguest recollection.

"Essentially Peter, in common with many others, demanded that converts accept numerous aspects of Jewish law. Paul argued that this was unnecessary. In the end Peter accepted Paul's view and made a public retraction of his previous position. Heady stuff at the time and with significant lessons for us today. First, there is the fact that Peter, the Pope, although the term had yet to be minted, could admit of error on a major aspect of doctrine. Second, that he could actually admit to such error publicly and not simply allow his position to erode quietly over time. Third, that Jerome in trying to white wash both Peter's error and the possibility of any disagreement in the early Church, could claim that the whole episode was an amusing game played by two people who really saw eye to eye."

Now Peroni was really worried. He could see exactly where the Pope was heading and, in his mind, the signpost was labelled 'disaster'. "Holiness, the matters of which you speak have been raked over many times throughout Church history and not always to the benefit of the Faithful. Doubt is the arch enemy of faith and should be avoided at all costs."

"And what if the cost is to embrace Satan and not Christ. Remember that Jesus called Satan the 'father of lies'?" Suddenly the Pope looked old. "I don't think we should try to beget good out of evil."

"So where do we proceed from here?"

"I believe that we have to cut the ropes in which we have trussed ourselves. Having declared ourselves infallible we cannot admit error without renouncing infallibility. If Peter, Christ's anointed successor, could be wrong how can Peter's successors be consistently superior judges? Yet, when new knowledge or other development cast doubt on an aspect of the Magisterium, we begin an elaborate strategy of defence. New rules are invented so that the justification under assault is replaced by a different justification or some such device. Like a conventional war, truth has become the first casualty."

"Are you then about to declare yourself fallible?"

The Pope relaxed a little. "No, Stephano. I concede the need for some mechanism by which doctrine can be developed and proclaimed in a way which is more profound that a simple statement of opinion. But we have gone way, way beyond that requirement. Let me ask you a question. How many infallible teachings are there?"

"Well we have the Immaculate Conception and one or two others." Peroni wasn't about to play some childish game.

"If you believe Bishop Gasser, a staunch supporter of Pius IX, there are many thousands of definitive teachings all of which demand the unequivocal allegiance of the Faithful. Opinions vary as to what constitutes an infallible statement.. In 1994 my predecessor issued a statement reaffirming the Church's ban on ordaining women priests. The CDF followed by adding that 'definitive assent' was required to this doctrine which was 'irrevocable, irreformable and infallible'. Is the CDF, then, also infallible? If the doctrine was infallible why was this not made clear in the Pope's original statement? Pius XIII spoke out strongly and courageously against the war in Iraq. Was this an infallible statement and, if so, should Catholic servicemen and women refuse to fight in an unjust war? Whichever way you look at the issue, we seem to have created more fog than light. One could argue that infallibility covers a few well publicised dogma or that it covers virtually everything that has come out of the Vatican. If you take the strong form of the argument, the vast majority of Catholics spend their entire lives blissfully unaware of the many doctrines which require their unequivocal allegiance. A cynic might conclude that the Church gains from such vagaries in that they are open to as many interpretations and reinterpretations as the situation requires."

The Pope raised his hands towards heaven. "I am sorry, Stephano, I got carried away. But, harking back to the fundamental question of truth, one cannot but be sceptical about the circumstances in which the present doctrine of infallibility was promulgated."

"I would prefer to describe the circumstances of the First Vatican Council as involving robust debate out of which arose consensus."

"I beg to differ. Pius IX was duplicitous in his stated reasons for calling the Council, namely pronouncing on his preferred topic of 'modern errors' and identifying necessary reforms. No prior warning was given that infallibility was to be an agenda item. Bishops were bullied, rules were bent, majority votes were allowed to replace the consensus requirements of previous Councils. Discussions were in Latin, effectively giving the Curia and the Italian bishops an additional advantage when they already had grossly disproportionate numbers relative to their constituencies. I do not think that Augustine would have recognised Pius's actions as a genuine attempt to establish the truth."

"With great respect, Holiness, I think you are expanding the concept of truth to embrace other aspects of the Council."

"Perhaps I am. But let me end on one frightening note. The Archbishop of Bologna argued, in a speech which received enormous support, that the Pope could never be infallible when acting on his own. Pius was so incensed that he summoned Guidi and yelled at him that he, Pius, was 'the tradition, the Church'. Subsequently Pius demanded that Guidi deny the altercation. I hate to say this but I find Pius' statement to the Archbishop far closer to megalomania than infallibility. Judged by the yardstick of truth, the First Vatican Council was severely lacking. Yet, here am I, lecturing politicians and the media on the need for truth when, on a whole range of issues, the Church has been found wanting. When an ill-defined infallibility lurks below the surface of every Vatican utterance, the admission of error becomes virtually impossible."

Peroni was being pulled in two directions. The majority of his life had been given over to diplomatic niceties: the use of language to hide a conflict, to gain an advantage, to confound an enemy. While he readily assented to the Magisterium, outside of that most truth was subjective. Now this eccentric man was challenging the basis of his career. It was frightening but, somehow, exhilarating. He recognised the energy and thrill he had felt when first ordained, when he was more the revolutionary and less the revisionist. He decided to take a risk.

"Holiness, you scare me. No! You terrify me."

The Pope laughed bleakly. "Stephano, I terrify myself. No! I think......I pray that it is the Spirit that is opening us up. When you have been closed for a long time it is bound to be painful." The Pope paused and looked directly at Peroni. " I will never ask anyone to act against their conscience but, if you can in conscience travel with me, the journey will be the easier for your companionship. Jesus said that he was 'the way, the truth and the light'. He did not say that he was an arch sophistic. Again he told us that 'the truth will make you free', not that prevarication will get you off the hook. I want the council to reconsider the whole question of infallibility, without any pressures from either myself or the Curia, and I will abide by whatever decision is reached."

CHAPTER 24

Castel Gandolfo has been the Pope's summer residence since the eighteenth century. Situated in the Alban Hills at over 400 metres, the castle itself is relatively unimposing but the scenery across a lake, formed from an extinct volcano, is dramatic. After Rome the air is fresh with the scent of country and, apart from occasions when an entertainment takes place in the courtyard, all is peaceful. A small town has grown up nearby, largely to service the needs of tourists. Swiss guards are on duty in costumes apocryphally attributed to Michelangelo. The souvenirs in the tourist's shops claim no such provenance. Members of the public are admitted to the castle by invitation and some are selected to meet the Pope, but only after strict security screening.

The amenities bear witness to the interests of previous popes. Pius XI was responsible for the billiard tables and John XXIII for the bowling alley. The complex is serviced by around 100 workers and, in the summer months, attracts up 10000 visitors for the pope's Sunday blessing. Two twentieth century popes have died at Gandolfo, Pius XII and Paul VI, but as though to balance the books, many thousands of refugees from fascism were protected here during the Second World War. Though German troops were in a position to seize the castle the order to attack was never given. The Vatican City enjoyed the same curious immunity.

Today there is no orchestra in the courtyard and there are no tourists present. The Pope is meeting privately with Stephen Carterton.

"I can't get over having a brother as a pope. I just wish I had gone to Ladbroke's twenty years ago and put a hundred quid on you. I could have bought this place with the winnings."

"I can't get over having a brother who is a confirmed atheist but who may be just the objective counsellor I need."

"I'm flattered, and looking at all this, I hope you can make the appointment permanent."

"I want you to give me an outsider's assessment of the Vatican, the Curia. A psychological perspective on this rather curious beast."

"Then you'd better fill me in. I haven't taken much interest in your curious beast."

Based on Franelli's brief and his own knowledge, the Pope explained how the Roman Catholic Civil Service operated. When he had finished, Stephen grinned.

"Tight as a drum. No wonder you've lasted two millennia."

"I hope longevity is also a sign of authenticity."

"Well you must be doing something right but, joking apart, it is scarcely a model for rapid reaction or absorbing new ideas…. and we live a fast changing world. Maybe it has exceeded its shelf life."

"So what is your professional assessment.?"

"You're in for a bit of a lecture."

"Take your time."

"Let's begin with reality. Something which doesn't really exist since everyone's perceived reality is different from everyone else's. Sometimes by a small margin, sometimes by a great gulf. We tend to seek out people who share a reality similar to our own: it is more comfortable. Comfortable but dangerous. We see the tendency at its worst in extremist groups where criticism of behaviour, no matter how aberrant, does not exist because the members share the same distorted vision and the group norms exclude the possibility of critical analysis. So incidents, such as Jonestown, can occur or those of September 11th in New York. From what I glean from the media, the reaction of the Church to child sexual abuse showed little capacity for self-criticism. At a systemic level such conformity eliminates an effective feedback mechanism. So it is that Stalin's Five Year Plans may appear to be working because, at every level in the communication chain, it is in the interests of the reporter to say that all is well. The fact that the peasants are starving in their millions is simply ignored."

"I don't think the Curia is quite so callous."

"Maybe, maybe not, but let's stick with this idea of reality for the time being. Organisations, families even, can manufacture their own reality which may bear little resemblance to that of the outside world. Put a strong minded CEO into an organisation, let him recruit clones as they so often do and, over time, everyone sings the CEO's song regardless of how discordant it may sound to an outside listener. You may know the dubious story of how Spanish came to be spoken with a lisp."

The Pope shook his head.

"One of the Spanish kings was, allegedly, born with a lisp but, rather than permit the king's speech to sound imperfect, the whole population was compelled to imitate him. It's not a bad metaphor for what can happen when conformity replaces sanity."

"I see no popular movement within the Curia to conform to John XXIV's ideas."

"And a good thing too provided that the non-conformity is out of a genuine spirit of debate rather than a slavish adherence to what has gone before."

"I suspect much of it is the latter."

"It could scarcely be otherwise from what you have told me. It is virtually inevitable in any organisation where there is little staff turnover and little regular contact with those outside. What usually happens is that those in the inner circle come to regard those in the outer circle as a sort of barbarian horde against whom the purity of the inner circle must be protected. You see it all the time with governments. They claim and often set out to be the servants of the people, but quickly come to regard the same people as impediments to government. Disraeli said, 'We must educate our masters'. But I don't think he meant it. You know, years ago when I taught management psychology, a theorist called McGregor categorised managers as being

'Theory Y' or 'Theory X'. The Theory Y managers were democratic, trusted their workers to be inventive and self-motivated,
saw their job as providing a climate which encouraged creativity
and believed that managers were responsible when an organisation was failing. Theory X managers took the opposite line.
To them workers were idle, ignorant and needed to be kept in
a state of fear if they were to do anything useful. If an enterprise failed, the workers were the culprits. I was naïve enough
to believe that Theory X managers were few in numbers, an
endangered species that would die out before the end of the
century. I never expected the resurgence. Short term contracts, casual employment, outsourcing and downsizing. We
haven't yet begun to start the day with the company song but it
can't be far round the corner. Workers as pawns rather than as
partners. I haven't taken much interest in Church affairs but I
don't think too many popes have been of the Theory Y school
of management, John XXIII and probably John Paul I if he'd
lived. Maybe even you, Bill, if the power of the Curia doesn't
divert you first."

"Vatican II showed some signs of Theory Y influence."

"I get the impression that it has been quietly buried. I think
you've got a tough job. All organisations are under some form
of pressure to hear only what they want to hear. To block out the
bad news. What about the weapons of mass destruction? It's a
classic case study in group think. Gather together like minded
people. Use peer pressure to blackmail any weaker members.
Make it absolutely clear as to what information is acceptable and
what is not. Massage the information to justify what you have
always intended to do. If the information proves to be faulty you
can always blame the provider and gradually alter the basis on
which the decision was made."

"But people are not fools. They can see what is happening."

"Some do. Some are not interested. Many are in denial.
The man they voted into office is a liar but they don't want to
admit electing a liar. Worse still a lunatic. Who wants to go to
bed at night believing the President is seriously unbalanced? In
any case, memories are short and tomorrow's news may be far

more engaging. Then there is the impact of the Authoritarian Personality."

"We have more than a few of those."

"I'm sure you do but I was talking about some specific research. After the Second World War academics turned to the whole question of anti-Semitism and set out to study the phenomenon. Curiously they concluded their studies by declaring that 'anti-Semitism has nothing to do with Jews'. What they believed they had unearthed was a specific personality type that was predisposed to analyse relationships in terms of 'in groups' and 'out groups'. The in groups represent all that is good and noble, the out groups all that is bad and venal. So, when things go wrong, as they undoubtedly had done in pre-war Germany, rather than indulge in the rather painful practice of personal accountability, you simply blamed the Jews who happened to be a convenient out group. To put it another way, had the Jews not existed they would had have to have been replaced by some other marginalised sector of the population."

"I don't think we have any Jews in the Vatican." The Pope joked.

Stephen laughed. "Some might question whether you have any Christians in view of some pronouncements on the human condition. But going back to the Authoritarian Personality. It is manifest in attitudes such as ethnocentricity, conservatism and authoritarianism. Authoritarianism particularly. For example, when surveyed the Authoritarian Personality will nominate obedience and respect for authority as the most important virtues for children to acquire whereas others might argue that tolerance and respect for the truth were more critical. The Authoritarian Personality tends to be against inter-faith or interracial marriages, resents too much being spent on the inherently incapable members of society and admires leaders who are themselves autocratic." Stephen paused. "I know little about the Curia, but it is hard to imagine that being part of the government of a Church, which claims ultimate teaching authority on earth, would not hold its attractions for someone with an authoritarian bent. I am in no position to say whether and to what extend this is rampant but, if it is, and you have a significant number who place a premium on obedience and respect for authority rather than on tolerance and truth....well?"

"Returning to the Curia. What do I do?"

"I think you have to break the logjam. What was it, John XXIII said: 'Open the window and let the air in'. Personally I would avoid having anyone in the Vatican for too long. Maybe five years' maximum, then back to some sort of parish work. Maybe a week every six months in a parish while they are in the Curia. Get some women into the place. It must be the very last all male preserve in the free world and women tend to be less authoritarian. Change the rules so that Cognitive Dissonance doesn't get in the way of sensible decision making."

"Explain that last one."

"Cognitive Dissonance occurs when we are trying to reconcile contradictory attitudes or behaviours. Going back to the idea of having elected a liar or a maniac. Not a belief which helps you to sleep at night. So what do you do? Admit to making a mistake and learn from the admission? Difficult if you don't like to be wrong. Even more difficult if you believe that admitting to being wrong will undermine all the other decisions you have ever made, publicly and privately. Almost impossible if your office confers upon you the mantle of infallibility. Easier to say you were right first time round and that the President is a man of honour whose duplicitous justifications for action are perfectly credible. Trouble is that the crazier the President behaves, the greater the ongoing dissonance and the more credulity has to be stretched." Stephen looked directly at his brother. "Is there an analogy in there somewhere?"

The Pope nodded sadly. "I think I have been suffering from a form of Cognitive Dissonance. With respect, you haven't really told me anything new though you have given me a new label for what I already sensed. What you have done is made me face up to something I have been trying to avoid."

"Don't be too hard on yourself. Dissonance makes cowards of us all. We don't want to face the fact that life can be cruel, random and very partial. Why, if it weren't for dissonance the need for religion would probably disappear. Marx wasn't wrong when he called it the opiate of the people. It allows them to accept conditions now on the basis that heaven will be a compensation. That resolves the dissonance they experience in being asked to believe in a benevolent God when they are having shit for dinner. Remember what Blake wrote, 'Every morn and every night, some are born to sheer delight. Every night and every morn, some to misery are born. Some are born to sheer delight. Some are born to endless night'. How do you resolve the dissonance in relation to a supposedly loving God. If you are born to sheer delight, no problem. You have ample evidence in this life. If you are born to endless night, big problem. However, the promise of paradise after this vale of tears may just tip the scales in His favour. In fact, without the prospect of some reward in the hereafter, life in the 'endless night' stream becomes intolerable."

"It keeps coming back to this." The Pope shook his head. "To this whole concept of infallibility. I won't bore you with the theological arguments but, even given that some teachings are infallible, there are many which have, deliberately or otherwise, been marketed to imply infallibility. It's Pandora's box to the power of ten."

"But Bill, you are a theologian. You must have known these things a long time ago."

The Pope smiled. "Should have known. I kept well out of the more practical areas. Amused myself with concepts of grace and the Trinity. Nothing too likely to blow up in my face. No! Cardinal Caution would have suited me well but, and I know you will think I have gone mad, the Spirit had other ideas. That's what my papacy has to be about and it scares the hell out of me. Yet, at the same time, I never felt more alive."

Stephen fell silent and the Pope gazed at a rose. A flower devoid of free will could be perfect. Not so mortal man.

"You've given me your time, Stephen. Now it's your turn. How are you travelling?"

"As well as can be expected for a man who has two failed marriages behind him and rather strained relations with his kids. I envy you...anyone who has faith, no matter how weird. Never having doubts must be a constant comfort."

"I'm sure it must though I haven't met too many who enjoy that luxury."

Stephen laughed. "You old fraud! The Pope has doubts! What a lead story that would make in the Star. Good job you didn't use it in your election manifesto."

"Sometimes I'm sorry I didn't but I don't think It's unhealthy. Maybe the reverse. Some of the great saints have had doubts, the dark night of the soul as it is sometimes called. You know, St Vincent de Paul is supposed to have spent two years when his faith had almost wholly deserted him, except for a copy of the Creed which he kept in his pocket and touched, periodically, for reassurance. Doubts keep you in good company."

"They didn't teach me that at school."

"But that was in a different era. Doubting was unfashionable. You didn't doubt the wisdom and probity of your leaders. You didn't doubt the critical importance of fasting on Fridays. You didn't doubt that Catholicism was superior to all other Faiths. In fact you didn't doubt that Protestants and others had a one way ticket to Hell and you certainly didn't doubt that Hell was full to overflowing with small boys who had abused their bodies. Looking back you wonder how we could have been so gullible and looking forward you wonder how certain our current certainties will appear twenty years hence."

Stephen gasped. "You might make a convert of me yet. Joking, of course. But it's refreshing to hear you talk like that and you know why? Because when two people have shared a common background, it's reassuring to know that their respective realities are not too far apart. If they are, it suggests that at least one must be seriously wrong and paradigm shifts are hard work."

"Cognitive Dissonance!" The Pope chortled. "You see, you've taught me something."

"There is one other thought I might mention. Not so much a thought as a metaphor and what you have just told me helped crystallise it. The Church in which we were brought up acted like a big parent. The parent issued orders and we, the children, obeyed without question. As you suggest, it was pretty much the same with all authority. As people became better educated, as the discipline of nations at or preparing for war collapsed, so the children began to question parent's wisdom. Most parent figures, sensing the change, relaxed somewhat. In fact, if I look at it from a child rearing viewpoint, many relaxed to the point of irresponsibility. From what little I know, I don't think the Curia relaxed, quite the reverse. The only problem is that most of the Faithful had ceased to behave like children and were trying to behave like adults."

"I think you have just given me an important insight. The Church is like a family coping with its adolescents. The Curia, the hierarchy.....whoever....needs to loosen the reigns of childhood while retaining the basic family values. The substantive issue is not whether the kids dye their hair orange or even whether they go to Sunday Mass. It is whether they deal decently with other people. In essence, whether they love their neighbour as themselves. We can get too tangled up in external at the expense of the internal."

"Given the right sort of leadership people are pretty humane and trustworthy. But with the wrong sort, the big parent instilling fear, they tend to become self-centred and inward looking. Fear drives out humanity. That is why so many politicians like to beat the terrorist drum. Then they can curtail civil liberties, portray oppositions as disloyal and generally, avoid the scrutiny which comes from a self-confident electorate." Stephen laughed. "Think of all those paintings depicting the horrors of Hell and how effective they must have been at keeping the Faithful in line."

"I can think of a few luminaries who would bring all that back tomorrow, given half a chance." The Pope stopped and looked out across the valley. The scent was intoxicating and a far cry from the banks of the Mersey. In his heart he would love to have stayed here. Pursued a daily round of study and writing but he knew he had to return to Rome.

"Any last thoughts, Stephen?"

"I was wondering. Do you know anything about Pius IX's background? His childhood?"

"Not a thing but I know a good deal about his eccentric behaviour as Pope. Why do you ask?"

"It just occurred to me that he had a particular devotion to the Virgin and I wondered why?"

"That's easy. He narrowly escaped an accident when visiting a convent. I can't recall the exact details but he attributed his escape to Our Lady and paid a special visit to one of her shrines to acknowledge the fact."

"Your predecessor had a similar experience. I recall how he believed she had intervened to save him from the assassin's bullet."

"I think his devotion preceded that event. After his mother died his father took him on a pilgrimage to the Black Madonna of Czestochowa and I think he then claimed her as his surrogate mother. The assassination attempt only strengthened an existing devotion. But I am curious as to your interest?"

"Oh! Just a random thought. Most psychologists would connect Pius XIII's devotion with mother substitution but I wondered whether Pius IX also needed a mother figure arising out of early childhood experience. Extrapolating, how often are spiritual manifestations rooted in very mundane events?"

"Quite often, I suspect, but don't become too sceptical. God uses mundane events to further His grand design."

"I knew you'd have an answer." Stephen replied, laughing.

"You look refreshed, Holiness. You should make greater use of the summer residence."

"Thank you, Stephano. It certainly helps to clear one's mind being out of the office, so to speak."

Peroni winced privately. Papal mind clearing sounded ominous. He waited without responding. The Pope gestured to a chair.

"I have been thinking about the Curia. Not just thinking, I have been taking some advice from my brother, Stephen."

"I didn't know that you had a brother a priest. Or a monsignor perhaps?" Peroni prided himself that he knew the name of every bishop, at least the names of those which did not consist of fifteen consonants and only two vowels.

"Neither. He is not even a Catholic though I pray that he may find his Faith again."

"And he is your adviser on the subject of the Curia? It is, if your Holiness will permit me, rather unusual. Is he, perhaps, some academic who has made a lifetime's study of Church governance?"

The Pope laughed. "You are making fun of me, Stephano."

"Holiness, I would never do that."

The Pope laughed again. "I am delighted if you do. It is a sign that we like each other and it helps stop me from becoming self-important."

Against his will, Peroni smiled back. This man had got under his Curial skin and he did not like it, but his humility was more powerful than any resort to authority.

"Perhaps you will do me the same favour."

"My brother is a psychologist, a retired psychologist. I believe he was...is... quite a good one. I asked him to give me a professional evaluation of the Curia. Not of individuals but of its structure and what that might imply. I think he had some useful things to say."

"Which were.?"

"To summarise doesn't really do justice to the theoretical basis of Stephen's observations but I will give you the main points and elaborate if you so wish. He believes that the Curia has evolved in a way which promotes authoritarianism in terms of both recruitment and retention. Those of an authoritarian bent are attracted to Curial jobs and then reinforced in their attitudes by colleagues who share those attitudes."

"Understandable and in many ways admirable. The Church is the custodian of God's authority on earth."

"I agree, but not every issue needs the jack boot of authority behind it. Stephen talked about something called Cognitive Dissonance and connected it with authority. For example, say the Church had made a wrong decision, a Cognitive Dissonance would exist between the attitude that the Church is the authority of God on earth and the contradiction of a wrong decision. The dissonance can only be resolved by owning up or by denying the error on the basis that the Church can never be wrong. Not a comfortable situation for anyone but, for the Authoritarian Personality, the pressure to deny the error and proclaim the Church to be right is overwhelming. Their whole psyche relies upon the rightness of authority. To go against that....that compulsion requires rebuilding a personality from the ground up. Add to this peer pressure from authoritarian colleagues and what chance do you have of ever admitting any error? No wonder dissenting theologian have to be disciplined harshly. They don't just represent a threat to the Church but to the personalities of many of the Curia and that includes popes."

Peroni was confused. He seemed to have caught this Cognitive Dissonance. To admit that the Pope had a point, no matter how exaggerated, called into account his own stewardship as the effective head of the Curia. He needed time to think. "Did he have other observations, Holiness?"

"His other points were less esoteric, more practical. Again, to paraphrase him, he felt that to remain in the Curia for more than, say, five years was to entrench an organisational reality which bore little relationship to the reality of the non-Curial world. This, in turn, accentuates the sense of hostility towards those who might question Curial wisdom. Regular movement of personnel in and out should remedy that failing."

"I had better pack my bags immediately. I have long overstayed my welcome."

"Not in my view. I need you to help me approach Curial reform in a humane and efficient manner. There are some things which we can implement quickly and others which can only occur over time. If we have been wrong on doctrine I believe we should have the courage to admit error as soon as it is apparent. I do not think the same immediacy need apply to all reform and the rotation of staff will only be one element. I also want to give women an initial and increasing role in the bureaucracy. It will mean a further commission. One which I would like to chair and have Stephen as an outside consultant."

Peroni raised an eyebrow. "Don't worry. He has no axe to grind. He doesn't believe in God. He will be there to provide analysis purely from the organisational viewpoint. He has agreed to work for his attendance expenses and no more so there can be no question of papal nepotism."

CHAPTER 25

Stephen's observations on the cloistered nature of the Curia had confirmed the Pope's own reservations. He determined that all should have regular exposure to the working of the non-Curial Church and that included himself.

"Sister Catherine, I appreciate your chairing the commission on birth control and now I have another favour to ask of you. I want to visit one of your houses in the third world. I have spent too a comfortable life and I am in need of a reality check."

"I take it this would be as part of an official Papal visit?"

"Not at all. I think the expense is difficult to justify and, in any event, I don't want any special treatment, I simply want an unscripted experience. No crowds, no fanfares, just what your sisters deal with on a daily basis."

"You know they are calling you the Pope of Surprises and not always in a flattering way. I can now see why. However, there are some practical considerations."

The Pope nodded. "There is my passport. I renewed it for the Conclave and it gives my occupation as cardinal. I don't want anything like that to draw attention to the visit. I can get round that by having a Vatican City passport issued."

"Occupation, pope?"

"No. Chaplain! Chaplain to the Sister of Hope. With your permission."

"We wouldn't accept anyone less than a pope as our chaplain."

"Good. No need to inform the local hierarchy since I am a mere chaplain, not worthy of notice."

"That seems to about cover it. How about absence from Rome. The Pope's whereabouts are public knowledge."

"I shall be at Castel Gandolfo, resting. Only Cardinal Peroni need know."

"I can't imagine he'll be enthusiastic."

Sister Catherine's remark proved prophetic. "Holiness, it is a quiet mad idea. I can organise a perfectly good briefing on any aspect of the Church anywhere in the world by the nuncio. That is why we have them: they are the eyes, ears and voice of the pope in their respective spheres, our ambassadors. A clandestine visit is totally unnecessary. What's more, it is potentially dangerous. If word leaked out and, in my experience it always does, the local hierarchy and probably the political leadership would be enraged."

"I am sorry to be such a nuisance to you, Stephano."

"Being a nuisance to me is not the point. The point is that popes have to behave within certain norms, not invent their own. I beg of you to re-think the idea. If you must go and visit poor people try Naples, there is no shortage of them there and I can ensure your security. Where does this nun intend to take you?"

"Not just me but Father Nolan as well and she hasn't told us yet."

"So you are determined?" The Pope nodded. "Then take Franelli and a Swiss Guard or two, not in uniform."

"Pat will be sufficient. And could you please arrange two passports describing us as chaplains."

Peroni was about to leave when the Pope asked. "Talking of nuncios, how is the United Kingdom Nuncio progressing over the election of the Archbishop of Westminster?"

"He is recovering from shock along with a number of other senior clerics."

"And the priests and the people?"

"I'm told they rather like the idea but let us await the outcome before we consider it a success."

The Pope's instruction, that his proposed visit to South America should remain a secret between the three participants and the Secretary of State, was obeyed in full except for one small and seemingly inconsequential detail. Namely, the issue of the Vatican City passports for the two chaplains. The matter was handled by a quiet, self-effacing priest who reported the incident to his superiors in the Organisation. The information was quickly transmitted to the leadership and a hurried conference was called at the Villa Palermo.

"Our Father must be turning in his grave to know that the Church which he so loved is being destroyed by the Englishman." He could not bear to use the Pope's title in case it suggested acceptance. "Is nothing sacred to him? We have commissions considering the traditional teaching on birth control, on women priests, on married priests, on homosexuality, on increased links with non-Christian religions. In a clearly connected manifestation of liberality gone mad we have the Congregation for the Defence of the Faith re-named the Congregation for the Development of the Faith. Not only that but he has put it in the hands of a man who came close to a charge of heresy and is a public critic of the old establishment. It is obvious where it will all end. He will dispense with discipline and replace it with conscience. A conscience educated by the desires of the flesh and dismissive of any allegiance to a higher morality."

"Of even greater concern to the Organisation and as a act of deliberate arrogance, he has reversed the decision of Pius regarding the process for canonisation, an act which many of us believe is directly aimed at our own blessed founder. Not that we in the Organisation require an outside endorsement of his sanctity, it is simply that our weaker brethren are in dire need of such authenticated role models."

"To say we have reached crisis point would be an understatement. Those of us who lived through Vatican II know just how easy it is to misguide the masses and convince them that all they need do is obey the so called 'internal forum'. But the wilder aspirations of Vatican II were mild compared to what we now face."

"I was informed today that he is shortly to visit South America along with the Superior of the Sisters of Hope, an Australian nun of intemperate character, and his Irish import, a priest of dubious practice and with a significant drinking problem. They are to travel incognito to what purpose we can only guess. But, given the presence of the nun and the disposition of her order, it seems likely that they are to amuse themselves by cavorting with the lower orders. Probably in an attempt to revive another dormant cancer, Liberation Theology."

"The question is this. Do we stand aside and allow the cancer to spread and spread rapidly or do we decide that our duty is to rid the Mystical Body of Christ, which Our Father so loved, by all the means at our disposal? I now invite your opinions."

The practical discussion which followed was outwardly cautious in keeping with the culture of the Organisation but, for those who understood the code, it was unusually passionate. For them the sub-text was very clear: over seventy years of progress must not disappear by default. A high ranking South America prelate, sympathetic to both the Organisation and to his country's dictatorship, would be alerted as to the Pope's visit. A courtesy to the man as well as practical intelligence.

The nun and the two chaplains, all in civilian clothes, boarded the flight without incident and took their seats in Economy. When the plane reached it's cruising altitude, Sister Catherine provided some background.

"The favelas are not a modern invention though they have increased in size, quantity and in the general consciousness in the last fifty years. They were first established on a hillside in Rio by African-Brazilian war veterans in the late nineteenth century. The name comes from a tree found on that same hillside. However, it was only in the second half of the last century that they expanded dramatically as Brazil and other countries had their industrial revolution and agricultural workers crowded into the cities. Now they can be found all over the developing world and even in some developed countries. I have, myself, seen them around Lisbon."

"Today they probably account for about twenty to twenty five per cent of the population of cities like Rio, Sao Paulo and Belo Horizonte, north west of Rio. The favelas are by no means identical but they all share some common characteristics notably poverty, limited access to utilities, unemployment, crime and lack of equality before the law."

"And your sisters? Tell me how they operate?"

"First and foremost they largely share the conditions of the poor. They are a contrast to the celebrities, and occasionally church figures, who make well publicised visits to the favelas only to lose interest once the media has departed. At a symbolic level their role is to represent Christ in his compassion for the poor. Beyond that, depending upon their skills, they assist with education, health care and, quite often, mediation with the authorities." Catherine laughed. "Conflict resolution is an expanding area but it can be dangerous especially when it involves the narco-gangs. A UN survey declared Jardim Angela in Sao Paulo as the most violent place on earth with an annual murder rate in excess of one per 1000."

"The burn out rate for your nuns must also be very high."

"Less than you might think." Catherine paused and hoped the tears would remain invisible. "When you have given your heart to the poor it seems to find its home there."

The Pope reached across and gently patted her hand.

Lunch was served. Fr Nolan asked for Guinness but had to make do with Peroni. "Fancy naming a beer after the Secretary of State! Or was it the other way round?"

"You know it's not such a bad drink after all." He announced, drank two more and fell soundly asleep.

"How about relations with the secular clergy and the hierarchy?"

"Like the favelas themselves, variable. Some are our greatest supporters, some see us as a fifth column. One cardinal told me quite openly that, 'Your sisters are here to do what I tell them to do, no less and no more'. He went on to say that when you mixed exclusively with the people of the favelas you became like them and this was a real danger for any religious, particularly women. Presumably he was referring to our under-developed ability to discriminate."

"How did you respond to that?"

"It required more than my usual degree of self-control but I had to keep in mind our purpose. So I replied that the sisters took their vow of obedience very seriously and were particularly diligent in seeking the advice of male clerics when dealing with all but the simplest of moral issues."

"And the cardinal?"

"As with most self-important people, he could not conceive of anyone being mildly sarcastic. He dismissed me politely and said that he was pleased that we understood each other so well. As far as the nuns were concerned it was business as usual."

"I think you are having more fun as a Sister Superior than I am as a Pope."

"Only if you choose to let it be so. I think it was Woody Allen who said that comedy was tragedy plus time. It's not a bad way of looking at life's difficulties. Australians pride themselves on having a BS indicator which helps them take others and, hopefully, themselves less seriously."

"What is a BS indicator? Where do you buy one?"

Catherine laughed so loud that Fr Nolan woke momentarily before relapsing.

"It's not a thing. It's an attitude towards people big noting themselves, being drama queens or kings, believing their own propaganda. It's a bullshit indicator, Holiness." She said with mock formality.

"I think his Holiness needs one, an extra-large one. It can be your job to provide it."

"I'll see what I can do. It should go well with the beard. Add a beret and you'd have the makings of a genuine revolutionary"

"Is it much further?" Pat Nolan pleaded, regretting his walks with Kyrie had been restricted to level ground. Rome might be built on seven hills but Rio must be built on hundreds, all of alpine gradient and six Peronis did not constitute suitable training.

"Five minutes, maybe less."

The sun was immediately overhead and, in the narrow, winding alleyways of Rochinha, there was no semblance of a breeze. Catherine seemed unaffected, the Pope puffed but Pat sounded like a steam locomotive. Sweat poured into his eyes making them sting, his legs dragged and he anticipated a heart attack at any moment. They kept slowing for him to catch up. Suddenly it all stopped and they entered a small wattle and daub shack which a large fan kept relatively cool. Not waiting to be asked, Fr Nolan collapsed on an ancient chair.

"This is Sister Juanita." Catherine introduced the small, black nun with the amazing smile. She gave Catherine a big hug and shook hands with the Pope and the recumbent Nolan.

"Welcome." She said, in broken English. "Today very hot." Her eyes flicking to Nolan. "He needs rest." Nolan nodded, speech had yet to return.

Sister Juanita served cool drinks and small cakes. All sat. Catherine opened the conversation.

"Juanita, what I now tell you is in the very strictest confidence." Juanita nodded. "This man." She pointed and lapsed into Portuguese. Juanita looked stunned then, as she absorbed the information, she fell to her knees and started to cross the dirt floor towards the Pope.

"Please! Please, Sister!." The Pope rose and reached down to help her up, taking both her hands in his and smiling at her. "I am so pleased to be here and to learn something of your wonderful work."

Catherine translated and asked Juanita to sit. Quickly she explained the purpose of the visit and why secrecy was necessary. She asked Juanita to tell the Pope about her life and work in the favela. She told her story in a mixture of Portuguese and English with Catherine translating when necessary.

"I came to work here after seven years in Recife where I had worked with Sister Catherine and two other nuns. Altogether there are three sisters. Sister Maria is from Portugal and is visiting her family there at present. This we are allowed to do every five years. Sister Louisa is an American. She is teaching the little children today. She does this most days. I trained as a nurse and try to help the people when they cannot afford the doctor. I also help the young mothers with their babies. Hygiene is not so good in the favela and many children suffer from sores and gastric complaints. Some die and some live. Families are very large and it is hard to look after everyone. Young girls are sometimes raped and they may be forced out of home because an illegitimate child is a disgrace. We try to help them and we have a small hostel for them. Sometimes the priest does not want to baptise illegitimate babies so we baptise them. Now we have AIDS and we advise the people about treatment but the drugs are very expensive. We have orphans whose parents have both died of AIDS but not so bad here as in Africa."

The Pope was surprised at how much her story was moving him. In principle he knew much of what she had to say but here, in the very place where it all happened and hearing it first hand, was an emotionally different experience.

"Sister, do you ever get depressed? Feel that the needs are so many and the resources so few that it is all pointless?"

"We never think of what we have not achieved, only what we have achieved. That way it is OK and God is very good. The closer things get to hopeless, the more certain we know that He will intervene. That is our experience."

Being a pope felt rather insignificant. "If all I take away from this visit is your faith, it will have been more than worthwhile."

Suddenly there was a loud commotion outside the hut. With the exception of Fr Nolan they went to investigate. Some metres away a man lay with a knife protruding from his chest. Nearby, a woman was sobbing and screaming. Sister Juanita disappeared and re-appeared with a medicine box and dealt with the wounded man. The woman continued to scream. The police arrived and questioned the onlookers. They spoke to the prostrate woman and took her away with them. After Juanita had examined the man and dressed the wound he was carried off on a stretcher. Life returned to normal. Back in the shack Juanita explained.

The wife had caught her husband with another woman. She had chased him and knifed him. The onlookers would not tell the police what had happened but the wife confessed immediately. This was how most violence occurred. It was very personal and did not require huge provocation. Infidelity, theft, insults could all result in a physical response. There were few random killings such as take place in less deprived places. Here it was all very practical.

Sister Louisa arrived straight from her junior class. She had up to forty five children when all actually turned up but there were many barriers to education in the favela. Larger children had to look after smaller children. Some were too weak from malnutrition to attend. Protein deficiency in infancy left brains underdeveloped and unable to cope with much information. Narcogangs recruited school children as inconspicuous lookouts. With the onset of puberty, the attractions of gang membership outbid those of academe. More than anything, perhaps, was the survival mechanism of the very poor, the capacity to live only for the day. This way they retained their sanity but at a high cost. What they had they consumed or wasted. As Orwell once wrote, 'They console themselves with luxuries since they cannot afford necessities'.

"It is a sad reflection," said Sister Louisa, "that we have to try to teach middle class values to help some of them escape a cycle of poverty. To persuade children, who have no realistic view of how to enter a better world, that it makes sense to mortgage today to pay for tomorrow is a mighty big job. They want the fruits of affluence but see them as either unobtainable or as being delivered by crime. A third way is too difficult a concept, at least for most. You know! Today I saw one boy throw away food at recess. He told me it was because he was full already. But by this evening you will be empty. He just smiled at my innocence."

"If such a large number of the population lives in the favelas, surely there must be some government assistance. You know, piped water, electricity, sewage?"

Louisa laughed. "Technically yes, practically no. About 15 years ago Rio received $180 million US dollars and Sao Paulo close to $250 million. It was a bank loan, though not at reduced rates. Very little filtered down to the streets and in Jaguare three buildings constructed with the money had all collapsed within six years. Yet Brazil is a rich country. It has a per capita GNP of about $10000 US dollars annually but half the population lives on less than $100 a month. Like so many of the world's problems, it is not a matter of resources but a matter of a more fair distribution."

"Your new President Lula. Perhaps he will change things."

"There are high hopes but we have known these before. He is popular and has a working class background but, as one man told me, 'I did not vote for him in the first round for fear he would win too easily, only in the second so that he would not take our votes for granted.'"

"What about Liberation Theology. Could that have helped?"

The nuns looked uncomfortable then Catherine spoke. "It covered a broad spectrum. Some priests, frustrated by years of corrupt government and institutionalised violence, were moving in the direction of an armed struggle. This we could never support. The majority aimed at a non-violent movement which would force governments to deal fairly with the poor. Some bishops supported the movement but they have been largely replaced by conservatives, often with connections to the ruling classes. To be blunt, I think the Vatican took the diplomatic option and not the poor option. In so doing we lost some excellent priest and nuns. Pius detested communism but seemed far less troubled by fascism."

Lunch restored Fr Nolan to his usual good spirits though he declined to join the others for a tour of the area.

The Pope had never seen such a mixture of races, from skin colour to facial features it was as though all human DNA had been through a mixer prior to embodiment. Catherine read his mind.

"It is the result of waves of immigration, some voluntary, some not. To the aboriginal population came the Portuguese.

They brought the slaves from Africa. These were followed by Italians, Japanese, Spaniards and Arabs. More recently Peruvians, Bolivians and Columbians. Not to mention fugitive Nazis, British train robbers and a melange of other worthies. 170 million of what must be the most polyglot nation on earth."

"Yet you have, I believe, relatively little racial tension."

"True but that is not to say that race or, more often colour, doesn't matter. 'White good, black bad', just about sums it up."

They walked further up the hill and Sister Juanita led them into a hut. It was dark inside and there was neither fan nor light. The heat was oppressive.

"This is Bonaventure Remedios." She indicated a woman lying on a stretcher in a corner. The woman made as if to rise but fell back on the bed. "She has AIDS and not long to live." Two small children slept on the floor.

The Pope was aware of a stale smell and could feel the sweat running down his back. Instinctively he knelt by her side and blessed her. The woman smiled weakly and said something he could not catch.

"She is thanking you, Holiness." Juanita translated.

The woman spoke again. "She apologises that she cannot stand up for the father nor offer him a cool drink."

The Pope shook his head sadly. Her humility was unbearable. Again he knelt and took her hand, trying hard to control his emotions. How could a nuncio convey such knowledge?

"She wishes to confess to you. She has not got long"

"But I do not speak her language."

"I can translate."

What was he thinking of? "That won't be necessary. Tell her to ask God for his forgiveness while I absolve her."

Juanita translated, the woman smiled again and the Pope murmured: "Ego te absolvo".

"May I tell her, who has heard her confession. It would make her death a happy one?"

"Of course and please tell her that her sufferings are almost over. She has nothing more to fear."

Outside in the bright light the Pope felt dizzy. He steadied himself and turned to Juanita. "What is her story?"

"Her husband was an addict. He contracted AIDS, probably from a shared needle. She got AIDS from him. He died last year and she will die soon leaving seven children. She is 26 years old."

"The children? Who will care for them?"

"We are not sure. Maybe the grandmother. We have sent her a message. If not, we will have to try elsewhere. It is not easy. There are too many orphans in Rochinha."

"We could show you many more such situations, some even worse. I think we should go back now."

Father Nolan seemed sound asleep when they return until they noticed the trickle of blood on his shirt.

"Pat!" The Pope said, feeling for a pulse. There was none. "Dear God, what has happened? He looked round the hut. There was no sign of a robbery. "Has anything been taken?"

"No. It was not a robbery." Juanita said shaking her head. "Everything is still here."

"Dear God, then why?"

Catherine summed up the situation. "I think it is a case of mistaken identity. We have to get you out of here. I think it was you and not Fr Nolan who was the target. Your visit has not remained a secret."

"That is preposterous. Why would anyone want to kill me?"

"Why did they want to kill Jesus? Power is far too seductive to give up without a struggle. Your papacy threatens to shift the balance of power and you cannot expect everyone to approve. Change always brings winners and losers. Clearly the losers don't intend to go quietly."

The Pope regarded the journey back as the worst experience of his life. The numbness he experienced in the favela and later in the police station had departed and he was left with the full horror of what had happened. Catherine had been magnificent. She had dealt with the formalities without ever involving the Pope. Fortunately, being the Superior of an order engaged in charitable work in Brazil, counted for something. The senior police officer treated her with great courtesy and promised to personally take charge of the corpse and it's return to Rome. He even arranged for their transportation to the airport to catch the next available flight.

The Pope tried to pray but found no words. He could only reflect that it was he who had brought Pat to Rome. It was he who had asked him to come to Rio and it was he who should be lying in a mortuary. Without him, Pat would still have been saying Mass for the prostitutes, walking Kyrie and drinking Guinness. Getting out of a warm bed on a cold night to administer the sacraments. In his cowardice and selfishness he had caused a good priest to die and he was the Pope. In reality he was a joke. He was a rather ineffectual academic who had mistakenly been chosen to lead a billion Catholics. If only they knew the truth of it.

Catherine seemed to sense his despair. How do you deal with a depressed Pope? Her practical self told her, like a depressed anyone else. She reached over and took his hand.

"It's not your fault. Don't let it stop you. You have no idea what your visit did for my sisters. But much more than that, you have no idea what hope your pontificate has given to so many."

"Thank you, Catherine. I know you mean well but Pat was my responsibility and, in many ways, my rock. All he wanted to be was a parish priest in Liverpool in a parish most priest try to avoid. I brought him to the Vatican and now to his death. To say that he died for me is nothing more than the bare truth. I am a hollow man, unfit to be Pope."

Catherine's fury came from nowhere. She withdrew her hand. "I won't have you wallowing in self- pity. If Pat's death is to mean anything, then it must mean that we have a Pope who inspires hope, who acts as though he really does love the world with all its cruelty and pain. Do you think for one moment that Pat would want you to be paralysed with guilt? You don't realise the impact you have had on so many of us. We, who expected so much to follow from Vatican II. We, the People of God, were to be given back our Church. To quote Augustine, we were 'To love God and do what we like'. But no, the Curia had other ideas and we quickly became the Abandoned People. Told to get back in our place. Hand in our consciences and obey the rules. Then, when everyone thought the battle was lost, along came Bill Carterton and again there was excitement. We'd been ordered to come to a funeral and, suddenly, we were invited to attend a wedding. Don't tell me you're going to turn round and say It's to be a funeral after all. I don't think we could take a second slap in the face."

She stopped as suddenly as she had started and, uncertain what to do next, summoned the stewardess. "Two large whiskies, please. Ice only."

The Pope was speechless. He had never before been treated like this, even as an assistant priest. He wasn't even sure as to how he felt about Catherine's attack. Did nuns usually give popes a good dressing down? He suspected not. Did he deserve one? Undoubtedly yes. Was his self-pity a betrayal of Pat? Yes, again. He accepted the whisky gratefully. His sense of the ridiculous had returned. He recalled how he had asked Pat not to let him take himself too seriously. Now he had lost one mentor and, seemingly, found another.

Catherine had subsided. She, too, speechless. What had she done? Why had she done it? Where had it all come from? She had taken advantage of this man's good will, made him the target of years of frustration. He had tried to relate personally, had dispensed with the barriers of rank, and she had returned the compliment by behaving like a fishwife. Perhaps he would excommunicate her. Anything was possible. Good job the Inquisition was no longer in business.

The Pope leant across and tipped her glass with his. "To Pat, may he rest in peace and may my pontificate be a fitting memorial to him. Oh! And to the BS indicator."

"To Pat and to his friend, the Pope." She closed her eyes and that decided that she had escaped Armageddon.

CHAPTER 26

Less than a week after the conversation on infallibility had taken place events in Washington DC ensured a radical re-ordering of papal priorities. President Grant Winthrop Bennett met with his inner cabinet to discuss a series of ever more gloomy opinion polls. With a little less than eighteen months to the next election drastic measures were needed to arrest the decline in his support. The leakage of traditional Democratic support, which had led to his controversial election, had ceased as tax cuts were increasingly seen to favour the rich. The terrorism card was no longer a guaranteed rallying point, as memories of the devastating attack faded. Even the notoriously insular American public was beginning to realise that world opinion increasingly saw the only remaining super power as motivated largely by self-interest. The financial scandals of the past years, some not too distant from the President and his Executive, had replaced patriotism with cynicism. To quote Bennett's own words: "We need a circuit breaker and quick".

"Perceptions! Mr President. The voters see you as a strong leader, an aggressive leader but, perhaps like Churchill after his war, they don't see you in quite the same light as a peacetime leader."

"Is that so?" Bennett was showing his non-public irritation. "You could have fooled me when I'm out there meeting them."

"That is different. They respect the office and how you led the country after the New York tragedy but their minds are now on more humdrum issues."

Vice President Collins interrupted. "Then they've got short memories. Can you imagine how Bordello Bill would have dealt with it?"

"That's true, they do have short memories. Just look at how they treated Dad. Ungrateful rabble."

"So what is the answer?"

"We need a war. "

"You're joking. We've not long finished one."

"Choose the right one and your ratings will return."

"I must protest, most strongly. We can't wage war just to ensure an election."

The President raised his hand. "Just as an exercise let's suppose we did have a war. We'd need an enemy and a reason."

"That's easy. Everyone hates Yusuf and he has oil." Collins mimed embarrassment. "Let me re-phrase that. He's a dangerous tyrant who threatens our security and that of the Middle East, consorts with terrorists and has failed to obey the UN resolution." The VP smiled in self-satisfaction.

"We'd be seen as doing the world a favour and liberating his poor, oppressed people."

"Industry would approve. Contributions would flow."

"Financial scandals would disappear off the public radar."

"The Democrats would be again seen as un-American."

"Get me the Chairman of the Joint Chiefs."

"My fellow Americans, I have been in receipt of disturbing intelligence which suggests that the terrorist attack on New York, appalling as it was, may simply have been the start of a much more serious threat to our security. Indications are that Yusuf bin Hashim is not only manufacturing weapons of mass destruction, as forbidden by UN resolution 965, but is planning to supply them to terrorist groups hostile to the Western democracies. As your President I believe that it is my responsibility to pre-empt any such threat rather than react after another tragedy has occurred. I know that my oppo-

nents will seize on this pre-emptive doctrine as evidence that I seek war rather than peace, but that is a risk I must accept. As a family man myself I ask the question, is it better to confront the home invader outside my house or wait until my wife and children are in his grasp? I have only one answer."

"My allegedly peace loving opponents will tell me that I should call the police rather than take the law into my own hands. But what if the police are unavailable or unable or unwilling to act quickly for whatever reason. Do I sacrifice my family on the basis of an unrealistic alternative? This country was not built into the greatest nation on earth by forefathers who procrastinated and waited for others to do the work they knew they must do themselves. It was their spirit of self-reliance which placed America in the forefront of the family of nations. Even laying aside our own protection, that pre-eminent position gives us additional responsibilities. Pax Americana is the true hope of weaker nations and oppressed peoples as well as of ourselves."

"So, tonight, I wish to place on notice those who would conspire with terror and flaunt international opinion. America will use all of her formidable resources to destroy any threat to world order. We will seek peace diligently but our patience will be strictly limited. Our first resort will be to the Security Council but, if that fails, we will act quickly in collaboration with other freedom loving nations or, if necessary, we will act alone. For the tyrants and terrorists of this world there is to be no hiding place."

"May God bless America, her people and her armed forces."

As agreed in telephone conversations, the British Prime Minister and his Australian counterpart made supportive speeches to their respective parliaments within the next twenty four hours. The reaction of other nations was less positive. The Canadian Prime Minister stressed the need for UN approval and hinted that domestic considerations rather than terrorist threats might be responsible for such a belligerent speech. The European Union, though not united in its reaction, showed little enthusiasm for the pre-emptive doctrine. While Bennett would have liked greater Western support its absence was far outweighed by his resurgent popularity in the polls. Not only that but the Democrats sounded especially feeble with their mantra of 'No war without UN approval'. In different circumstances, such a response might have received a fair hearing but capricious fate intervened when the People's Republic of Laefa took its place as the Chair of the UN Human Rights Commission, an oxymoron of elephantine proportions. Sebastian Hart, who had decided to support the GOP for entirely commercial reasons, ensured that his editors were alive to the contradiction

DRACULA RUNS THE BLOOD BANK

The United Nations has never commanded universal enthusiasm. Sometimes this has been due to the self-interest of individual nations, sometimes to failures within the organisation itself. But never, to date, has it attracted such ridicule and disillusionment as it has in the appointment of Laefa to the chair of the Human Rights Commission. The Laefan regime of Colonel Gustapha is one of the most closed and repressive in the world. Not only that but it has long used its oil revenues to support terrorist activities. It is the equivalent of putting Count Dracula in charge of the blood bank. How can an organisation, which allows such an outrage to occur, claim the moral authority to instruct the nations of the world on how to behave?

It is no wonder that, when the national interest is seriously threatened, the UN is seen more as an impediment to effective action rather than a promoter of effective action. Those political opponents who were quick to criticise President Bennett's speech as potentially by-passing the UN should clean their political spectacles before they rush to judgement. What President worth his salt is going to risk American lives in order to pay lip service to an organisation which is increasingly seen as impotent or deranged or both?

It is time for politicians to present a common front against an ever increasing threat, to have the courage to act decisively and in time rather than hide behind a non-existent mandate from a dysfunctional UN.

The Pope summoned Peroni to discuss the worsening situation.

"I need your advice, Stephano. President Bennett's speech is worrying and perhaps more worrying is the seeming absence of moderating voices in the United States. I do not hear the Catholic bishops making a case for peaceful negotiations. Should I speak out?"

"The situation is delicate, Holiness. There is still a lingering suspicion in America that Catholics are more loyal to the Pope than to the Constitution. It has been dormant since the Kennedy presidency but it is not dead. The bishops are aware of this. In addition their credibility has been undermined by the recent child abuse cases. Those who would speak out for peace are conscious that an intervention might be counterproductive. Others take a more robust attitude and are generally supportive of a military solution to the problem of terrorism. So there is a lack of both unity and certainty not to mention credibility."

"I see, but doesn't military action simply deal with the effects of terrorism rather than the causes? Aren't we allowing our behaviour to be shaped by the barbaric behaviour of the terrorist when we resort to war?"

"Holiness, to deal with the causes would require a whole new moral order and a long term strategy. It would entail the sacrifice of power in undemocratic countries and the sacrifice of living standards in the democracies. I do not think mankind has yet evolved to a point where such sacrifices are feasible."

"Yet a war will probably involve exactly those sacrifices and much more."

"As your English philosopher, Bertrand Russell, once remarked, "Men will sooner die than think".

"Then should not the Pope speak out?"

"I would not advise a public statement at this stage but quiet diplomacy."

"Holiness, this is an unexpected honour. I trust life in the Eternal City is to your liking?"

"Prime Minister, thank you for taking my call. I have not yet explored the Eternal City but I am look forward to the opportunity. My immediate concern is the prospect of a war with Sambre.'

"A terrible prospect but one which must be faced if we are to protect our own citizens and liberate Yusuf's suffering people."

"Perhaps war will, in the longer term, increase the danger to all people and lead to even greater suffering."

"Holiness, politics is not an exact science. If politicians waited for certainty before acting they would never act. Political decisions have to be based on the balance of probabilities. Yusuf is a dictator without conscience. He has demonstrated that fact in dealing with his neighbours as well as his own subjects. Do we give him even more time to increase his ability to hold the world to ransom or do we deprive him of that power? In this country, we know only too well the rewards of appeasement. Our backing for a military solution is to minimise future casualties not to increase them by inaction now."

"And there is no other way?"

"Sadly it would appear not. He has been given many chances to disarm but continues to defy both the UN and world opinion. Unless of course you, Holiness, have something in mind."

"I have nothing specific except to say that I will do anything in my power to avert a conflict. If you or President Bennett can see a way of using the papacy in the cause of peace, I will put myself at your service."

"A generous offer, Holiness. I will discuss it with the Cabinet and inform the President. I hope we can make use of it for we would all prefer a peaceful outcome."

The Pope had no counter argument. "I will pray that war may be averted even at this late stage."

"I think it is a question of rendering unto Caesar. I appreciate your concern and your prayers but there are some decisions some which are legitimately theological and some which must remain political."

Trent replaced the phone with some satisfaction. "He may think twice now about rejecting my offer of a partnership." He remarked to a confused secretary. "Arrange for me to speak with Bennett."

"The last thing we want is a dotty Pope involving himself in politics. Why can't he stick to beating the birth control drum and leave the real world to the professionals."

"We have to be seen to take the offer seriously. Maybe we could use him."

"I've got it. Why not a papal visit to Sambre. A peace gesture. If he gets assassinated we get rid of a thorn in our side and the French and Italians and other doubters will have no excuse for backsliding."

"What if he gets assassinated? What if he doesn't?"

"Why leave matters to chance? About accepting his offer, I mean."

"That's what I took you to mean."

"Quite so, but Yusuf may not jump at the idea."

"He will, anything to delay the inevitable. That's what he's been doing for years."

"But the military. They're living under pretty grim conditions waiting for the order. This means more delays."

"So it means more delays. They're still getting paid."

Trent was in self-congratulatory mode as he put down the phone. The Pope was certainly no politician. Not only had he accepted Trent's suggestion of a visit to Sambre, he was happy for Trent to make the first announcement. Thus the Prime Minister's prestige as both peacemaker and statesman was advanced at no cost to himself. What other world leader could claim to influence the Pope? The Catholic vote was now firmly in his pocket. He relished the prospect of his announcement to the House.

"The Leader of the Opposition rose, looking confident. "Can the Prime Minister enlighten the house as to why our brave servicemen and women have been enduring the heat and discomfort of the desert together with the psychological tension of waiting endlessly for an invasion which seems never to occur? Does he intend to emulate forever the Grand Old Duke of York who marched his armies up to the top of the hill before marching them down again? If he is incapable of making a decision, why does he not hand over the leadership to his ever-ready Chancellor?"

Trent felt that all his Christmases had come at once. He looked about him at the government benches. "Mr Speaker, if only we could all be blessed with the reductionist view of life held by the Leader of the Opposition. Decision making would come so easily and doubt would be banished from the earth. I would willingly embrace such a character if I had to run a sweet shop but, in reality, I have to run the country. Clearly the Leader of the Opposition has served his apprenticeship for the former but not for the latter." This was a reference to Charles Spencer's parents who had owned a mixed business. It was greeted with cries of shame from the Opposition benches and guffaws from the Government. "Let me assure the House," Trent continued, "I am only too conscious of the conditions of our forces but, behind the scenes, an area which appears not to exist for my honourable friend, we have been pursuing every possible initiative which might avert war. In any event, I am sure our service personnel would prefer discomfort as an alternative to having to kill and possibly be killed. Now, as part of this quiet diplomatic activity, I am able to advise the House that I have been in regular touch with Pope John XXIV and he has agreed to offer his services as a mediator with President Yusuf."

There was a stunned silence followed by some cheering. Someone called out that Sambre was Muslim country.

"Thank you for reminding me and, of course, the Holy Father. However, the Holy Father has made a special point during his papacy of reaching out to non-Christian faiths, Islam in particular. I can think of no man or woman more suited to such a delicate mission. Both President Bennett and myself are one hundred per cent behind what must be the last opportunity to avert war. A war which would be already in progress if the Leader of the Opposition was in a position to apply his simplistic approach to statesmanship. Fortunately, for the good of both the United Kingdom and the rest of the world, he is unlikely

ever to be in a position to run anything demanding more imagination than the aforementioned sweet shop."

Trent sat back to the applause of his party, trying hard not
to look smug. At the same time he was aware of his Chancellor's
lack of enthusiasm: Brian, he concluded, was coming to the
realisation that he just wasn't Prime Minister material. A glori-
fied book keeper but not a world class statesman. He decided to
rub salt in the wound.

"Are you feeling OK, Brian? You not looking your normal
self?"

"It's shock, Alex. I am amazed at what I've just heard. You
certainly had me fooled."

Trent hid his satisfaction. "Well I had my serious doubts about
Carterton, as you well know, but it seems that the responsibilities
of being Pope have brought him back to earth and a good thing
too. I think he's come to realise that my advice is worth taking.
Quite a coup don't you think?"

"My thinking exactly! But I do wonder who was the subject if
this coup."

"You're too cryptic."

"Let's say that his mission succeeds in some way. We'll have a
Pope on our hands who has achieved what the United States, the
United Kingdom and the United Nations have failed to achieve
and all without ever firing a shot. I think you've taken a huge
gamble, Alex, and one which is out of character. I've always
rated you as a man who wanted to keep rivals in their place and
definitely not one to promote their cause."

Trent was furious. This was typical of Fellows. The man had
the imagination of a koala. Totally unappreciative of Trent's ability to think outside of the square. Able to find fault in what the
rest of the House recognised as real leadership. Yet he had still
managed to implant the worm of doubt. Once you had been
Prime Minister, there was only one other goal, that of world
statesman. The deep vein of American isolationism militated
against US presidents being pre-eminent statesmen which really
left only Trent or, if Fellows was right, the Pope. Fellows was
certainly right about one thing, he wasn't in the business of creating rivals.

"I feel powerless, Stephano. Worse than that I am confused. The gospel tells us to turn the other cheek, to love our enemies. St Thomas advances the case for a 'just war'. The principle of double effect states that good cannot be justified if it flows out of evil. The politicians claim a moral imperative when an ounce of cynicism suggests that resources or electoral considerations may be paramount. And the Pope, the supposed leader of a billion Catholics, is neither omniscient nor omnipotent. In fact the very politicians whom he criticises are at least decisive when he dithers."

"Holiness, I have spoken with President Bennett. We believe that there is a way in which you may be able to assist in the peace process. It is not without dangers, both for your person and for your authority."

"Lives are more important, Prime Minister."

"If you were to visit Sambre, as a gesture of goodwill from the Christian-Western world, it would increase Yusuf's personal standing and could provide him with an excuse to cooperate with the inspectors. Instead of being seen to capitulate to the UN he could claim a reciprocal gesture.'

"You believe that it could work?"

"There are no guarantees but we don't have many options left."

"Then I'll do it…..if Yusuf agrees."

CHAPTER 27

"I think you are being used, Holiness. Yusef will take advantage of further delays without becoming any more cooperative. The President will have a stick with which to beat the unenthusiastic Catholic nations. The prestige of the Papacy will be reduced."

"You may well be right but any chance is worth taking and who can say, once the door is open, where the Spirit will alight. What do you think, Catherine?"

"I think the Cardinal is probably correct but Jesus didn't calculate the odds before acting. I don't think the Pope should either."

Peroni shrugged. "Then I will try to make the arrangements."

JOHN XXIV AND THE DEVIL

The Vatican confirmed today that Pope John XXIV is to make a personal visit to President Yusuf bin Hashim in an attempt to avoid a war. While this is a noble gesture on the part of the Pope it is also a naïve one. To quote Stalin, "How many divisions does the Pope have?". Yusuf may delight in the further delays, which the visit ensures, but he is unlikely to take notice of the words of a good but eccentric pontiff when he will not take notice of the firepower of the United States and its allies. It is also questionable whether a papal visit to an Arab country is prudent at this turbulent time in relations between the Western and Arab worlds. On the one hand, Moslems may see it as an intrusion of Christianity into what is, nominally at least, a Muslim country: a modern version of the Crusades. On the other, it raises security dangers with their attendant potential for further deterioration in East-West relations.

Meanwhile Alliance forces are increasingly frustrated, waiting for the order to attack which, seemingly, is forever postponed. A combination of falling morale and rising temperatures do not present the optimum conditions for an invasion should the already flawed peace efforts finally collapse.

The Pope's intentions are not in question but his judgement is in doubt. We have already seen a series of 'do gooders' and posturing politicians visit Sambre in misguided efforts to frustrate the Alliance and give comfort to Yusuf. Let the Pope remember the old adage, "When you sup with the devil use a long spoon".

Other papers took a more positive view including the Catholic Sentinel.

HOLY FATHER TO INTERCEDE FOR PEACE

Pope John XXIV's peace mission to Sambre is a courageous effort to avert war at the eleventh hour. It is not without its dangers, both personal and in terms of Christianity. However, Jesus brought a message of peace on earth and the Pope is attempting, in probably the only way open to him, to act out that message. Though fanatics, be they Christian or Moslem, may be critical of his visit, most people will accept that it arises out of a genuine love for mankind and a desire to avoid further suffering.

The fact that President Yusuf has welcomed the visit is a positive sign, even though there may be practical advantages for him in further delaying military action. The fact that President

Bennett, Prime Minister Trent and other senior Alliance figures have endorsed the visit is a further reason for optimism, even though they may gain some political advantage. In fact, the only player likely to lose from the initiative is the Pope himself. It is he who risks his life and his standing in the world. For that reason it is wholly in keeping with the precedent set by the founder of Christianity: Jesus was never averse to risking his safety or his dignity. The manner of his death provides the unquestionable evidence of that fact. In his pilgrimage to Sambre, the Holy Father is walking in the very steps of his master.

"We live in interesting times, Karl. A peacemaker Pope and a Middle Eastern tyrant. What would Shakespeare have done with such a cast?"

Maier smiled cynically. "I think he'd have turned it into his greatest tragedy. More bloody than Macbeth and more devious than Lear."

"What makes you think it will end so badly? It might just get Yusuf off the hook. Give him the excuse he needs to disarm without seeming to bow to the Americans."

"A few years ago he might have thought that way but recently he's been setting himself up as an Islamic icon. Somehow cozing up to the Pope wouldn't quite fit."

Hart nodded. "I take your point. What a dilemma for him. Accept the Pope's offer and he buys time with the Americans but loses face with Islam. Reject it and he keeps his iconic status until he loses the war."

"There is always the wild card and no one can be quite sure how that would affect the outcome."

Hart showed his annoyance. Maier's games did not amuse him. He gestured at Maier to explain himself.

"Another assassination attempt, perhaps a successful one. It could easily happen. He's had one near miss already."

"And we still don't know?"

"We know who carried it out. A nobody. Now a dead nobody. We're making progress but I don't think we'll end up blaming Yusuf."

"What a story. If there was a second attempt, we'd have a worldwide scoop. The only people able to expose the first and link the second. Do you think Yusuf would risk it?"

"Yusuf! Probably not but there are others who will. I can think of a whole range of players who could benefit from a dead Pope."

"Go on."

"The Coalition of the Willing for starters. An assassinated Pope would ratchet up the case for war by several notches. Then there is Al Qaeda. What a coupe if they could knock off the world's most senior Christian. It would be their best recruiting ticket ever. "

"Not to mention various other Arab terrorist groups. You are right and, if Yusuf got the blame, how much better. He's never been a favourite with the Muslim extremists."

"Then there are his non-military enemies amongst whom I suppose we would number ourselves and one or two other media conglomerates. The Organisation is hostile and not a few politicians. When you add it all up he's a potential target for a whole battery of missiles. The more you think about it the less likely he is to come out alive, rather a consoling thought, no pun intended."

Hart frowned mockingly. "Come now Karl, we shouldn't let our imaginations get overheated. I'm sure we all wish John XXIV a long and active pontificate. Perhaps you should take a greater interest in his personal security."

The Organisation's reaction to the papal visit was as Maier had predicted. The spirit of ecumenism had never taken root in relation even to the mainstream Protestant churches and the Pope's overtures to other faiths had been viewed with absolute horror. Not to put too fine a point on it, the Organisation was suspicious of the broad majority of Catholics.

Discretely, the powerful network was mobilised and Peroni was inundated with advice from all quarters as to the inadvisability of the visit to Sambre. Not that he needed to be convinced. In the wake of Pat Nolan's murder, or heart attack as was made public, he was against any unnecessary risks. Nor was the risk simply physical. Mixing religion and politics had a long and unhappy history in the Catholic Church. Too close an identification with the latter led to a loss of control. Loss of control led to the Church being besmirched by political expediency. You had to look no further than Italy and the Christian Democrat's association with Catholicism. What began as a united front to defeat communism had degenerated into a maelstrom of bribery, corruption and murder. No! So far as Peroni was concerned religion and politics was a cocktail with a guaranteed hangover.

"Holiness, every day I am beseeched by a whole range of persons in the hope that you will withdraw your offer of mediation. Not only do you risk your life but, if it fails or is somehow distorted, your ability to influence events in the future."

"Stephano, I appreciate your opinion and that of other well-wishers, though," the Pope chortled, "I cannot believe that they all arise out of concern for my welfare. However, I began my papacy in a royal funk, as you well know, and I am determined not to revert to cowardice."

Peroni's face darkened. He made as if to speak but remained silent.

"Spit it out! We agreed to deal honestly with each other."

"Very well. " For a moment he broke eye contact. "I cannot help wondering whether this visit and the one to the favela are not as much to do with therapy for the Pope as for their stated purpose."

"I share your suspicions and it is not a question I can answer myself, except to say that Jesus taught us that the weak could confound the strong. So my cowardice can be put at his disposal. If therapy for the Pope is a by-product, so be it."

"Holiness, I cannot argue with that except to say that you are not a coward. On the contrary I think you make cowards of us all."

Peroni rose and was about to leave the room. Suddenly he turned. "Holiness, be safe! When you were elected I prayed that your pontificate would be short. I do not pray that anymore."

Shortly after leaving the Pope, Peroni had a phone call from Monsignor Gomez, enquiring on behalf of the Organisation as to whether the visit to Sambre would proceed.

"There have been no changes in the Holy Father's plans." Peroni replied abruptly. "So any further requests for him to change those plans will be most unwelcome. I hope you disseminate that point, Monsignor. The position is not negotiable."

The Monsignor did exactly as instructed. In New York, the offices of Consol were not the only ones where the impact of the visit was discussed. Within the Organisation the consensus was slightly different.

"The situation continues to deteriorate. First, the Conclave elects a radical Pope. Second, the sobering effect of high office fails to temper his behaviour. Third, he begins to resuscitate the corpse of Vatican II. Fourth, he orders a new council which can only convene with the anticipation of still further erosion of the Magisterium. Fifth, he reconstitutes the Devil's Advocate and delays, perhaps even prevents, the canonisation of our blessed founder. Sixth, he goes over the heads of the hierarchy in order to communicate his revolutionary ideas to ordinary Catholics who have not the capacity to distinguish between substance and fantasy. Seventh, he has replaced his 'personal counsellor', the late, lunatic Fr Nolan, with an even less acceptable import, Sister Catherine of the Sisters of Hope. A woman in the Vatican and not just as a cook or cleaner! I can tell you, gentlemen, the Curia is in shock. No! That is too mild a word, it is traumatised. But, to continue. Eighth, he seems to have corrupted one of the most reliably conservative cardinals, namely Cardinal Peroni, the Secretary of State. Once a spiritual ally of the Organisation, he has now become as radical as his master. Ninth, he has accepted the resignation of Cardinal Kirst, Prefect of the Congregation for the Doctrine of the Faith, re-named this bulwark against heresy as the Congregation for the Development of the Faith and appointed a card carrying heretic to replace Kirst. I refer to the Franciscan, Fr Pereira, who was himself under investigation by the same Congregation. If that is not a sign of the future then I am as detached from reality as the Pope himself."

The leader paused. "Gentlemen, I could go on and on but, suffice to say, we are facing the biggest crisis since Monsignor Estoria founded us. As he looks down from heaven he must weep for the Church he so loved, but he must also thank God than he left us as his legacy. An Organisation uniquely able to react to the present danger. This we must do with all our strength and without delay. Time is of the essence. Within days the Pope is likely to visit Sambre. If his visit is successful his authority will be enhanced and his reforms become more acceptable to the Faithful. If, on the other hand his visit fails, for whatever reason, our task will be less onerous. We may even be able to put our energies into preparations for the next Conclave."

It took a moment for the last remark to register. Noting this, the leader raised his hand. "This Pope has made many enemies. You can never be too sure that they all restrict themselves to prayer and persuasion."

CHAPTER 28

The Pope, accompanied only by an interpreter, touched down at Bandan airport. They were met by Yusuf's Prime Minister, the only Christian in the cabinet, and driven under escort to one of the many presidential palaces. There were no crowds along the route as the government had imposed a media blackout and those with illegal radios and World Service access did not wish to advertise the fact. If the visit proved useful propaganda it would become newsworthy, if not it would never have occurred. The Pope was aware of this aspect of totalitarianism and it reinforced his resolve to keep media honesty as an ongoing concern.

"Why should you, a Christian, be concerned for the well-being of a Muslim nation? It was your Church which launched the Crusades."

"I understand your reservations. Yes, it is true that Christians inflicted terrible suffering on Muslims. The opposite is also true. However, what we have all often failed to do is to show love towards each other. That is what we are commanded to do. A command which, sadly, we have often ignored. To answer your question, my Faith tells me that all human life is equally precious to God. If there is a war, many will die, old scars will be re-opened, the world will have become less safe. If war can be avoided we will have shown that good will can overcome prejudice."

"I have already made many concessions. I have allowed inspectors into my country. Each time I grant a concession, more is asked. If I ask the American President to have my inspectors visit his country, what sort of reply will I receive? He is not concerned with the so called weapons of mass destruction, he is concerned with protecting his oil supplies and Israel. There is nothing I can do to stop this war." Yusuf paused briefly. "Unless the Pope can perform a miracle."

"In one sense a small miracle has already occurred. People have come from many countries to offer themselves as human shields. Perhaps that miracle could be built upon."

"A gesture but no more than that. At most a hundred and some have already left. A few idealists cannot shield a country the size of Sambre."

"But if you had thousands and, especially if those thousands came from all the nations of the Coalition, that might prove sufficient deterrent."

"And where would these thousands of volunteers come from?"

"There are almost a billion Catholics and many of other Faiths who are against this war. I do not believe that volunteers would be hard to come by. All it needs is a well-publicised request and a pope should be able to achieve that. I have little doubt that Muslim countries would encourage participation, too, in the face of a major Christian response."

Yusuf was beginning to see the possibilities. If war came his whole life would end in ruins. Instead of a second Saladin he would go down as a failed dictator. The Pope was an unlikely ally but no one else was showing enthusiasm for the role. Even a delay was an improvement on the present situation. The morale of the coalition forces would decline as the mercury rose, an encouraging development.

"Very well. If you think you can dramatically increase the number of human shields to a level where they are a real deterrent, we will welcome them."

"For your part you will cooperate with the inspectors. If they report a lack of such cooperation, the shields will be asked to withdraw."

The Pope and the dictator shook hands.

The papal flight reached 30000 feet. The Pope, anxious to finalise the details of what would be a major operation, spoke to Peroni by phone. Within two hours of the handshake a small team in the Vatican was already working on the plan.

The contents of the phone call were pick up by satellites, relayed to ground stations in Cyprus and Turkey, and thence for intelligence analysis. Hurried conferences were called and the implications of the Pope's agreement assessed. Any political ambivalence was more than balanced by military opposition. Delay had already had an adverse effect on troop preparedness. The Rules of Engagement were restrictive enough without adding thousands of young idealists eagerly seeking glory.

"I have an army ready for battle not for babysitting duties." A four star general thundered.

"The mums and dads may accept a son or daughter in uniform being killed by the enemy and buried with full military honours What they won't accept is the same son or daughter being killed by their own side and being dubbed a traitor. I mean no disrespect but we, the military, are likely to have the political rug pulled from under us when that starts to happen."

"He has to be stopped. Maybe his plane will crash and the problem will disappear."

"Wishful thinking."

"Not necessarily."

The papal flight was still in Turkish airspace when it exploded. The wreckage was scattered over the mountains. As for the pilot and his two passengers and the black box, there was no trace. The Coalition accused Yusuf of an act of unparalleled bastardry. Yusuf accused the Coalition of subverting the last opportunity of avoiding war. The Russian President accused Chechnya rebels of firing a missile and claimed that Christianity as well as Russia was now under this terrorist threat. Two days later the pre-invasion bombardment of Sambre began and Russia mounted a new offensive in Chechnya.

Conspiracy theorists, dependent upon their particular prejudice, variously accused the American President, the Vice-

President and other administrative notables. Several spread the blame between the US and British Security Services. At the fringes of suspicion, the Italian Prime Minister, the Organisation and Sebastian Hart were all awarded conspiratorial status. Not since the Kennedy assassination had a crime stirred up so much conjecture but conjecture it remained. No charge was ever laid, no warrant ever issued and no suspect arraigned before the courts.

As time passed, it became fashionable to doubt whether the plane had actually exploded or, indeed, had ever taken off. Or, if it had taken off, whether it might not have landed somewhere and its occupants gone into hiding. This curious theory was backed up by an alleged interview with an ancient Turkish farmer, who claimed to have sheltered the Pope and his companions for several days, prior to the party leaving for an undisclosed destination.

This claim became the basis for a book in which the Pope was said to be living in a monastery and devoting his life to prayer and penance, having concluded that he could better serve his God and mankind in the capacity of a humble monk.

Needless to say, efforts to trace the Turkish farmer and the monastery all failed but the book still sold over a million copies and was made into a film

CHAPTER 29

The death of Pope John XXIV became one of the great unsolved mysteries of the new century. Politicians proclaimed how a great a loss had occurred, not just for the Catholic Church but for all people of good will. The Coalition leaders expressed sorrow that his peace mission had failed with his untimely death, and claimed that he was yet another victim of the terrorism which they were so determined to eradicate.

Sebastian Hart let it be known that the late Pope, though a man of personal holiness and courage, was too naïve to govern as complex an institution as the Catholic Church. By implication, his successor should be a more worldly prelate. His editors rapidly reached the same conclusion. In private Hart asked Maier whether he had any personal knowledge of the plane crash.

"None that you should wish to know about except to say that we need to bury US$2.5m in the accounts."

Hart was sure Maier was using the episode to siphon off the money for himself but he could not be absolutely certain. Maier had an amazing intelligence network and it was just…just possible. He'd pay up for now without questions but the matter would not rest there.

The Organisation was caught in a dilemma. The Pope's death brought the prospect of a new pontiff of more conservative disposition and a rapid canonisation of their founder. Yet to express satisfaction at the death of a pope was somehow anathema to the whole rationale of the Organisation. After much discussion, the leadership arrived at a formula which honoured the office without being too enthusiastic about its most recent occupant. Pope John XXIV would be mourned as the Pope who, as though aware of his impending death, had tackled too many issues with too little experience: a man of noble spirit but intemperate personality. This settled, they embarked on the next election campaign.

As with Pius XIII, reactions to the brief papacy of John XXIV were extremely mixed. Consol's Post expressed one side of the spectrum.

REQUIUM FOR A MERCURIAL POPE

The tragic death, assassination perhaps, of Pope John XXIV provides the College of Cardinals, shortly to assemble in Rome, with a difficult decision. John XXIV's brief papacy had already threatened to provoke a schism in that most disciplined of bodies, the Roman Catholic Church. William Carterton's promotion to cardinal was a curious act by his long reigning conservative predecessor. His election as Pope was equally curious. Finally, his papacy was the most curious of all.

In less than two years, he had signalled major changes in the traditional teaching on birth control, celibacy, women priests, the treatment of divorced Catholics and, quite possibly, was going to relax attitudes towards homosexual unions. He had begun to lecture politicians, business and the media on their moral responsibilities which he clearly saw as far bigger issues than boudoir behaviour. His website had enraged many bishops as usurping their role as the intermediate communicators between the Vatican and the Faithful. His decision to hold another Vatican Council and to place infallibility on the agenda was a further sign of a man saw himself, at best, as one amongst equals.

While many in the Church applauded this new style papacy, just as many realised that the expectations brought about by the

Second Vatican Council had caused sufficient anxiety for several generations to accommodate. While the outside world is
changing at breakneck speed, it is surely reassuring to belong
to an organisation which is inherently stable. The flight of many
Catholics and, indeed, many Anglicans to more fundamentalist
creeds supports this notion. If Vatican II began the erosion of
the Rock of Peter, Vatican III under the influence of John XXIV
was likely to replace it with quicksand. Amongst groups alienated
was the powerful and secretive Organisation.

Outside of the Church, too, his habit of commenting
adversely on the work of politicians, the media and business,
took him into an area where he had no experience and, it
often seemed, resulted in judgements which betrayed a lack of
understanding of the constraints under which such professionals have to work. If a politician demanded that the Pope justify
murder, he would be ridiculed for asking the impossible. At
times the Pope's demands of other professionals were similarly
unreasonable.

The final act of his papacy, the one which cost him his life,
was wholly admirable and wholly naïve. The idea of giving Yusuf
what amounted to thousands of hostages was nothing short of
insane. Yusuf, the arch prevaricator, would have been able to
delay still further the destruction of his terrorist regime. It is a
sad comment to make but, in that context, the Pope's death may
well have saved the lives of many high minded and equally naïve
young people.

To describe someone a 'well intentioned' is tantamount to
damning them with faint praise. No one doubts that John XXIV
was 'well intentioned'. Let us hope that his successor will also be
'well intentioned' but with a greater capacity for dealing with the
reality of life rather than the fantasy.

The Sentinel reflected a different perspective.

A DEATH TOO SOON

Whether Pope John XXIV was murdered or simply the victim of a tragic accident we may never know with any certainty.
What we do know with certainty is that he set in motion a train

of events which will be difficult to stop. It is quite possible that the cardinals now assembling in Rome will choose a conservative successor out of fear, a fear being promulgated by various interests both inside and outside the Church. They have, admittedly, a difficult task since John XXIV polarised Catholics as no other pope of recent times. However, what he did convey unequivocally was a love of mankind, Catholics, Protestants, Muslims, Hindus, Jews and other faiths were all equally precious creations of God in his eyes. That he met his death in trying to prevent a war, in which Muslim casualties were bound to be the most numerous, was proof positive of his universal love. He was in the tradition of John Donne and Thomas Merton and others who were 'involved in mankind'.

He spoke out against vested interests, where he believed these to be detrimental to ordinary people in the exercise of their moral judgement. He had little time for politicians, media magnates or business men in general if they were guilty of lies and deceit. He was essentially a democrat, perhaps the first genuine democrat ever to occupy the throne of Peter. He was the absolute antithesis of Lord Acton's dictum about absolute power corrupting absolutely. He spoke directly to the people, not in order to undermine bishops, but to involve them in their Church. He breathed new life into the phrase 'People of God' after its steady devaluation since Vatican II. He had already announced that infallibility was to be considered at the Third Vatican Council and, in absolute contrast to Pius IX, he would abide by the bishop's unfettered vote. He did not just give lip service to subsidiarily and collegiality: he practiced both.

Like his master, he was critical of a priesthood which placed heavy burdens on men's shoulders. He believed that the Faithful were mature enough to act morally with minimal guidance from the Church. In a Church which includes two schools of morality: the school of conscience and the school of blind obedience, he was very clearly of the former. Treat the Faithful as irresponsible children and you will get back irresponsible behaviour. Trust the Faithful as morally competent adults and you will get back responsible behaviour.

His impact on the Curia is still a matter of speculation. However, Cardinal Kirst's sudden transfer from Prefect of the Congregation for the Doctrine of the Faith (now re-named for the Development of the Faith) to be Cardinal Archbishop of Cologne suggests that he, at least, could not come to terms with the new wind blowing down the Vatican corridors. His replacement by the controversial theologian, Fr Pereira, must have sent shudders down a few bureaucratic spines. Cardinal Peroni, the Secretary of State, has remained loyally in post and, it is rumoured, become something of a disciple of the late Holy Father. The Spirit surely works in a mysterious way.

His predecessor had the second longest reign of any Pope, being exceeded only by Pius IX. John XXIV had one of the shortest. In our view, both had a massive impact of the Church and the world beyond. Pius' greatest achievement, when the history books are written, will probably be his hand in the demise of the Soviet Union and the liberation of Eastern Europe: truly a major triumph. John's greatest achievement may well come to be regarded as that sublime moment when a pope and countless other Catholics, priests and people, knelt in penance for the Church's unconscionable abuse of children. A small gesture, perhaps, in comparison with the end of Soviet hegemony yet, in so many ways, so much closer to the actions of a God who became man and dwelt amongst us. If Newman were alive today, perhaps he would raise his glass first to Pope John XXIV then to his conscience.

Pius XIII stretched a long arm out of the grave when it came to electing his successor in that he had appointed so many of the Cardinal Electors. John XXIV had appointed none and was awaiting a more democratic process for filling existing and future vacancies. The composition of the last conclave is virtually identical to this one. Will it again demonstrate Its capacity to surprise with another Pope of Surprises or will it elect a Pope of Predictability?

Vatican watchers reported a curious stillness about the Conclave which was to elect the new Pope. Whether it was the shock of the accident or assassination, or simply a disinclination to engage in electioneering so soon after the tragedy is hard to say. Perhaps a little of both as most events and even non-events in life have multiple causes. This uncanny silence was unwelcomed by the media which relied on a diet of rumours as to who was in favour and hints of scandal as to who was considered unelectable.

Of course, such absence of hard currency did not prevent the less respectable journalists from a little creative speculation. Kirst was promoted as a right wing candidate, on the basis that he was believed to have resigned out of opposition to John's liberalism, and had proven his credentials as a revisionist while heading the Congregation for the Doctrine of the Faith. In order to provide something of a two horse race, Cardinal Murengo was touted as the doyen of the Third World possibilities. Finally, since that still left a liberal vacancy amongst the alleged competitors, Montalban, Cardinal Archbishop of Lyon, was chosen by a small element of the press corps. A three cornered race would provide plenty of copy, no matter how devoid of truth. "Who can tell, we may be more powerful in electing the next pope than all the red hats in St Peter's." One journalist had cheerfully remarked prior to embarking on a little relaxation with a young lady recently arrived from North Africa and trying desperately to repay the people smugglers.

In anticipation that the First Ballot was nothing more than a dummy run, several reporters stayed comfortably in bars outside the Vatican City. Time enough to sharpen their pencils when the serious business began. This, in hindsight, proved an unwise decision and caused more than one to seek new employment.

Two hours after the cardinals met, white smoke emerged from the chimney to a great shout of "Habemus papam". Inside the Sistine Chapel, the Dean of the College of Cardinals repeated the question which he seemed to have asked only yesterday. "Do you accept your canonical election as supreme pontiff?" "I do." By what name shall you be known?" "John XXV." Peroni's answer was virtually inaudible as the applause broke out. John XXIV appeared to have longer arms than most had ever suspected.

POPE JOHN XXIV –
GLOSSARY OF TERMS

Bishop. In essence the highest rank in the Church. The pope, himself, is Bishop of Rome and bishop of the whole Church. The pope is the first amongst bishops. Titles such as archbishop and cardinal may indicate greater prestige but, in theory at least, they are merely bishops in terms of institutional weight.

Church Councils. There have been a total of 21 councils up to and including the Second Vatican Council, roughly one per century. They are usually called when there is significant disagreement of some point of doctrine or in response to schism. In theory such councils reinforce the importance of the bishops as the supreme governing body of the Church but, as with their civilian counterparts, those who control the agenda and produce the minutes hold a disproportionate power.

College of Cardinals. A collective term for a meeting of cardinals

Conclave. A meeting of all cardinals, usually at the Vatican, when all those younger than 75 years are authorised to elect a new pope

Encyclical. Encyclical letters are one means by which a pope may comment on matters which he perceives to be of pressing importance. This may involve no more than re-emphasis on received doctrine or may deal with new issues which arise out of new knowledge

Ex Cathedra. A teaching issued 'ex cathedra' is considered to be infallible and becomes a mandatory belief for all Catholics

Infallibility. Based on the promise that the Spirit would guide the Church in the truth, the implication is that, under certain circumstances, Church teaching is, in effect, direct from God. An Ecumenical Council of bishops is generally accepted as the appropriate medium for such pronouncements. However Pius IX, using tactics which would put most politicians to shame, managed to have the pope declared as infallible when making certain pronouncements, with or without the concurrence of a bishop's council. Infallibility remains a highly contentious issue. Popes have largely avoided 'ex cathedra' pronouncements rendering acceptance of a particular doctrinal point a prerequisite for Church membership. However, according to some sources, virtually all Vatican statements carry infallible status. In British military circles, good tactics is cynically defined as the "Opinion of the most senior officer present". What constitutes an infallible statement can sometimes appear to occupy a similar status

Magisterium. The complete teaching of the Church based either on direct scriptural sources or as interpreted by the bishops in council and, depending upon the legitimacy of papal infallibility, on the pope acting with or without the bishops' concurrence

Natural Law. A concept developed by St Thomas Aquinas. While a clear definition is difficult to find, the Natural Law is a moral guide which is determined by studying humanity in context. It is distinct from man-made laws but should provide the principles on which they are based

Papacy. The institution of pope

Papability. The degree to which a candidate is seen as standing a chance of being elected as pope

Pontificate. Normally refers to the reign of a pope

Principle of Double Effect. Concerns the morality of an action which may have both good and bad consequences. The principle states that for such an act to remain morally justifiable the bad effect must not be intended, the good effect must not flow directly from the bad effect and the good effect must be sufficiently important to outweigh the bad effect. For example, a man using reasonable force to protect self or other from serious harm might, inadvertently, severely injury or kill an attacker. According to the principle (and most law) the act would remain moral and would not be considered culpable.

Second Vatican Council. Called by Pope John XXIII with the aim of "opening a window on the Church" and allowing the Spirit to enter. A gesture not designed to find favour with conservative forces and one which caused, according to the more liberally minded, "The Empire to strike back".

Subsidiarity. As defined by the Second Vatican Council, the principle states that it is "..........an injustice, a serious harm, and a disturbance of proper order to turn over to a greater society, of higher rank, functions and services which can be performed by smaller communities on a lower plane". "In accordance with the principle of subsidiarity, decisions should be made at the lowest possible level in order to enlarge freedom and broaden participation in responsible action." (The Teaching of Christ). A principle more honoured in the breach than the observance

Syllabus of Errors. A document issued by Pius IX which, in essence, attacked 'modernism' and purported, amongst other things, to have the pope acknowledged as superior to all rulers of nation states and to suppress freedom of religious belief. Unsurprisingly it gained no support amongst non-Catholics and very little among Catholics

Synod of Bishops. Instituted by the Second Vatican Council and consisting of a representative body of bishops called together by the pope to provide him with advice. Seen by many as a threat to Curia domination

About the Novel

The novel is set in the early 21st century. The unexpected appointment of a panic stricken but ultimately revolutionary Pope John XXIV re-kindles the expectations generated by the Second Vatican Council. But it does so at the cost of antagonizing powerful interests, both inside and outside of the Catholic Church. An unholy alliance of reactionary forces begins to form, as politicians and media barons realise that the Pope is not going to restrict his reform agenda to matters ecclesiastical. An assassination attempt fails, both to kill the Pope and to cause him to change direction.

Alarmed at the imminent prospect of war in the Middle East, John XXIV undertakes a peace mission, further alienating existing enemies. His trip ends in tragedy but....out of the ashes!

ABOUT THE AUTHOR

John Cogley has led a varied life. Born in Liverpool England he has lived in Europe, Asia, Africa and, currently, in Australia. His career has included service as an officer in the British Army and he currently works as a psychologist. He is a practicing Catholic. Pope John XXIV is his first published novel.

9 781461 123620